AF328698

"Change—big, disruptive, eye-popping change—is headed your way, as it is for every organization. Remember that Sears was the leading retailer in 1995. Ari Lightman, Rafeh Masood, and Gary Hirsch have crafted a delightful discussion of the innovation imperative, using real-world examples to illustrate potential issues and likely fixes. You'll appreciate this chatty, supremely interesting read, and your organization will be better for it."

—CATHY HOTKA,
principal, Cathy Hotka & Associates

"Finally, a business book that gets it: transformations fail or succeed because of people, not tech. *Monster Transformation* is the book business leaders need to disrupt their way of thinking, to unleash the Monster Slayers within their teams, and to achieve transformational wins in ever-changing markets."

—BRENDAN WITCHER,
principal analyst, Forrester

"Transformation isn't stopped by a lack of ideas. It's undone by the hidden forces inside every company—the monsters of complexity, silos, and ego. *Monster Transformation* doesn't sugarcoat that reality. It names those monsters, gives us the courage to face them, and shows us how to find the monster slayers already in our teams.

This book is honest, practical, and deeply needed for leaders who want lasting impact in the age of AI and beyond."

—SANDY CARTER,
bestselling author of *AI First, Human Always*

MON STER
TRANSFORMATION

CONQUER YOUR DIGITAL FEARS,
BE AI READY, AND FOCUS
ON WHAT MATTERS TO YOUR
ORGANIZATION

MONSTER TRANSFORMATION

ARI LIGHTMAN

RAFEH MASOOD

GARY HIRSCH

WILEY

A Note of Thanks

We are deeply grateful to Carnegie Mellon University for creating the space and spark for this book. The opportunity to learn, teach, and engage with some of the world's sharpest minds inspired much of what follows.

To our students, colleagues across industries, faculty peers, and our ever-patient friends and family, thank you. Your questions, insights, and encouragement shaped every chapter.

Contents

Foreword

Being part of a transformation at any organization is really hard, and that's certainly not for a lack of desire or ideas or ambition. Rather, transformations often stumble or fail because of the barriers that present themselves, many of them self-imposed. No one likes to talk about these obstacles or put them into a presentation deck. Instead, they get overlooked and glossed over. "We'll deal with them eventually," people say.

The problem is that change is not something most companies can afford to ignore. Digital transformation, generative AI, and agentic AI are just a few capabilities that are driving change in every organization I'm involved with. A recent UN Trade and Development (UNCTAD) report projects the global AI market to increase 25-fold from \$183B in 2023 to \$4.8T in 2033. This growth is also being met with growing concern. According to TechRadar, 98% of organizations intend to expand AI agents, yet 96% also see them as security risks. Global spending on digital transformation alone is expected to hit \$3.9T by 2027, according to International Data Corporation. Yet despite this high price tag, around two in three digital transformation efforts end in failure, according to Boston Consulting Group. Why? Because the real blockers to success aren't technical or external. They're cultural, structural, and human woven into the fabric of your company.

That's where *Monster Transformation* comes in.

This is not another business book filled with buzzwords and frameworks you might have seen or heard about before. The authors don't offer a quick fix or claim to have all the answers. What the book does present is something far more valuable: a fresh, honest take on the hidden forces, or what the authors call *monsters*, that typically derail transformation efforts. These monsters show up in various forms – such as complexity that grows quietly, silos that stifle collaboration and integration, or hubris that keeps leaders from facing hard truths. We've all seen them. And too often, we've ignored them as well.

What I love about this book is that it gives us language, tools, and, most importantly, permission to talk about what's really getting in our way. The book doesn't pretend transformation is easy but constantly reminds us that, despite the challenges, it's definitely possible. Yes, there are monsters lurking in the shadows of your company, but the authors show that there are also monster *slayers* – those best skilled to defeat the monsters – likely present at your business as well.

The authors bring this to life with real insight and lived experience. Sure, they teach students and working professionals at Carnegie Mellon University, but they're not just academics. They're in the trenches with leaders at some of the world's most iconic companies. One is a builder and operator who has guided major digital transformations at several organizations. Another is a strategist and researcher who studies human behavior and what makes change stick. The third draws from the world of performance and the visual arts to help leaders connect with clarity and conviction. Together, they create a powerful blend of analysis, insight, and heart.

They've interviewed more than 100 senior executives across different industries, gathered data, and, most importantly, listened to pragmatic and impactful advice. What they've created is a story-driven rationale for how to use your most readily available resource – your employees – to have the best possible chance at a successful transformation.

Because transformation doesn't begin with a budget. It begins with courage.

If you are trying to create real, lasting, and impactful change, this book is for you. It will help you stop chasing silver bullets and start doing the hard, human work of transformation. The kind of work that makes a difference.

It's time to name the monsters. It's time to start slaying them.

—Shellye Archambeau
Author, *Unapologetically Ambitious*
Former CEO, MetricStream

Introduction

—**Anil Aggarwal, founder of Money2020 and Shoptalk**

Change, as the saying goes, is inevitable. As trite as this may sound, the truth is that the imperative for businesses to transform is increasing while the willingness to put in effective and effort is only decreasing. All organizations are going through a fire drill of re-organizing themselves, adapting to shifting expectations and trying to become more innovative, resilient, and agile. They are continually bombarded by new technology vendors and service providers that promise efficiencies, collaboration, compliance, discovery, or the ability to generate new revenues from data, markets, products, or services.

Artificial intelligence (AI) is just the latest example of a technology that forces organizations into the age-old transformation question – how do we do it successfully? Can consultants help us get up to speed to become AI proficient and enabled and at what cost? What should we address first that might throw up roadblocks, causing delays, false starts, and failed implementations? Some organizations are reaching an existential point – although they might not even know it – where they must evolve or risk becoming stagnant, inefficient, irrelevant, or, even worse, extinct.

Like the technologies that preceded AI (the cloud, metaverse, blockchain, to name a few), AI dominates the conversation around transformation. However, unlike previous technological shifts, AI is considered a game-changer transforming how we work, live, and interact with technology. For organizations, AI impacts many of the decisions companies make and drives change in an unprecedented way. Organizations, particularly legacy ones, faced with this new AI-driven landscape, must come to terms with what transformation means for them and rethink, well, just about everything.

And yet, transformation is not something an organization can fix by simply buying an AI-enabled application, attending a webinar or certification course ("Transform your Business Using AI in Just Three Days"), or hiring a new C-level executive. True transformation involves rolling up your sleeves, getting to work, and addressing many of the challenges and issues that were put off for whatever reason. Many executives have been sold on the idea that there is a perfect playbook or guaranteed path to transformation success. Strategic advisors arrive with frameworks. Vendors pitch silver-bullet solutions. And yet challenges still persist. Why? Because real change is hard. It requires continuous assessment, tactical maneuvering, self-awareness, and a willingness to face uncomfortable truths about our organizations and ourselves.

Another Book on Transformation?

This book began from a place of shared woe, lament, and exasperation. Through our work with hundreds of organizations, we have seen the same patterns emerge: unrealized expectations, stalled initiatives, and a growing gap between transformation ambitions and reality. The three authors of this book have designed and taught classes and workshops and consulted for and put in place programs to understand digital and organizational transformation, disruption, and innovation. Students, participants, clients, and employees have then made strides associated with transformative thinking, only to go back to work and encounter roadblocks and hurdles leading to more frustration. The results? Market share erodes. Innovation slows. Employee engagement plummets. What starts with the promise of transformative change becomes a bottleneck of stalled efforts with the associated impacts rippling out in waves, from customer dissatisfaction and poor bottom lines to employee displacement and cultural disruption.

Just how pervasive is this sense of frustration? During a recent executive education class, we asked participants to describe their digital transformation efforts in one word or emoji. The overwhelming response? The poop emoji. This was not just gallows humor – it was a literal expression of the difficulties that permeate many of these efforts.

Why? Because transformation demands active participation and clear expectations. It requires people to change how they think, work, and lead, navigating a maze of technology, people, and processes, all while trying to keep the organization running. And now, with generative AI emerging as the Ozempic of the corporate world, helping organizations shed inefficiencies like pounds on the scale, the divide is growing even starker. Some organizations transform speedily, while others fall behind without the right tools, processes, people, and approaches. Those organizations with well-designed AI systems are accelerating their transformation at unprecedented rates, while others risk becoming the eight-track of today's digital world.

A Fork in the Road

Many legacy companies find themselves in what can only be described as a midlife crisis. They have the wisdom of experience and the weight of success, but they are watching younger, more agile companies make technological leaps. Sure, they want the nimbleness of a startup but are still weighed down by the anchor of established processes and archaic systems. They might have attended seminars, used frameworks, and even attended some of our workshops, and yet their transformation efforts often remain isolated to specific activities (AI chatbots, anyone?) or relegated to certain divisions like customer service or fulfillment, creating more rifts and divisions than any actual benefits.

In our research into why organizations struggle with transformation, we discovered something powerful: when we openly share and identify our transformation fears – when we name the monsters that stand in our way – we take the first step toward overcoming them. Here's what we've recognized about transformation challenges: every organization is experiencing them to some extent. Naming and understanding why they exist is the first step, but to tame them we need to understand them within each organization's unique context. It's not just about identifying generic obstacles. Each organization's history, culture, current state, and simultaneous internal and external pressures create their own unique transformation landscape. It is like trying to navigate a complex journey without a map customized to your specific situation. It's just a fact. There is no "one-size-fits-all" solution. Understanding this reality is the first step toward making progress.

Some Want It, Most Resist It, All Face It

That is exactly where this book began. Picture this: an operator (a battle-scarred digital transformation veteran), an academic (a Carnegie Mellon professor), and an artist (and pioneer of applied improvisation) walk into a bar. No, this is not the setup for a joke. It's how we started our journey to decipher why transformations so often go sideways or even reverse course. Between rounds and rounds of debates, we realized something fundamental: the first step to solving any problem is defining it. When you understand how the issue came about and how it impedes your efforts, you gain power over it. When you name your fears, they become challenges to overcome rather than invisible forces holding you back.

This is not just bar talk. Through our work founding, developing, and teaching several executive education programs, we have had a front-row seat to the transformation circus. We were fortunate to speak with professionals, industry analysts, futurists, practitioners, academics, and consultants across multiple industries (n = 105). Others, we surveyed to get their thoughts on hurdles to successful transformation (n = 50). We gathered data, insights, and listened to battle stories. What emerged was a pattern of recurring monsters – each unique, each frightening, and each absolutely defeatable once you acknowledge and understand what you are up against. We also heard encouraging stories of folks who are going up against these monsters and winning slowly but surely. They made us think of people we have worked with who have unique skills (competencies) that are important to consider in slaying transformation monsters. So, we developed a list of these competencies – Monster Slayers – that we believe are foundational for reducing barriers and having the best chance at transformational success.

The good news is you don't need to go out and hire a bunch of new people; they already exist within your organization. The bad news is that because of a number of factors like organizational inertia, they have not been able to practice and share their Monster Slaying talents. This is what we will be conveying throughout this book – understanding the critical need to identify, activate, and engage these slayers to have the greatest chance of success.

Here is what else we learned along our journey: transformation is not about checking boxes or implementing technology. It is about creating value and building competencies. Full stop. You cannot create change when you are paralyzed by unnamed monsters. You cannot build competencies without understanding how they emerge from different skill sets while simultaneously suppressing them. True transformational competency involves: acknowledging the barriers that hamper success; bringing an attitude of openness and honesty; sharing and collaborating; building coalitions across divisions; and scaling transformation in spite of all the obstacles in your way.

Frankenstein Was Fiction; These Monsters Wear Badges

In this book, we identify 10 unique monsters that lurk in the shadows of every transformation journey. These monsters represent hurdles or barriers that are stalling or derailing your transformation efforts or causing them to be less successful than planned. From the FOMO Monster that pushes you to chase every shiny new technology or trend to the Hydra Monster that multiplies complexity faster than you can cut it down to the Reckless Monster that tempts you to rush in without a plan, each one represents a tangible obstacle that can derail your transformation efforts.

But here is the good news: every monster has its weakness. Every fear, once named, becomes manageable. Every obstacle, once identified, can be overcome. Drawing from both quantitative analysis and qualitative insights, we will show you not just how to identify these monsters but how to defeat them. We will help you recognize the monster slayers within your own organization – people with the skills, mindset, and tools to turn transformation from a source of anxiety into a source of competent change. We will share with you inspiring stories of folks who have brought these competencies into their organizations.

We also suggest simple creative exercises called "Try This . . ." to spur critical and system thinking, getting different folks to share ideas, understand and assess monsters, and build consensus. To those readers who might be rolling their eyes right now at the thought of more team-building exercises, we hear you. We have developed and delivered these low-effort, socially designed, high-impact exercises successfully in a variety of environments for a diverse set of organizations and so can you.

This is not another theoretical textbook or another "Transform now or your money back" workshop. Nor is it a simple collection of case studies. It is a field guide for the modern business leader, written by people who have been in the trenches, taught in the classrooms, and, yes, occasionally figured things out in a Zoom riff session. We aim to cut through the bull**** and focus on the practical competencies and the empowerment your organization needs to build true transformation capacity.

So, whether you are just starting your transformation journey or stuck in the middle wondering what went wrong, this book is your monster-defeating manual. Because in the end, transformation does not have to be a source of endless frustration. It can be an opportunity to create real value, if you are brave enough to name your fears and face them head-on.

Welcome to your monster-slaying journey. Let's begin.

Chapter 1

WTF Just Happened

Why do companies experience FOMO (Fear of Missing Out)? Perhaps, they missed capitalizing on a key trend and now find themselves in the unenviable position of missing the boat, being deemed outdated, or simply feeling left behind. The challenge is not only the variety of trends that exist but also in trying to assess the maturation of the trend. Will it fizzle out or shift, leading to an expectation in consumers, partners, or employees? Some companies can catch up by acquiring the capacity to capitalize on a trend. For example, Meta paid $19.1B to acquire WhatsApp, which brought them firmly into the mobile messaging market. Some companies change their entire business model to capitalize on trends, while others ignore them and become irrelevant. The story of Netflix and Blockbuster is a cautionary tale. Netflix was a direct mail provider of DVDs to the home and pivoted to online streaming to accommodate the market shift to finding and watching content online. Consumer watching patterns shifted from linear programming (content coming out at scheduled dates and times) to streaming (content available on demand). A combination of consumer adoption resulted in the differentiation of services becoming the expectation. In contrast, the previous dominant service (DVD delivery to the home) was relegated to becoming differentiated. However, the critical factor became the supporting technology to support this shift to the mass market, including Internet-enabled television sets and high-speed bandwidth to the home. In addition, consumers were interested in recording shows and watching them at a later point without ads disrupting their viewing experience. On the other hand, Blockbuster stayed true to its roots, grounded in physical stores with lots of coverage. In the 1990s, Blockbuster had 9,000 stores worldwide across 25 countries. They invested in expanding their physical presence with video game rentals. However, it still involved having consumers visit the stores to return or rent. Blockbuster failed to see the signals that Netflix did on the convenience of renting entertainment and the move toward streaming content. There were many other missteps, but in the end, they filed for bankruptcy, and today, only one store still remains as a testament to ignoring trends.

Organizations don't want to become the next Blockbuster, Kodak, Sears, Toys "R" Us, Nokia, Xerox, or Yahoo. However, they also can't afford to shift their strategy or deploy resources to accommodate every trend. Can a trend kickstart, accelerate, or derail your transformation efforts? Should transformation even respond to trends? Trends have a life cycle similar to products. They emerge and grow in popularity, may become adopted by the masses, and mature and evolve to a de facto standard; however, in many cases, they decline or take much longer than envisioned to come into the mainstream. Trends can be an indicator of change and a signal of what's on the mind of the consumer. Missing out on the latest trend and your company risk being left behind. Follow the wrong trend and your company can head down the wrong – and often expensive – trendy rabbit hole. In the face of all these trends, many executives are often left wondering, WTF just happened?

The Robots Are Coming/The Robots Are Here

As we mentioned, spotting trends is "relatively" easy. It is one part observation, one part curiosity. You should also apply different perspectives – *sky* view, a panoramic view of what's happening;

eye view, a focus on what's immediately visible; and *your* view, a personal interpretation or opinion of what's happening. We can use smart cities as an example of a sky view. As urban areas increase in population, cities are focusing on how to become more intelligent and are associated with the effective delivery of services as well as the movement of people and goods safely and efficiently. The eye view might look at Intelligent Transportation Systems (ITS) that use machine learning to improve traffic flows. An example of your view is that these systems will use less gas and help you get to work faster.

Reading through any technical newsletter or blog like TLDR, Medium, or personal substacks, you will be inundated with predictions of soon-to-be game-changing technologies. Visit any technology-focused conference like the Consumer Electronics Show (CES), SXSW, or Dreamforce, and your head will be swimming with ideas of how technology will shape the future. These are inspiring and energizing but usually meet the cold, hard reality of capacity and willingness within your organization, competing projects, limited resources and interest, and "organizational memory" of attempting similar efforts before that failed to realize any significant scale or impact. This can be deflating. In other situations, companies have chased trends without significant planning, capacity understanding, or market adoption assessment. This led to wasted resources (capital and personnel) that could have been deployed elsewhere, potentially impacting the company's ability to adequately compete. It also might lead to frustration and intractability. Our research found that companies that get spurned by chasing trends become less likely to do so in the future. Chasing trends is similar to a dog chasing its tail; it can be a useless exercise without adequate planning, assessment, and categorization. What you need are Trend Spotters . . .

The FOMO Monster Slayers

THE TREND SPOTTER

Trend Spotters spot trends (kind of obvious) and also categorize them into types (technical, consumer, regulatory, etc.). They can also go the next step and map those trends to business needs within the organization and address their potential impact. This isn't done in a silo but by bringing different teams together to assess based on consensus building how trends are viewed, organized, and of relative importance to the organization. The key consideration is not the trend in itself but the value it might bring to the organization. Generative AI (Gen AI) can be thought of as a technical trend with different use cases. You might use it to make people, departments, and functions more productive, or you might use it to create customized and highly targeted content for consumers. Gen AI could also be used internally to make employees more collaborative, engaged, innovative, etc. In this example, there are two trends central to the issue being discussed: a consumer trend (focus on personalization) and a technical trend (incorporation of Gen AI). The consumer trend could be met without the incorporation of the technology. This is why it's critical to start with a business need; identify, assess, and organize trends, map those trends to use cases; and try to quantify value, risk, infrastructure needs, and capacity.

Once trends are mapped and assessed and there is consensus on value to the organization, there is still a necessary competency to include to make sure trends align with capacity and competency. Say hello to the . . . .

The Organizational Pragmatist is not a blocker (far from it). They provide the balance for the Trend Spotter to make sure they are as successful as possible. They push through organizational idealism, politics, and over-planning to bring realism, adaptability, and results orientation into the process of assessing and acting on important trends to take into consideration for transformation. But what is important? This might be a fundamental shift in consumer expectations, where if the company does not execute to meet the need, it might hamper its ability to compete in the market. So, the Organizational Pragmatism helps in putting together assessment, mapping, and consensus on what the organization might be able to achieve or need to develop in order to be able to capitalize on the trend. They are also aware of other projects and how those might compete with or complement the proposed efforts. Think of these two folks working together on a fundamental question: How can the organization position itself to capitalize on trends without always seeing them fly by and struggling to keep up? In other words, how can we become responsive to the market, customers, and employees while neutralizing the FOMO Monster?

That question isn't theoretical. We have seen it play out in the real world. Sanjay Srivastava knows something about being an organizational pragmatist. As an investor, a connector, and the chief digital strategist of Genpact, a global professional services and solutions firm, he continually discusses and examines trends but remains practical in choosing which to invest time and effort in.

Most employees don't walk into work thinking "How can I disrupt myself today?" A finance department isn't going to suddenly decide to reinvent its operating model just because a consultant's slide said transformation is urgent. That's not how change happens. It's why trend mapping and organizational pragmatism, two of our most important FOMO Monster-slaying competencies, often show up quietly. You don't need fireworks. You need people who are tuned into signals, fluent in constraints, and wired to move before the system tells them.

Because here's the truth: creativity is often born out of constraints. The best organizational pragmatists don't see limitations as blockers. They treat them as raw material. They notice patterns others overlook. They ask questions that sound simple but open doors. Where's the friction? What's about to break? What's worth fixing before it does?

When Sanjay Srivastava joined Genpact, he didn't have a transformation mandate or a big title. He had experience, having built and sold four start-ups, and he had a trained eye for pattern recognition. Instead of launching a bold initiative, he started by listening. He paid attention to emerging signals. He spoke with clients, start-up founders, technologists, and skeptics. He looked for trends that weren't fully formed yet. What was bubbling beneath the surface? What were others dismissing too quickly?

That was phase one. Spotting the trends. Not chasing the obvious ones, but sensing what might actually matter. He didn't just follow headlines. He connected signals across industries and asked what they meant in context.

Phase two was all about assessment. Not everything he spotted was worth acting on. So he filtered ideas through both qualitative and quantitative lenses. Was the infrastructure ready? Did the culture support it? Was the value clear enough to avoid a six-month debate? If the answer was no, he parked it. If the answer was maybe, he tested just enough to learn. The goal wasn't to roll out. The goal was insight.

Phase three was translation. Long before AI dominated agendas, Sanjay saw its potential to reshape enterprise transformation. He led Genpact's first acquisition in AI seven years ahead of the current wave of GenAI. That move laid the groundwork for their Cora AI platform, which now anchors the company's transformation into Agentic AI. What counts is a practiced sense of timing, a willingness to act when the signals line up – even if no one else is watching.

None of this was accidental. Over time, Sanjay formalized what he had been doing. He created lightweight frameworks. He built a trusted network across industries to compare notes. Eventually, the organization gave him the room to do what he was already doing. He didn't disrupt the system. He earned his way into it. Today, he also runs a global think tank of senior executives across industries, a community he built to exchange signals, pressure test ideas, and stay ahead of the noise.

Sanjay's example is not about being a visionary. It's about paying attention. He didn't come in to save the company. He just kept asking the right questions until the organization started listening. This is what it looks like to cultivate trend mapping and pragmatism. Not through slogans. Through repetition. Through constraints. Through care.

Sanjay's approach isn't flashy, but it's foundational. It shows how organizations don't just need more ideas; they need better filters, braver listeners, and people willing to act at the right moment. This is what trend mapping and organizational pragmatism look like in practice.

The Organizational Pragmatist is the needed "voice of reason" that:

- Bridges the gap between strategy and execution and helps translate lofty goals into actionable steps.
- Keeps things grounded and prevents the organization from "chasing trends." Cuts through the noise with data-informed decision-making and common sense.
- Navigates complexity and creates clarity in ambiguous situations.
- Focuses on outcomes, not optics, and cares about what works versus what looks good. Bringing an honest, unfiltered assessment of FOMO and its impact on the organization.
- Balances unbridled enthusiasm with reality and continually asks the question, "With everything going on, can we actually pull this off?"

Pulse Check: What's Trending?

The ability to spot, assess, map, follow, and respond to trends is an essential skill in your organization's efforts to meet market needs and expectations. It is also critical to be responsive to what employees expect. Successful organizations assess and react to trends to be innovation leaders and critical thinkers while also being aware of their capacity and ability. Rather than chasing trends to try to keep up with competition, these organizations become hyperresponsive, even predictive, to stakeholder needs, developing an environment where transformation capacity can address trends as they shift from fads to expectations. Those who dismiss the opportunity to innovate, fail to recognize shifting patterns in expectations, or simply do not place an emphasis on building capacity to spot and assess trends often underestimate the impact of aligning transformation with changing expectation patterns.

Of course, spotting trends – particularly ones that are in the mainstream – is relatively easy. The world is filled with experts looking to see what's trending. Understanding, categorizing, and evaluating trends, as well as assessing the need to act on them in terms of their impact on an organization's business, by contrast – now that's challenging. It can be frustrating trying to convince management to dedicate resources and capacity, just to have it fall on deaf ears. On the other hand, a green light without the right contingencies, measures, or timelines in place may result in a failed implementation, costing the organization time and money as well as eroding trust. Like everything we will discuss in the book, transformation exists in a balance between responding and strategizing. Having the capability and wherewithal in place to move quickly is a skill that's critical, especially in a turbulent and continually evolving space.

To become more responsive to trends, organizations need to:

- Stay vigilant in spotting trends.
- Identify appropriate use cases.
- Evaluate the benefit/risk trade-off.
- Execute efficiently and effectively with shared purpose.

The Trend Is Your Friend – Well, Sometimes

It can be exhausting to consider all the current and potential trends and try to organize, categorize, and map them according to a company's needs, interests, and availability. Trends, especially technology-based trends, follow a hype cycle developed by Gartner, the IT consultancy firm.[1] Understanding where the trend may be within the hype cycle is important for planning and development. A Trend Spotter recognizes the larger superset of trends, works with others to narrow the field, and looks for ways to incorporate policies, procedures, or practices that will help drive transformation. In other words, they incorporate *foresight* into their trend assessment. Foresight takes into consideration market research, cultural understanding, and the recognition that trends can be time-bound (i.e., seasonal), geographical, consumer-oriented, technology-specific, etc.

Many are intertwined, as we mentioned, with Gen AI. Another example is the trend toward immersive experiences using virtual reality (VR). There is the technology trend of VR and all the associated challenges with introducing new technology – user interaction, form factor, integration issues, and power limitations. There is a consumer trend focused on immersive and personalized experiences. Of course, you can have that without VR, but the technology allows for customization as well as measuring to quickly optimize the experience. With the addition of the technical component, new issues arise, like consumer privacy. VR headsets collect a slew of information that companies can use to optimize the experience. That said, certain trends can accelerate or impose barriers to adoption. Macroeconomic and societal factors can also play a role. Take COVID-19 and the pandemic, for example, which resulted in a renewed focus on remote work practices, further accelerating infrastructure and developing VR applications for employees to remain engaged and productive.

The pandemic also created a heightened focus, not just on work modality (remote versus in-place versus hybrid) but also on employee health and well-being, which is another complex and intertwined space. In 2021, Microsoft launched Viva, an employee experience platform that brings together communication, well-being, learning, and knowledge. It was launched in direct response to address employee burnout, disconnection from team culture, and loss of informal learning and collaboration that accelerated during the pandemic. Modules like Insights were designed to provide analytics to support well-being and productivity, while connections were an internal recourse to spur connection across the organization. The benefit associated with the development and incorporation of Viva was to promote well-being with a focus on mindful breaks to reduce burnout, improve employee engagement to foster inclusion, help employees feel more connected, and boost productivity by focusing on nudging users to disconnect after hours. Viva became an integral part of the Microsoft Teams platform to lead a shift toward employee experience and well-being. Insight into well-being allowed companies to rethink work, working, and the workplace to make sure that they focused on employee quality of life, not solely on productivity.

Well-being, though, is a broad space and can be broken down into several subcategories, including:

- Physical wellness: Physical activity, sleep, and preventing illness.
- Social wellness: Sense of connection and well-being.
- Spiritual wellness: Sense of purpose and meaning.
- Emotional wellness: Creating satisfying relationships.
- Vocational wellness: Satisfaction and enrichment from work.
- Intellectual wellness: Expanding knowledge, creative abilities.
- Environmental wellness: Environments that support well-being.

This trend focused on health and wellness might be considered within a corporate setting (employee benefit) but also as a value proposition incorporated into new products, features, or process changes for customers. How might you test these new ideas based on trend exploration? Many organizations test them internally to understand usage and adoption prior to delivering them externally. Google is a well-known company where employees try products and services prior to release to the general public. Waymo, which is Google's self-driving car, was initially tested by offering rides to employees and their families. This allowed the company to get real-world information in a controlled environment.

But which trends should be addressed and why? What happens if it turns out not to be a trend but a fad that fades away? To what extent can the organization address the trend? In the previous example on health and wellness, we might look at high-end air filtering and monitoring systems as a technological trend that has the potential to provide better air quality and awareness of air quality improvement. How, though, does the value of this trend intersect with an increasingly remote workforce? Exercises like Trend Mapping often help, not just identify what might be feasible and practical but also how trends interact across different dimensions to deliver value while avoiding competing efforts to try to achieve similar results.

Moments Versus Movements

In trend assessment, one of the deadliest pitfalls is confusing moments with movements. A moment, like the sudden explosion of QR code menus during COVID-19, creates temporary urgency but may not signal lasting change. A movement, like the shift toward digital payments or sustainability, fundamentally reshapes how businesses operate and customers behave.

Organizations paralyzed by FOMO often fall into one of two traps: either they chase every moment as if it's a movement, spreading resources thin on temporary trends, or they dismiss actual movements as passing moments until it's too late to respond. Recent history offers a sobering example: companies that dismissed mobile commerce as just another digital "moment" in the early 2000s learned the hard way that they were witnessing a movement that would fundamentally reshape consumer behavior and business operations.

Success requires both the telescope to spot potential movements early and the microscope to assess their true impact, distinguishing between what's trending and what's transforming.

Look to the Future, Learn from the Past

The future is uncertain; the past is known. Of course, history isn't a static entity. While there may be a historical record of what happened at any organization, it's crucial to remember that perspectives muddy the waters. Winston Churchill famously said that "history is written by the winners," suggesting that history isn't objective but rather favors the version of events of those in power. Your organization too has a history and events that are perceived differently by those impacted. The danger is that this historical context becomes the kind of "organizational memory" that might be used as a blocker for future transformative efforts.

Trend analysis relies on a combination of historical research and future projections to generate and test hypotheses (we will be discussing more about hypotheses in Chapter 6) and seek out strategic business opportunities. However, once again, the future contains many unknowns. It's also hard to predict timing. Trends that were accelerated because of necessity during COVID-19, like telemedicine, experience a retraction when folks return to physical visits. It does not negate the importance of telemedicine; the use cases go from the general population to specific situations where telemedicine is a better option than a physical appointment. As a result, it's often hard to get different folks on the same page about what's in store and how certain scenarios might impact current efforts. These different variables result in a multitude of if/then scenarios that are subject to interpretation and can become an obstacle to experimenting with new initiatives, with the hope of implementing them and driving change throughout the organization. Sometimes trends follow a cycle of weak signals focused on a niche community and then grow in appeal to become a shift in expectations. The key is to regularly practice trend spotting, classification, mapping to business needs, and assessment. However, you always need to be on the lookout for common internal issues.

Our research showed that there are several challenges companies face in assessing and acting on trends, including:

- **Unrealistic expectations:** Don't over-promise and under-deliver. Experimentation, accessible test markets (like employees), and prototype development can provide a sense of what is achievable.
- **Overinvestment in hype:** Pay close attention to the hype cycle, and filter out noise from the market. Get consensus from a diverse audience on timing, especially trend maturation.
- **Underestimating cost and complexity:** Learn to simplify and develop a testable proof of concept. We'll cover this in Chapter 6 and understand how process complexity slows down innovation.
- **Clearly articulating the business value:** Make sure there is consensus on this and on how to deal effectively with naysayers.

Many organizations still find themselves complacent. This might be a result of a culture that values predictability and routine, perceived lack of urgency or motivation, or a tendency to focus on short-term gains versus long-term strategic thinking. The one issue that was mentioned to us over and over again was dealing with "organizational memory." Naysayers often use examples of failed efforts from the past as a rationale for not moving forward despite that the market has evolved and the organization may have developed new competencies, infrastructure, and services to support the transformation. Leaders traumatized by previous attempts to embrace trends can become blockers in moving to address trends. Even though there is urgency to address customer needs and achieve competitive parity, folks remain rooted in the struggles of previous generations, find rationale not to move forward, and are afraid to embrace change.

How can you shrug off failed implementations of the past, learn from them, and embrace new opportunities? This is where the organizational pragmatist comes to the aid of the Trend

Spotter in helping to identify impediments to transformation. Trend Spotters focus on either near-term or long-term adoption of trends. They can articulate and demonstrate inter-dependencies of trends in relation to technology adoption, consumer expectations, and societal needs. Along with the Organizational Pragmatist, they can develop a comprehensive plan to communicate organizational capacity, market interest, and mapping to business value. Without that, trend analysis will stay relegated to just that – trend spotting and waving as they pass you by.

The Trend Factor: What's Shaping Tomorrow

When does a trend mature into a fundamental shift in customer expectations? Organizations need to respond to shifts in consumer (and employee) expectations to stay relevant and competitive. With so many trends, how do you know which ones to track and which ones to disregard? For those that you are following, do you have the organizational capacity to address the trend? How do you ensure it will be beneficial for the company? How does it impact transformational efforts?

Trends, especially technology trends, are challenging to assess since there have been so many that have fizzled out or failed to meet expectations (anyone remember the Segway?). The Metaverse, for example, has been commercially and publicly available for several decades. Second life, the user-created virtual community developed by Linden Labs, has been providing users with a multi-player online experience since 2006. That said, there was not widespread usage until technology, specifically, higher speed connections and graphic processing, caught up, which allowed for a more seamless user experience. Using the technology prior to that involved a great deal of patience and fortitude. Even now, with a variety of wearables, ample computing power, and a plethora of practical use cases, we are still not seeing widespread adoption of the Metaverse within the corporate space. Yes, ardent gamers have been playing in virtual worlds for a long time. Manufacturing specialists have been aided by augmented and virtual reality to assist them in their jobs. Even physicians and medical students are starting to use VR/AR to assist in and provide training on complicated procedures. And yet, it still has not achieved widespread adoption for corporate business use for a variety of reasons: it's still considered a novelty and not a significant business driver. Except perhaps in specialty manufacturing, no one has demonstrated practical use cases for mainstream business applications. The price point is too high, and the learning curve is steep. Ultimately, the value/risk trade-off does not warrant its incorporation. For many companies, the organizational memory surrounding the adoption of new technology may be too fraught to even consider trying something so new and unfamiliar.

Analysts and consultants continually publish research on future trends. Venture capitalists make bets on companies that will be able to push technologies into the mainstream. Academic researchers receive funding from governmental agencies looking to advance science and technological advancement for societal benefit. What these initiatives do not take into consideration is the capacity of the organization to develop competency and infrastructure for implementing these trends successfully and in a sustainable way.

Spotting trends takes a curious mind. Timing trends take controlled patience. Finding the optimal time to incorporate trends takes a holistic understanding of the organization's ability to adapt. If the Trend Spotter overshoots the technological shift, the organization may be viewed as a laggard, slow adopter. However, if the

Trend Spotter urges the adoption of a nascent technology prior to its maturation, the organization risks wasting time and resources and eroding trust. Depending on the deployment, the new technological trend may also open the organization to potential threats, cybersecurity incidents, and regulatory issues.

The Four Lenses of Trend Spotting

To really assess trends, organizations need to examine them through four different lenses. Of course, there is the *technology* lens, which takes into account usability, infrastructure, utility, etc. However, you also need to consider them through a *socio-economic* lens, not just the totality of cost to develop a product or service to meet the trend but also ongoing costs to support and update products and services. This lens also should take into account income levels and affordability. Another important lens is *regulatory,* especially as more products and services contain digital traces of user information. The really challenging lens is *behavioral,* mainly because it fundamentally relies on people and the adoption of new processes and technology. The lenses are critical when assessing trends and can be paired with perspectives. We already mentioned the sky view, eye view, and my view, but in the case of understanding capability, we think of the telescope and the microscope.

We use the analogy of the telescope and the microscope. A telescope assists folks to look outward to try to understand the impact of current and future trends. The microscope, by contrast, is a tool for looking inward, assessing internal capacity and capabilities, but also understanding the impediments (like organizational memory) that might put the brakes on implementing new policies, processes, and technologies before they even have a chance to see the light of day. The Organizational Pragmatist helps provide some grounding for our Trend Spotter. This is not to say that the Organizational Pragmatist's role is to function as a constant contrarian, always trying to shut down initiatives, but rather to offer practical advice and wisdom on how to enable shifts and provide the best chance for success.

When it comes down to assessing transformation initiatives, assessing technology is often the most well-understood. Enterprise architects, user interface designers, and application engineers often develop prototypes that can be tested, ported, and scaled, adhering to specifications that meet the proposed demand and success measures of an organization. This is by no means an easy feat, but largely understood. When the implementation becomes available, understanding and predicting behavioral patterns and socioeconomic conditions, as well as the regulatory and policy landscape, is a real challenge. In one example told to us, a group was developing an application but failed to assess the evolution of technology in their target market to access and use the application effectively. The key takeaway is to know your market's needs and technical capacity prior to beginning development. In addition, are there any barriers associated with current and future proposed regulations? For example, how might privacy regulation impact your market's perception of your application or service? How will the organization adhere? At a high level, organizations find themselves in one of four quadrants dominated by readiness versus response, as shown in Figure 1.1. With a high level of readiness but a low level of response, organizations are optimizing processes and capabilities but not necessarily jumping in. On the other hand, high response with low readiness means organizations are just chasing trends with a low probability of capitalizing on them. To transform themselves with high purpose and intent, organizations need to have a high level of readiness and response.

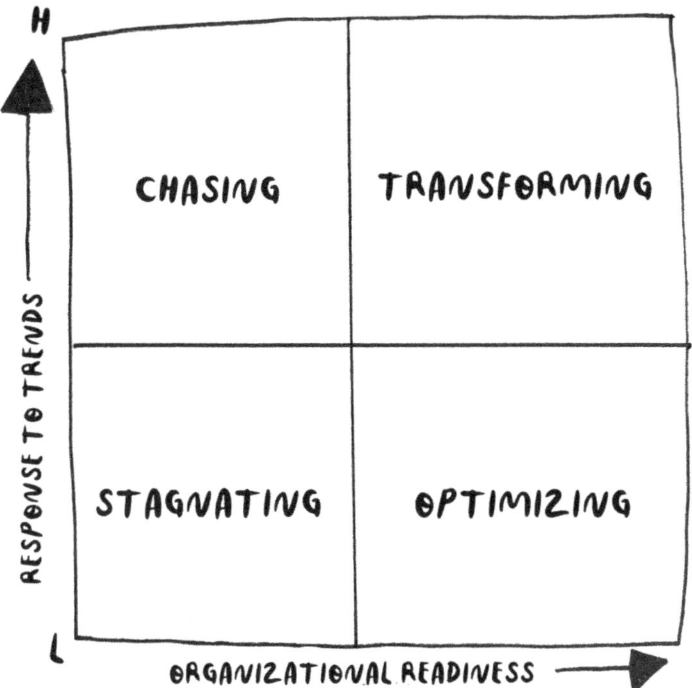

Figure 1.1 From stagnation to transformation.

See the Forest Through the Trees

Tapping into tens of thousands of conversations about your brand, products, and industry can be done through social listening. In addition, it can help organizations assess how consumers perceive value, what they might be looking for in the future, and how they would like to interact and engage. When context is taken into consideration – when was it said, what prompted the conversation, on what platform, how many times, by whom – you obtain a richer understanding of how to filter and assess this information. Social intelligence combines this data with other relevant datasets while applying machine learning (ML) or AI to understand key online constituents, influence patterns, and connections between one online audience and another, as well as how and what is trending.

There are a slew of social listening platforms available that provide an interface (window) into all this social data and deploy algorithmic means to sort, filter, and display the data for public consumption and understanding. They can provide insight into consumer, technology, societal, and regulatory trends. They can map trends with specific hyper-targeted audiences. Perhaps your apparel brand would like to know the styling trends important to underrepresented audiences. Perhaps a CPG organization focused on snack products might be interested in dietary trends to assess what ingredients they might need to procure to be in compliance with one of these trending diets. Social listening can be incredibly useful to spot trends and watch their maturation. Social intelligence can assist the Trend Spotter to combine other sources of consumer data and audience analysis to understand where the trend originated, why it might be growing in appeal, how organizations are developing to meet the trend, and with what success. Organizing and assessing trends, as well as getting consensus on the trend, is done through the process of trend mapping.

Trend Mapping

A trend map is a visual depiction of trends that can be assessed according to the impact on a given system. A quick, easy exercise of building a trend map can be done to identify an issue and possible ways to address it, either with process change, technology adoption, or simply reframing the situation. For example, let's say you are experiencing diminishing satisfaction associated with customer service. There are several things that might be done to address this, including:

- Customer relationship management (CRM) provide insights on customer segments and issues.
- If you have a CRM in place, how would you leverage advanced analytics to uncover insights to address the issue?
- Chatbots or virtual assistants can learn over time and be deployed to augment customer service representatives.
- Omnichannel support looks at integrating all the different touchpoints a customer has with the organization.
- Use different social platforms to engage and develop support-based communities where consumer advocates provide support and direct seekers to appropriate resources.

Each of these ways of addressing the issues might have several implications from the perspective of resources, costs, time to implement, risks, etc. These all can be highlighted and assessed to find what might be the optimal solution. In this way, our trend mapper and organizational pragmatist can work together to identify how to address different types of trends. Bear in mind that a good practice is to bring in employees representing different departments and functions within the organization. This not only brings in their viewpoint and assessment but also helps to achieve consensus on the impact of the trend associated with competitive parity, strategic business value, and the capability of the organization to address.

Your Blind Spots Are Where Surprises Live

Understanding the associated macroeconomic environment helps determine whether a trend is substantial, sustainable, and worth paying attention to or not. The retail industry saw a plethora of new trends emerge during COVID-19. Live shopping uses live streaming where retail companies present products to consumers in real time to spur commerce activity in a remote fashion. During the height of COVID-19, brands and retailers were experimenting with the model to provide a way for consumers to engage with products that they could not physically interact with. This has been in place for a while (i.e., QVC), but the combination of streaming vendors, technology capabilities, social influence, and the inability of consumers to shop physically, heightened interest. Further, the combination of virtual reality and the promise of the metaverse had future-thinking retailers developing strategies to host virtual live shopping with digital avatars presenting virtual goods that represent real products. This brought up several questions and issues; namely, is this a fad? Will we see a return to a balance between traditional e-commerce and physical commerce? Is this geared to only a specific demographic, and are they growing or diminishing in purchasing power? Are there any cultural issues we need to address/adhere to that might strengthen or weaken our case? What supporting infrastructure needs to be in place to make sure there is a consistent and value-added user experience?

Mapping trends is not the difficult part; it's trying to assess if and how your company can pivot to adopt. Going back to the live shopping example, if your company has a culture of physical shopping and has invested significantly in physical stores and infrastructure, incorporating live shopping might be extremely challenging. It's not insurmountable, but there needs to be a well-thought-out plan to build support, experiment with the model, and engender trust that would enable this new modality of consumer experience and engagement.

Key Takeaways

As was mentioned in this chapter, it's critical to:

- Enable Trend Spotters to develop internal competencies in spotting, categorizing, assessing, and interpreting trends. It's also critical to be ready to act on these trends before they shift into expectations.
- Engage Organizational Pragmatists to develop expertise in categorizing trends and mapping organization capacity and needs to trends.
- Address the FOMO Monster by obtaining consensus on trend assessment, bringing in folks representing different departments and groups across your organization.
- Regularly map trends to strategic initiatives while also ensuring you have the capacity to effectively address the trend.

Organizations need to ask themselves what trends are important to track and assess, how organizational readiness can be developed so that transformation addresses the trend as it shifts to an expectation, recognize "organizational memory," and make sure that it does not become a future barrier to innovation. Remember, not all trends are worth chasing. The best companies don't say yes more often – they say no more effectively.

Case Story: Instacart

Caught Between Hunger and Hype

Apoorva Mehta started Instacart in 2012 after working for two years at Amazon as a supply chain engineer. There, he had learned that books and electronics were easy to ship, but groceries just didn't work online. Groceries were messy, temperature-sensitive, subject to personal preference, and wildly unpredictable from one store to the next. Conventional wisdom said it was impossible to deliver perishable food in a tight window. Other online retailers, like Webvan and HomeGrocer had tried, raising significant funding, only to fail during the dot-com crash.

Among the challenges these companies faced was building out their delivery infrastructure. To remedy this, Instacart took a page from Uber and the Airbnb platform model, connecting seekers with providers. With Instacart, the company paired retailers, shoppers, and consumers without having to develop and maintain costly infrastructure. Combined with an explosion of mobile apps and users following the launch of the iPhone in 2007 and Android in 2008, there was fertile ground for new mobile-first applications.

Instacart's native mobile environment appealed to its early adopter community of young urban dwellers and affluent families, who could easily access the application and order groceries from virtually anywhere.

By 2014, Instacart had launched same-day delivery in San Francisco and began signing with major grocery chains. The model worked: app users clicked to fill carts, shoppers scoured local aisles, and retailers saw orders spike overnight. Flows of data began pouring in, giving insight into customer preferences, store stocking patterns, and regional trends. To create revenue, Instacart's business model included a service and delivery fee for each order, as well as a fee for grocery stores and retailers for using the platform. In addition, the company launched Instacart Express (now Instacart+), a subscription service, providing customers with $0 delivery fees on orders over $35 (now, orders over $10). Lastly, since the platform was generating data on consumption and shopping patterns, Instacart saw an opportunity to collaborate with CPG brands offering them targeted advertising solutions to promote their food, drink, and household products across the platform.

The FOMO Monster in the Aisles

As the company grew and expanded, new opportunities presented themselves. Consumers were becoming increasingly comfortable using and making payment via mobile apps and their phones. Today, the company serves 7.7 million monthly active customers, provides flexible earning opportunities to more than 600,000 shoppers (who fulfill orders), and has become a critical growth engine for its top 20 retail partners – accounting for 5.0% of their total sales in 2022, up from just 0.6% in 2018.[2]

Within the online retail world, data and AI were driving innovation and offering new opportunities for platform-based companies like Instacart. Machine learning had historically been used to predict demand fluctuations, suggest products based on user data, and offer personalized experiences, while AI-powered chatbots provided instant customer service. Now AI could analyze browsing data, past purchases, and even dietary needs, resulting in personalized grocery lists.

Pandemic: Retail Innovation Accelerator

When the pandemic struck in spring 2020, grocery delivery demand exploded, and Instacart was under pressure to deliver even more. Over the course of the pandemic, Instacart's business quadrupled. For those in the industry, the rapid growth was both exhilarating and terrifying. Companies had to act fast or watch another company like Amazon or DoorDash leap forward and take their market share.

At Instacart, engineering teams pushed to open application programming interfaces to increase order volumes and spur data-informed innovation. Product teams wanted to roll out new services like curbside pick-up, order-ahead items, and new payment options, like SNAP, PayPal, and more. Marketing wanted to offer new ad formats for consumer packaged goods (CPG) hoping to reach families stuck at home. Retail partners wanted an easier way to market and sell high-margin prepared foods, as well as new ways to push their digital coupons and loyalty programs.

But this rapid success also bred tension within Instacart. Retailers worried about brand dilution. Management worried about profit margins. Every new idea brought additional new questions. The company was scaling fast but wanted to move smarter.

The FOMO Monster had officially arrived.

Grocery Meets Graph: Instacart as a Trend Engine

Andrew Nodes joined Instacart in 2014 as a business development lead eventually working his way to VP and GM of business and supply chain. He was one of the first business hires. Andrew had a background in management consulting working with clients on merchandising, procurement, and operations strategy. His day-one challenge was simple in theory: get grocers onboard the digital marketplace. In practice, his task felt like convincing giant incumbents to partner with a start-up that might potentially eat away at their margins, while also capturing their customer data. Imagine walking into a leadership meeting at a large supermarket chain with a presentation and saying "Trust me with your entire database." Most people would laugh.

Andrew did not try to convince them by selling the technology. Instead, he asked questions. Yes, e-commerce could help them move products, but how would they address substitution of one product for another? This integration could speed things up but what about margin pressure? He framed Instacart's potential features as direct answers to specific retail anxieties. It made him credible. Over the next few years, he crossed the country meeting regional managers, store directors, and IT leads. Each conversation taught him something new about how markets operated. He began to think of Instacart, not as a national chain but as a chain of hundreds of individual franchises.

Andrew and Instacart stuck by a simple model when it came to trend assessment — solve for the customer. With Instacart's four-sided marketplace — consumers, retailers, brand partners, and shoppers — this meant asking if potential projects, applications, acquisitions, and new business ventures benefit every partner in its ecosystem? The Instacart team was leveraging assets from the retailer business while building out assets and applications for shoppers. This resulted in a method of:

- Holistic data presentation and assessment. Time saved is important but recommendations and purchasing trends were as well.
- Forecast resourcing for both large bet projects and smaller projects.

- Iterative thinking, aka run a variety of experiments. Run them concurrently and focus on ease of use for the mobile space. What is the time and effort to get value for the user?
- Looking for the strategic places where others aren't focusing on.

From Pantry to Prediction: Tracking the New Grocery Graph

In 2020, Andrew noticed a couple of important trends:

- Elevated grocery costs were fueling demand for less expensive alternatives. Discount grocers (for example, Aldi and Save-A-Lot) were aggressively expanding while other grocers were investing in their private-label brand offerings to appeal to price-sensitive consumers.
- There was a clear need within marginalized and underserved communities, often with limited access to transportation options, for access to healthy grocery items.

At the time, online grocery delivery was often seen as a luxury – convenient for some but far from accessible or available to most households. Andrew considered overlooked markets and realized that grocery stores were supporting in-store customers using the Supplemental Nutrition Assistance Program (SNAP). Why couldn't Instacart? According to Feed America, SNAP's fact sheet,[3] SNAP is the largest federal nutrition assistance program in the United States. To qualify, household income must be at or below 130% of the federal poverty line. About two-thirds of SNAP recipients are children, elderly, or disabled limiting their ability to travel to find groceries. Benefits are provided via an electronic benefit transfer (EBT). SNAP benefits were an important trend to monitor and assess for Andrew. The societal benefits were many, including:

- Reducing food insecurity.
- Improving child health, school performance, and adult productivity.
- Stimulating the economy (very $1 in SNAP generates about $1.50–$1.80 in economic activity[4]).

The business model fit was another consideration, including the need for home grocery delivery and the ability to use platform dynamics, matching and advanced analytics to provide service to this community sustainably and economically.

During the pandemic, the government increased the dollar amount for SNAP benefits, but outdated legislation still restricted its use online. While many leaders focused on flashier growth levers, Andrew built a quiet conviction: this addition could unlock real value for Instacart and its partnered retailers alike, particularly at conventional and discount grocery stores. To build his case, Andrew collected data from grocers, surfacing how meaningful EBT/SNAP transactions were to their bottom line. Then, he made the case to Instacart execs, despite facing significant hurdles about policy, legal frameworks, and engineering complexity. With many still skeptical, he persuaded the CEO to greenlight a small tiger team.

What followed was a tour de force in stakeholder orchestration. Andrew worked with state governments, the USDA, trade associations, and even the Vice President's office to enable SNAP/EBT usage online a reality. He then helped architect the integration with a legacy payment processor and onboarded early retail partners to pilot the program. Eventually, what started as a scrappy side project became a cornerstone of Instacart's offering. Instacart now reaches nearly 98% of SNAP households, enabling delivery services for nearly 180 retail banners, including Publix, The Save Mart Companies, and Walgreens, spanning more than 30,000 stores across all 50 states and Washington D.C. Andrew handed the program off once the momentum was proven, turning a policy-choked constraint into a competitive differentiator.

Tensions That Changed the Game

By 2021 Instacart was deep in hyperscale mode. Competitors – DoorDash, GoPuff, Uber Eats, and more – were aggressively coming into Instacart's space. Data teams were building AI to recommend items that would pair well with avocados. Tech teams were integrating recent acquisitions like Unata, a Canadian start-up focused on providing grocers with white-label e-commerce websites, couponing, loyalty programs, digital circulars, and personalized grocery experiences. But on the ground, shoppers were still struggling to fulfill items that were shown as available. Store managers were voicing frustration with complaints about excess substitutions overload and distorted inventory data.

This was a moment of truth. Without cohesion, innovation would fracture the business. With discipline, innovation could sharpen it.

Andrew stepped in to ask three questions about every new idea:

- Is this solving a real problem on the ground for customers and partners?
- Can this be standardized across our retail footprint within 90 days?
- What is the fallback plan when things go wrong?

One top-of-funnel idea that generated intense internal debate was same-day, 15-minute delivery through retailer micro fulfillment locations to compete with well-funded competitors like GoPuff. It sounded sexy but required significant consumer interest, retailer buy-in, and radical reshuffling of priorities. Andrew asked, "If we could start with a trusted retail partner in a single market, we could jointly gain learnings and determine whether a micro-fulfillment model would provide additional benefit to all of Instacart's stakeholders." When metrics didn't add up, the idea was shelved. The fact was that Andrew didn't cancel ambition. He cooled it to mesh with reality.

Eventually, Instacart took this understanding and built a different version of ultrafast deliveries directly from retailers' existing stores, garnering the same-customer results, without the costs associated with micro-fulfillment. Instacart ultimately approached ultrafast in a more cost-effective and partner-centric way by leveraging existing retail infrastructure rather than building stand-alone dark stores, optimizing assortments for speed and efficiency, and integrating tightly with our retail partners' inventory and fulfillment systems. This allowed the company to deliver a fast and reliable experience without taking on the high fixed costs of vertically integrated models, like other players in the space.

The Dual Role of Trend Spotter and Pragmatist

Andrew understood the need to stay future-facing while rooted in the messy present. He loved the fact that Instacart data pointed to emerging trends in the grocery technology space. Whether it was grocers working to stand up their own e-commerce sites or companies developing unique technologies for brick-and-mortar stores or brands seeking to advertise to Instacart's unique user base, he kept his finger on the pulse.

But the only greenlit ideas that benefited all sides of Instacart's marketplace, which included customers, retailers, brands, and shoppers. When contemplating opportunities, he would ask:

- Is this something that customers want?
- Will this help our retailers grow their business?
- Will brands be better able to reach potential customers and drive sales?
- Can this optimize earning opportunities for shoppers?

It was also important for Andrew to address not just market opportunities, costs, and technical capabilities but potential regulatory (federal, state, and local) and compliance risks. Instacart had developed a community of shoppers who were contractors. The platform did not work without them, so understanding their unique desires and any legal and/or compliance risk was key.

Satisfying these conditions helped move any initiative to broader rollout. If the conditions weren't met, Andrew knew they needed more time to workshop and refine, rather than launch.

Retail Media and the Rise of a Platform

In 2022 Instacart significantly scaled its advertising business, which had initially launched in 2019. Imagine ads that appear when you add ice cream to your cart or customized coupons in smart carts while you shop. It felt futuristic even inside Instacart headquarters. Board members loved the revenue projections. Brands loved the targeting. Consumers responded well to prompts.

But inside the company, deploying ads required new alignment across engineering, pricing, analytics, shopper experience, and retailer privacy teams. Andrew facilitated "question sessions" with retailer leadership teams to ensure Instacart was aware of any concerns they had and retailers were educated about the types of ads that customers would see. He ensured this feedback was provided to product leads so they could focus on appropriate formats and customer targeting. He created running checklists for each new ad format that had to provide meaningful customer value, pass retailer criteria, and follow appropriate communication guidelines. Andrew mentioned that, in the early days, Instacart didn't want retailers to be surprised by new ad formats and wanted to ensure retailers carried the product that was being advertised. If any box failed, rollout was paused for iteration.

The growth that the ad business experienced over just a few years was remarkable. In 2025, when Instacart launched Universal Campaigns – a suite of new automation tools to help brands of all sizes create high-performing ad campaigns across retailers and surfaces, online and in-store – ad revenue saw a noticeable lift within the first few months of launch, while basket size and app satisfaction remained stable. The disciplined architecture and thoughtful rollout allowed Instacart to build a significant revenue stream without turning the app into a billboard.

Bringing Order to the Rapidly Expanding Platform

According to analysts and consultants tracking the space like Capgemini, 71% of consumers want generative AI in their shopping journeys.[5] AI has long been core to Instacart's business, especially in powering personalized recommendations across the app. In 2021, the team expanded this intelligence into the in-store experience as well, introducing smart shopping carts in physical stores. With Caper Carts, all customers need to do is grab an item and drop it into the cart and items – including produce – will automatically be added to an on-screen total. It's easy for customers to add, remove, or swap items as they go. When they're done, they can check out directly from the cart, avoiding lines altogether. An array of technology and integration development were needed to roll out the service, including:

- Smart sensors and computer vision cameras could recognize when a customer added a product, along with built-in scales to measure weights.
- E-commerce integration allowed users to build a shopping list and shop it from the cart.
- Personalized features offered location-based deals and check-listed items on sale.
- Integration with store loyalty programs ensured a holistic shopping experience.
- Integration into store infrastructure and point-of-sale systems (POS) provided enhanced benefit for retailers. E-commerce integration allows shoppers to pay right from their cart.
- Stackable charging stations ensured that carts are always powered and ready to go.

Through trend mapping, more acquisitions followed, like Foodstorm (2021), an order management system (OMS) designed specifically for grocery prepared foods and catering. It enables retailers to:

- Centralize and automate order-ahead, catering, bakery, and floral workflows.
- Support omnichannel ordering – via online, phone, in-store kiosks, and POS integration.
- Manage end-to-end processes: ordering, production, and payments.

At this point Instacart evolved into a multifaceted ecosystem, with multiple businesses operating across different surfaces and technologies. Underneath the high-growth veneer was a complex operating system working to keep pace with syncing inventory, multiple service-level metrics, marketplace governance, and post-order payment reconciliation.

As the business became more and more complex, Andrew had to rethink the best approach to work with Instacart's retail partners. He stood up a new team focused on how to go to market with new innovation while garnering critical feedback from partners. With this team, he created an operating rhythm to the business, ensuring product, engineering, and commercial teams were on the same page to flag friction, be radically transparent to ensure progress continued on the most important projects, and celebrate wins. He introduced new analytics teams that would work side-by-side with retailer partners to identify the right growth opportunities versus the retailer just following the FOMO Monster.

Slaying the FOMO Monster by Holding the Funnel Open and Closed

Saying yes without thinking creates waste. Saying no without nuance kills momentum. The Instacart team didn't shut down energy and creativity. It simply brokered new growth opportunities. Open submission forums for new ideas. Metrics required for each idea. Internal stakeholder meetings to triage proposals. If something represents a significant shift in strategy or approach like restaurant delivery, then Instacart considered partnering rather than building and competing, like in its partnership with Uber Eats.

Initiatives moved forward when there was broad alignment among stakeholders and key criteria were met. If not, the initiative was parked with a timeline for re-evaluation. This enabled the group to say yes to more than 30 new initiatives in a single year and scale more than a dozen.

The Payoff of Discipline

By Q1 2025, company-wide orders at Instacart grew 14% year-over-year, and gross transaction value reached $9.1 billion. Net income was more than $100 million, and adjusted EBITDA was nearly $250 million, showing that you can, in fact, invest in innovation without losing profitability.

More important for Instacart's long-term evolution is what disciplined alignment unlocked. New app features and network effects created delight for customers. Retailer trust increased, allowing Instacart to sell innovations, like enterprise storefronts, and in-store technologies, such as Caper Carts and Foodstorm. Retail media helped brands drive sales and became a high-margin business for Instacart. And shoppers earned more and more by serving Instacart customers.

Andrew and the Instacart team have learned to walk the tension line between anticipation and adaptation. Between seeking the next trend and making sure the last bet works. They didn't slay the FOMO Monster with fireworks. They slayed it with frameworks. It repurposed excitement into decisions. It converted speed into structured progress. Slowing the funnel is not failure. It allows for focus.

Key Takeaways from Andrew's Journey

- Trend spotting is useful only when paired with operational filters.
- Platform innovation must balance what retailers can operationalize with what consumers value.
- Saying no strategically protects organizational capacity.
- Habits of discipline are what make chaos repeatable.
- Stakeholder alignment is the operating system behind scalable innovation.

Try This: The Shiny Object Trap

The FOMO Monster thrives when teams chase every new idea, tool, or trend without a clear strategy. One way to weaken it is to expose the trap before you fall into it.

Step 1: Pick Your "Shiny Object"

As a team, think of the last big trend or tool your company jumped on . . . maybe it was AI, blockchain, the metaverse, a hot start-up partnership, or ways of working that promised transformation.

Step 2: Ask Three Brutal Questions

For that shiny object, answer the following:

1. What was the actual problem we were solving for? (Or were we just excited because everyone else was doing it?)
2. Did it make a measurable impact? (Or did we abandon it when the next big thing arrived?)
3. If we could rewind time, would we still invest in it? (Or should we have put resources elsewhere?)

Step 3: Make a "No-Fly List"

Based on your answers, create a "No-Fly List" that includes criteria for avoiding future distractions. For example:

- If we can't articulate the problem it solves, we don't invest.
- If it doesn't tie to our core business priorities, it's a pass.
- If success isn't measurable, it doesn't make the cut.

Use this exercise to keep your team's focus locked on what truly moves the needle – no more chasing shiny distractions.

Chapter 2

Press 9 and Wait in Purgatory

"Transformation starts with listening — if you're not hearing your customers, how can you solve their problems at scale?"
—Mario Ciabarra, Quantum Metric

Many of us have had the woeful experience of being routed through a hell of digitized backend customer service platforms.

Let's see if this sounds familiar to anyone:

AI BOT:	I'm sorry you haven't received your product yet. What's the order number?
YOU:	3OYZ7TTE.
AI BOT:	Three-oh-i-three-seven—
YOU:	No! 3. O.Y. Z. 7. T. T. E.
AI BOT:	I'm sorry, I didn't get that. Can you read the number again?
YOU:	OK. 3. O.Y. Z. 7. T. T. E.
AI BOT:	Great, here's what I have: O. K. 3. O. Z.—
YOU:	No!! I said OK, not OK. Agent! Agent!
AI BOT:	Would you like to speak to a customer service representative?
YOU:	Yes, please.
AI BOT:	Great! I'll transfer you.

(10 minutes later.)

AI BOT:	I'm sorry, all our representatives are busy right now. Perhaps you'd like to use our automated system?

Congratulations, you have entered digitized customer response purgatory.

Over the course of this book, we highlight many common reasons companies engage in transformation. Sometimes, it's about staying competitive. Other times, it's about achieving operational excellence for faster manufacturing, delivery, or reduced costs. Whatever the reason, we argue the rationale for transformational change should always be a renewed focus on the customer. After conducting interviews with 100+ executives, we heard the same overwhelming message: the primary rationale for transformation is to improve customer experience and increase customer value to retain and grow your customer base. Whether your customers are patients, clients, partners, passengers, subscribers, students, members, or users, these folks, after all, are the reason you are in business.

Yet, many companies still don't have a unified plan on how to optimize customer value and experience. They suffer from the Scatterbrain Monster. They lack alignment on customer value and experience, in many cases a comprehensive and holistic vision on "customer acquisition and retention strategies." Why is this challenging? Well, for one, you have different interpretations and perspectives on what customers need versus value. Also, you might have a different assessment of customers' changing relationships with your offering (product and/or service) over time. Lastly, you might have a difference of opinion on how to assess customer segments, loyalty preferences, or even customer perception of your brand. Ask yourself: What do your customers want? How do they engage with your products and services? Do you know their perception of your brand, products, and services in relation to what the competition offers? How do they acquire your goods? How would they prefer to acquire your goods? What level of customer service do they expect?

Without alignment on who your customers are and what they value, you're left trying to piece together random bits of data without a unified, strategic plan. You have, in other words, inadvertently fed the Scatterbrain Monster.

Are We Really Customer-Obsessed?

Companies that suffer from the Scatterbrain Monster have a hard time aligning on customer value or even coming up with a clear picture of who their customer is. As a result, they have difficulty building transformative capacity to develop customer-focused initiatives.

Take, for example, the omnichannel, which is used to describe aligning any customer touchpoints (customer service, physical sales, web) to provide a consistent customer experience. It does not matter which group or department you interact with; they will have a shared understanding of you, your history with the company, and your preferences in terms of engagement. Any interaction is recorded, shared, and used to provide a personalized experience. That sounds good but has significant challenges including integration issues across data silos, data management from different sources and resource allocation, and budgeting, not to mention operational challenges. Companies that are customer-centric realize that these issues need to be addressed to provide a seamless customer experience. Department-specific issues take a backseat to collaboration and integration to provide consistency across all channels and a highly personalized experience for interactions with customers.

Another factor that needs to be considered is incentives, which may not be aligned with customer satisfaction, retention, and acquisition. This divergence of opinion and effort on customer needs and values results in a lack of consensus on why we are engaging in transformational development focused on customer needs. This often leads to discontent. Are we all doing something together or having something done to us? To get consensus, we need individuals who can advocate on behalf of our customers and someone who can connect the dots between groups to enable a shared understanding and belief on how transformation delivers exceptional products and services that customers expect and value. You need a relentless advocate and a Dot Connector . . .

The Scatterbrain Monster Slayers

The Relentless Advocate is a customer champion within your organization. Their unique power is to provide a consistent view of different customers, their needs, and how they relate to different activities across the organization. Much like client relations specialists, who promote products and services externally, the Relentless Advocate has the unique ability to help others understand and get alignment on the changing dynamics of customer segments. Simply put, this is the person (or people) who make customer needs and expectations the driver for any transformational efforts. They make sure customers are heard, understood, and appreciated, and their issues are addressed sufficiently and promptly. They have a clear understanding of what motivates and delights customers, whether through purchase and ownership or through unique experiences. This might entail personalized attention that is meaningful for them, such as outreach on product-specific issues or recognition via loyalty rewards. It also entails representing the Voice Of the Customer (VOC) across the organization. VOC represents customer feedback about their experiences and expectations in interacting with your brand, products, and services. The Relentless Advocate goes further in making sure there is an understanding of the why, who, and how associated with impact via transformation activities. They represent the "meaning" for VOC data and ensure customer satisfaction is at the center of decision-making efforts.

The Relentless Advocate often accomplishes these goals through different methods, including (1) training programs on customer advocacy, showing how transformation should align with customer issues; (2) communicating customer stories to highlight experiences with various products and services; and (3) achieving consensus on customer segments, prioritization, and value. The Relentless Advocate, in other words, helps align customer-centric views across departments, groups, and divisions, and ensures that all parties understand the customer-focused rationale for transformation. To do this, of course, they need to make sure they are connected and bring in the right people into the conversation. For that, they need the help of a Dot Connector.

It seems everyone knows a Dot Connector. They have the innate ability to connect people to make things happen. You know them when you see them: that individual who seems to know everyone and can skillfully facilitate connections to accelerate initiatives. Within your organization, the Dot Connector is your force multiplier. Much like a matchmaker, the Dot Connector understands willingness, interest, and availability, and can find complementary people to work with the Relentless Advocate to drive consensus on transformation activities. While the Relentless Advocate develops the mechanisms and content for understanding VOC, the Dot Connector makes sure the right people are in the room.

Know Your Customers (KYC)

Are you customer-focused, customer-obsessed, customer-centric? There are myriad of terms to describe how companies service customers. In many cases, they often miss the mark. Why? Customer-centric companies focus on customer experience and needs by developing a comprehensive understanding of them, their behaviors, and what they value. As the title of this chapter suggests, if this is not orchestrated well and there is poor alignment of how to provide differentiated and valuable service, then experience might suffer, eroding trust and potentially leading to customer churn. Often companies struggle with providing personalized service versus automated responses that could lead to bad experiences, as we mentioned at the beginning of the chapter. Our Relentless Advocate builds an understanding of the VOC across the organization, helping them move from the chaotic to reactive zone (see Figure 2.1). The Dot Connector helps departments connect to rally around customer value (as well as achieving consensus) to move from reactive to a state of Alchemy. Alchemy represents a state organizations aspire to, where different disciplines come together to achieve a state of transformation and growth.

The challenge lies in moving farther away from typical customer touchpoints, which is an interface between a company and a customer, where perspectives differ on the customer and how to deliver customer value. Also, a change in consumer perception. Why? Well, this is similar to the telephone game where messages are whispered from one person to another. Errors eventually accumulate in the telling of the messages so that when the message

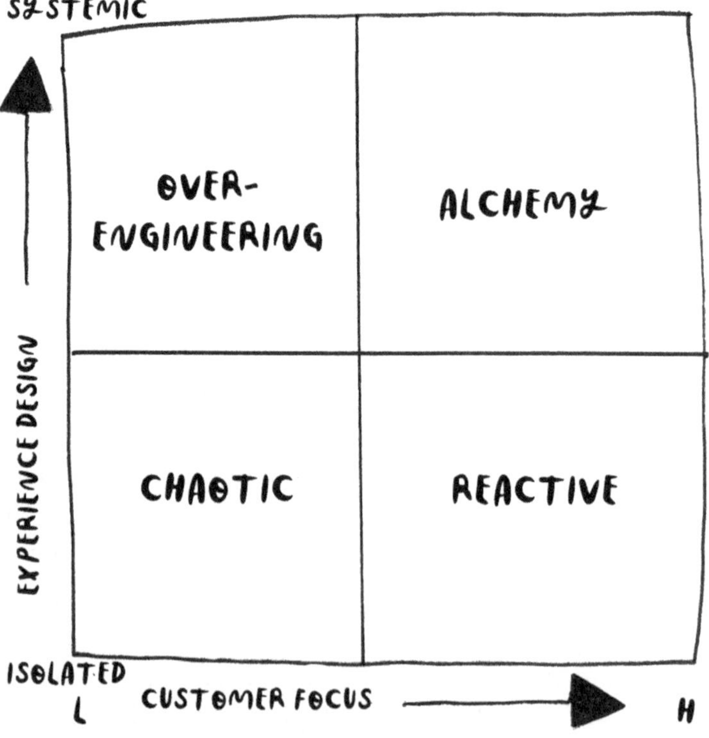

Figure 2.1   From chaos to alchemy.

finally gets to the last person, it's significantly different from the original message. Sales folks continually interact with customers and form ideas based on their scope and clientele, marketers are researching the market to identify the VOC as well as customer value and expectations, product management translates customer needs and value to features and functions associated with development, and customer service reps are helping consumers with service requests. They all have different views of the customer based on their job function. Most of the functions within the organization are removed from customers' operations, engineering, manufacturing, legal, IT, finance, and HR. How do they form an accurate and current depiction of customer value, need, and expectations? In many cases, they get information on customers from departments that spend most of their time interacting with consumers. However, in the absence of continuous interaction and communication, their views may be based on legacy thinking. After all, your customer base continuously shifts over time as the market changes and new competition enters the space.

Anything, Everywhere, All at Once

A pretty lofty initiative, but this is moving to what customers are demanding from companies. Can you provide it? How can you work toward it? When looking at customer service, customer interaction design needs to be addressed in terms of situation, cost, experience management, capacity, and even customer segment.

In some cases, an autogenerated interaction might suffice, even be preferred, whereas in other situations, you might have to have a human in the loop; this is the challenge of assessing piloted versus autopiloted interactions. An autopilot customer experience entails an automated agent or service like a chatbot providing basic information or directing customers to available services. A piloted interaction is one where you have a human working with you to resolve issues, answer questions, and provide personalized services. This becomes an important consideration when companies look at costs associated with customer service and support. A basic customer service and support call ranges between $3 and $5, while a technical support call might range from $7 to $12. Deciding how to provide the level of support in a cost-effective manner without diminishing the customer experience is challenging and an area where the Relentless Advocate can share the VOC. Many of us have had the experience of delayed or canceled flights. Trying to seek the help of an airline rep to rebook is a trying experience. Airlines have been directing travelers to digital channels and chatbots to get additional information, get rerouted, or even rebook travel. Some airlines are taking this a step further and automatically rerouting passengers on any airline that has a similar flight, taking autopilot interaction to a new level. This represents a significant development and, as we have mentioned in this chapter, needs to be viewed through a customer experience and value lens as well as carefully tracking issue management and resolution.

To be customer-obsessed means to understand customer experience across the product life cycle from awareness/discovery to assessment/consideration and then to acquisition, use, and disposal. Relentless Advocates and Dot Connectors ensure alignment across the organization on why and how transformation can enhance customer value, how to achieve it, and how to push forward the methods, tactics, and timelines to do so. Next, we will cover techniques and processes to better assess customer needs, but we will also make an argument that understanding, assessing, and predicting customer needs and wants (there is a difference) should be the primary motivator for any transformation effort.

It's important to note that companies that are customer-obsessed do the following:

- Continually assess and measure customer experience, engagement, and satisfaction.
- Adapt quickly to changing customer needs.
- Retain at-risk customers by assessing needs and competition and offering differentiated experiences.
- Use personalization to deeply engage with customers.
- Understand that fixing a customer-related issue solves that issue for all current and future customers.

Of course, all these efforts are predicated on customer consensus and enabling the efforts of the Relentless Advocate to make sure all groups align on customer prioritization and assessment, while the Dot Connector ensures that the right people are at the table.

Meet Them Where They're At

Understanding customer behavior is an essential job of the Relentless Advocate. After all, companies often develop all kinds of services, communication strategies, and engagement models to assess customer attitudes and actions. What happens, though, when the behavior isn't rational? How do times of stress and anxiety change the way consumers behave? How do these unexpected reactions impact brand perception?

Irrational behavior occurs when consumers engage in an activity that defies logic or expected behavior. For airline passengers, it can be about getting to the gate, waiting in the security line, and forgetting about protocols and procedures in the security line but acting surprised when banned items are confiscated. For patients, it can be during a diagnosis, forgetting vital information about treatment, and focusing on cost and care. For students, it's usually around exam time, through cheating, prioritizing short-term gain without thinking through potential risk and long-term repercussions in getting caught. For retail consumers, irrational behavior often occurs when deciding on the right product, waiting for it to arrive (if delivered), setting it up, and incorporating it into their lives.

What we know for sure is that irrational behavior is often exacerbated during times of macroeconomic or societal stress. Remember the binge buying of toilet paper and hand sanitizer during the pandemic? No one had planned for that. Becoming agile and adaptive, even during times of irrational behavior, is essential to a customer-centric atmosphere.

Nowhere is this more apparent than in relation to waiting in a queue, an activity few people enjoy. Studying the behavior of those waiting, in either a digital or real-world queue, has provided fundamental data on how to provide a less stressful environment. Perhaps not surprisingly, it turns out:

- Unoccupied time feels longer than occupied time. Customers who continue to move forward in some way feel less anxious than those who sit waiting to move in line. The solution: Show the customers their place in line.
- Uncertain waits are longer than known waits. The solution: Giving details about the wait time often provides some level of solace for customers.
- Unexplained waits are longer than known waits. The solution: Give customers a clear explanation of why they are waiting in the queue. That way, customers can assess the value/trade-off of waiting versus trying at another time or by another method.

Companies are trying all sorts of solutions to make sure wait times are manageable and no one is caught in customer service purgatory. AI assistants and chatbots, now the frontline of customer service for routine questions, can actually learn and become better at handling common customer requests. Customers are often offered the option to receive a callback rather than having to wait. Some companies are even exploring DIY online communities, which can provide assistance directly to consumers, thereby steering questions away from customer service. The Relentless Advocate can help map and evaluate any of these potential solutions to meet the different customer segments and experiences.

The fast-food "drive-thru" offers another great example of where customer expectations and behavior can be measured. How long does it take to get through the queue to pay and get your food? Would it have been quicker to park and go into the restaurant to order your food? Can the customer actually understand the voice coming through the speaker? Do they know which window is payment versus food pickup? Are they different? By assessing customer needs and segments, Quick Service Restaurants (QSRs) have been able to deploy different mechanisms to improve and enhance customer experience, including:

- Doubling capacity in the drive-through lanes.
- Personalized and digitized ordering board.
- Mobile ordering and either pick-up or delivery.
- Machine-vision camera to predict demand.
- AI-enabled voice assistance.
- Greater automation from online ordering to touchless pickup.

As we move from human customer service to cost-effective and scalable robotic/AI mechanisms, we run the risk of getting things wrong and failing to address consumer needs. Deploying the Relentless Advocate and Dot Connector to get consensus on different customer segments and where they exist on a spectrum from loving to hating your brand is a good starting point.

Hug Your Customers and Hug Them Well

All companies segment their customer base either implicitly or explicitly. There is a variety of data companies use to develop customer segmentation. Some companies may be tracking customer engagement and entering it into a customer relationship management (CRM) system. In addition, you can conduct focus groups, survey mechanisms, and field experiments, as well as use data from social platforms to develop segments. Personas can be used, which represent interesting customer segments to illustrate and develop stories around customer journeys.

Many organizations use a segmentation technique called RFM, which stands for recency, frequency, and monetization. This is a company-centered view, essentially asking the question, who are our best and most loyal customers? Customer-centric companies, in other words, put themselves in their customers' shoes (see "Case Story: Brooks Running"). That's great if you are a small service provider, because it's relatively easy to know your customers on a personal level. You can identify what provides them with value and offer targeted and specific service. It becomes vastly more challenging if you multiply the number and variety of customers. Suddenly, it's not as easy to keep track of what they might need. What if you need to build out your services to include new products and add to the number of people who work with you? What if you form a corporation with different departments, each with its own policies and agendas? Things can become incredibly complicated and messy. Customer segmentation allows companies to pool different traits and create segments that represent key customer groups.

The Relentless Advocate helps shift the focus from what customer segments provide to the company to how they think of themselves and what they value, then we might be able to understand behavior, perception, and needs. This is done through data collection and analysis, specifically focused on:

- **Demographic data:** Age, gender, ethnicity, income, location.
- **Behavioral data:** Activities, social interactions, purchases, website browsing.
- **Psychographics:** How people perceive the world around them, what motivates and interests them.
- **Attitudinal data:** User satisfaction and preferences.

Follow the Yellow Brick Road

Journey maps are one way companies understand how customers become aware of their products and brands, how they evaluate competing offers, and how they make decisions. After all, not all journeys are the same. When Dorothy set out from Munchkinland with the Scarecrow, Tin Man, and Cowardly Lion, they were all headed toward the same destination – Emerald City – but had different expectations and needs when they got there (heart, brain, courage, a way home). Customer-centric companies recognize the need to develop customer journeys specific to their different customer segments. These different journeys help illustrate the customer's end-to-end experience. However, a journey map goes further in understanding how customers become aware of products and brands, how they evaluate competing offers, how they make decisions, and what drives decision-making.

Companies that are customer-centric obsess over journey mapping, a process designed to consider the different ways customers engage, both digitally and in person, with the company. A physical touchpoint might be a sales associate in a store, while a digital touchpoint could be a direct email or an online AI-based chatbot. Relentless Advocates explain customer centricity through journey maps. A traditional journey map starts with the marketing funnel. It illustrates the movement from awareness to consideration to intent, followed by some type of conversion and then (ideally) loyalty and advocacy. These phases bring up a slew of questions for the Relentless Advocate to engage with others on, including how to increase brand *awareness*. How do consumers *consider* acquiring offerings? What actions constitute *intent* to acquire? How do you efficiently *convert* consumers to customers? The last phase of loyalty might be associated with who joins or signs up for your loyalty program, and status might help designate the degree of loyalty. In many ways, the company is going to be discovering who their Relentless Advocates will be outside the company itself, among their customer base. In addition to supporting the company through continued purchasing, these outside advocates are amenable to discussing the value, benefits, and positive experiences they have had with the company. These are the consumers sharing positive reviews, helping others understand the value of your offerings, or sticking up for your brand when there is negative sentiment. How do you engage effectively with different online segments?

The customer-centric flywheel (see Figure 2.2) developed by Hubspot[1] takes a cyclical approach to moving consumers along the path from strangers to prospects to customers and finally promoters (advocates). The mechanisms associated with moving folks along this path include attraction, engagement, and delight. Rather than a linear path, this path is circular because advocates or promoters influence the next set of strangers into the flywheel.

Consider, for example, someone making a long-awaited purchase from a brand they have researched and come to admire. They unbox the product, capture photos, and share their excitement on social platforms, tagging the brand. Others see the posts, comment, and

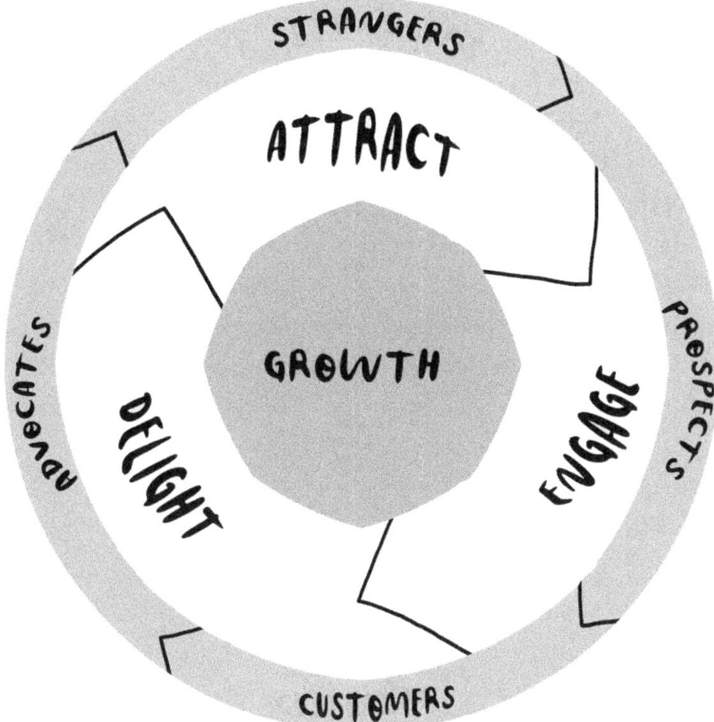

Figure 2.2 The reinforcement loop from strangers to advocates.

share. All of a sudden, there is now a group of delighted promoters and advocates.

But what happens when the experience doesn't go as planned? Perhaps the product arrived late, didn't perform as expected, or customer service was slow to respond and did not provide any real value. Suddenly, those same customers can turn into detractors and the positive sentiment turns dark as negative comments about your brand, product and service accelerate across social platforms. Do you respond with a sincere apology and offer something of value, like a replacement or credit toward a future purchase? Will that be sufficient to bring them back into the flywheel?

To satisfy changing customer expectations and provide a consistent, unique customer experience, companies need to be ready for the unexpected. Winston Churchill once said, "Never let a good crisis go to waste." This was on full display during COVID-19. The pandemic provided a stress test to gauge how companies could implement rapid transformation in service, customer expectations, and transformation. Companies rose to the occasion because they had no choice. Whether it was digital ordering and delivery, telemedicine or remote learning, organizations needed to transform to provide a successful customer experience. The questions: Without that sense of urgency, will companies still continue to transform to provide the digital experiences that consumers now expect? Will those experiences continue to develop loyalty?

Loyalty Is Good and Advocacy Is Great

How do you reward your most loyal customers? Do you provide some sort of loyalty program, incentivizing customers with everything from free products (food, beauty products) to free/upgraded travel and hotel stays? Your Relentless Advocate makes sure the organization understands the customer perspective when it comes to loyalty, including differentiated products, services, and experiences that create "stickiness" (retention) for consumer segments. Do consumers "buy to play" (paying a fee or subscription for access to exclusive benefits and rewards) or "spend to play" (earn rewards through spending money with the brand). Oftentimes, companies see these programs as marketing initiatives to spur loyalty, but what's the value we get in providing this? The Relentless Advocate changes collective thinking to help the organization assess the customer value in choosing and being loyal to one program over another. In some cases, these programs can provide customers with access to differentiated services like promotions, exclusive deals, or free shipping. It might even offer customers access to their own data, such as orders, product identification, and cost, providing the customers with a way to easily digest their purchase history.

Invite Them to Fall in Love with You

Sometimes, of course, things go wrong, and the customer experience doesn't live up to its promise. When that happens, we run the risk of losing customers aka customer churn. Retaining at-risk customers then becomes an additional challenge. Understanding how and where to apologize – or even make some kind of restitution – is another layer in creating customer loyalty.

Customer loyalty certainly helps if your business is the "only game in town." After all, if you want to stream Marvel movies, you'll need to subscribe to Disney+. If you're looking to vacation in a town serviced by only one airline, you know what company you're going to use. Other companies often lock in their customers through their loyalty programs, encouraging customers to maintain or increase their status ("platinum" or "elite") and add points or miles, which can then be used toward future purchases, and sometimes loyalty is dictated by consumer lock-in. If your entire family uses iPhones, you probably won't be running to get an Android device, even when your contract is up.

Our Relentless Advocate also needs to communicate the customer's experience in terms that everyone in the company can understand and assess. Experience is dictated by how our company engages with the customer during every stage of the buying journey. Consider the difference between an evolution versus a revolution. Amazon 1-Click – where members who have entered their credit card information simply hit a button to order or pay – might be considered an evolution or a logical extension of an existing tool for the world's largest e-commerce provider. This function provides greater ease and convenience for seamless transactions. You could also consider an evolution when restaurants add digital ordering. Patrons can scan a barcode to access a menu and order effortlessly from their mobile platforms.

A revolution represents the radical transformation from the norm. Conceived as a communication device, the iPhone soon sparked the imagination of developers interested in seeing what else the phone could accomplish. As mobile commerce exploded, Apple understood that its customers would be willing to make purchases from their phones. The iPhone, in other words, is a mobile computer with sensors that just so happen can also be used to call someone. That means you can store credit cards (even the Apple-branded credit card) and mobile payment services like iPay to pay for goods. This is a revolution since it represents a radical change in use and a fundamental change in how people view a product or service. Another revolution is Tesla bypassing the traditional dealership model and allowing users to order and purchase a car online.

Ultimately, customers are the reason you are in business. You should be obsessed with providing value, resolving issues, and delivering unique experiences for those customers. The Relentless Advocate and Dot Connector can help focus your understanding of your customer, whether they are fiercely loyal or at risk or somewhere in between. They can help you deliver what the customer expects and values most. They can, in other words, help defeat the Scatterbrain Monster. This, in turn, can help turn your customer into something even more valuable in the long run – a loyal advocate for your business.

Key Takeaways

1. Slaying the Scatterbrain Monster requires a unified vision on customer value, experience and becoming truly customer-centric.
2. Your Relentless Advocate shares the vision with the groups and departments that the Dot Connector brings together.
3. Continually sharing customer stories puts customers first when going through transformations.
4. AI implementation needs to hold up to a customer value lens – will the value outweigh any of the potential risks?

Case Story: Brooks Running

Focus on What Matters

The "perfect run" is an ideal, something all runners strive to achieve. It symbolizes running without pain, achieving a personal goal, communing with nature, feeling your stride, and so on. This perfect run might involve running with friends (like a running club) or enjoying the peace of a solo run. Whether on race day, a short jog, or a distance-timed run, runners count on their gear to help them achieve it. And nothing plays a larger part in helping runners achieve their perfect run than their most important running tool: the shoes. A footwear company that strives to inspire everyone to run and be active is *customer-focused*. A company that incorporates that ideal and drives it through every facet of the organization? That company is truly *customer-centric*.

Brooks Running, one of the most customer-centric companies in the industry, has been focused on the specialty footwear market for more than 100 years. Originally started in a small factory in Philadelphia, making bath and ballet shoes, Brooks was initially driven by a goal to create "specialized gear for a specialized activity." After forays in the 1930s and 1940s into other kinds of sports footwear, like baseball and football cleats, everything changed for the company because of the 1972 Munich Olympics. There, US runner and Yale graduate Frank Shorter won the gold medal in the marathon, propelling widespread interest in running as an activity. Brooks turned its focus to the running market, rolling out innovative and iconic shoe designs, like the Vantage, the Huger GT, the Kinetic Wedge, and the Beast.

Running Away from a Fragmented Market

During the time Brooks was busy creating innovative running footwear, running as an activity continued to grow in popularity around the world. Many aspiring and well-known athletes incorporated running into their training or as a central component of their exercise regimen. Muhammad Ali, the legendary boxer, was known to incorporate distance running as part of his workout regimen to build endurance and mental fortitude. Running clubs, local races, and track-and-field activities started popping up everywhere. And as more individuals got hooked on running, the specialty footwear space fragmented with new brands entering the market, such as Nike, New Balance, Saucony, and Mizuno. Some of these were pure-play running shoe and apparel companies, while others branched out into all different kinds of sporting activities.

During this period, Brooks also branched out into different athletic products such as tennis shoes to capture the growing popularity of the sport in the 1980s. It was difficult for the company to compete in different and crowded markets. As Brooks expanded into new product lines, trying to compete with different players, Brooks experienced issues trying to keep up with the competition, consumers' expectations, and focusing on what was important.

During this time, Jim Weber, CEO of Brooks from 2001 to 2024, helped steer the company through near bankruptcy into a phase of reduced product spread and laser-like focus on performance running. Prior to when Jim came in there had been four CEOs in two years, and Brooks had filed for Chapter 11. Weber helped orchestrate a decision, in other words, to stop being mediocre at many things and instead become excellent at one thing. Weber detailed these developments in his book *Running with Purpose*.

Organizational Focus on the Runner

In 2023, Brooks hit $1.2 billion in sales, a greater than 5% increase globally from the previous year. Much of that growth came in North America, where the company continues to take in about 80% of its total revenue. A large part of this success can be attributed to Brooks focusing on customer centricity, a practice that is embedded into the culture of the company and one of its core principles. How, then, is this reflected in operating practices? Several key ways:

- In **hiring,** Brooks makes sure new employees have a customer-first mentality and understand the importance of being customer-centric.

- In **leadership**, across the organization, Brooks demonstrates and incentivizes customer-centered and collaborative initiatives.
- Brooks always **strives** to do better. A "champion heart" means never being complacent. This ethos pushes Brooks' employees to always outdo themselves to continue to win with the customer.

Perhaps the greatest reflection is in Brooks' culture, which embodies the runner and literally puts Brooks' employees in the shoes of their customers. This includes:

- Cultural strength surveys that reflect employees' views on being connected to runners and how products meet customer needs.
- The 1st Thursday Run/Walk sponsored by departments and open to all employees to collectively engage in the activity the company promotes.
- Volunteering, including run-themed events.
- Symposiums focused on the "Future of Running."

The Digitized Run

Like so many other sports, running has become increasingly digitized. Companies use digital manufacturing processes to 3D print uppers and insoles and embed sensors into shoes to record running data. Companies have developed unique digital experiences for their customer base, like community-based running clubs. Digital models can show wear patterns in soles, runner gait analysis, and strike pattern information to enable better fit, comfort, and performance. In addition, the buying process has evolved alongside other retail operations to offer different shopping modalities. Physical *and* online retail channels are necessary to meet the needs of different customers in finding, assessing, comparing, and acquiring top-quality running shoes. Two factors really accelerated the push toward digital. One, the growing younger audience is more engaged in social media for their shopping experience. Two, COVID-19 accelerated the reliance on digital for finding, virtual fitting, reviewing, and receiving shoes.

Advocacy for the Runner

As one of the drivers behind the digital innovation programs at Brooks, Kristl Date-Dopps focuses her time and attention on making sure the company's programs reflect the primary core value of Brooks – a focus on inspiring everyone to run and be active. Kristl's background in partner management and digital product development helps her and the internal teams she works with understand the challenge and needs to build customer centricity. They are constantly surveying, interviewing, and researching Brooks' customers as well as competitors' customers to understand the customer journey. The different sequences or needs and engagement as runners learn about the company, investigate the various product lines, acquire particular items, and eventually wear out and dispose of these products. Such a full-cycle understanding helps Kristl and the teams develop an intimate understanding of what customers and prospective customers value, their pain points, and how they want to engage and their expectations of the Brooks brand. Understanding a unified experience for all stakeholders led to the development of Gurus, which are associates who are advocates for specialty running retailers.

As Brooks' leader of the IT department, Kathlyn Jones has a deep understanding of how applications, platforms, and technical projects get developed, adopted, and add value to the core business. While Kristl develops new digital tools and experiences for Brooks, Kathlyn makes sure that these new plans fit within the company's capabilities. She ensures that the company has adequate resources to see them through to fruition. However, Kathlyn and her team struggle with how to convey brand value and messaging in the right way to the community. The plethora of digital connection points and mediums provides a challenge on the best mechanism to engage with consumers on their needs and collect data to make science-based decisions.

Both Kristl and Kathlyn reflect the characteristics of the Relentless Advocate, use a lens of customer advocacy, and a focus on customer value as a decision criteria, which they then use to motivate their teams, assess future projects, and drive customer-centric initiatives.

Running in Different Directions

Consumers, like shoes, are not one-size-fits-all. Their needs change over time. Trends matter. Sometimes, changes occur based on consumer preference patterns. (Remember when running barefoot was a thing?) Runners, not surprisingly, share information freely on forums and blogs, but especially within product reviews. They offer detailed information about what they like or do not like about a shoe, offering opinions about everything from fit to wear to even customer service and warranty information. More than ever before, the consumer has substantial information about a product prior to moving forward with a purchase.

Many runners, considering the switch to Brooks, may rely heavily on such information. After all, the slightest variation in the shoe design may result in an uncomfortable run or, at worst, blisters, shin splints, or even plantar fasciitis. More often than not, such issues arise only after several runs. Imagine getting ready for a race and having that one nagging issue with your shoe fit result in a poor time or even dropping out of the race because of pain. Runners often scour through reviews looking for information that resonates with their experience. They look for similarities to themselves in terms of height, weight, arches, foot width, strike patterns, pronation, etc. This information is critical to assess and understand if these "unbiased" reviews describe issues important to them. Brooks management understands that they can provide mechanisms for prospective buyers to ease their fears and allow them to try the footwear to make sure it's the right shoe for them. Brooks provides prospective buyers more confidence in their purchase by encouraging them to give their footwear a real-world trial. If it doesn't meet the runner's satisfaction, the Brooks Run Happy Promise guarantees a 90-day return policy. Once again, they put the runner first in ensuring that their expectations are met.

Focus on the Runner and the Run

So, how do you satisfy different runners with varying wants and needs? Brooks' approach is to collect data on their runners and use those analytics within internal labs. The RunSight Lab, which dives deep into both qualitative and quantitative insights about a runner's motivation, hurdles, and pain points, helps to drive new product creation, optimization, and new marketing concepts that empower teams to make data-driven decisions. The other is the Run Research Lab, which explores the science of the run (performance data and biomechanics) to unlock ways to enable the runner to run further, faster, longer, and injury-free.

Biomechanics and runner-based personalization require greater levels of performance data to analyze. The findings bring about innovative new tools and capabilities like Shoe Finder, which helps runners find the right shoe for them based on several criteria grounded in science. In addition, a data-oriented approach can be applied to emotion around running. For example, how does someone feel after a run? What contributes to these emotions? Hypothesis testing is critical to identify and innovate around friction points for runners.

Still, how does an organization manage data collection effectively in an era where there is little trust and privacy infringement happening almost weekly? For Brooks, this requires taking the idea of data stewardship seriously, following consent management and policies focused on customer protections. Such protections include:

- Reconsenting with consumers when launching new initiatives like the Brooks Run Club.
- Involving the legal team and ensuring transparency as well as research into "value" that is provided back to the runner.
- Grounding initiatives in science, making it easier to get behind product direction.

Focusing on consumer protection is critical for Brooks in its quest to garner and sustain trust with the runner. Often, runners need help interpreting data. So, by turning the collection of data into something that benefits the runner, the information becomes value-added and actionable. Management at Brooks understands that there will be a willingness to provide data if value is apparent and understood.

Digital Programs to Reinforce Customer Centricity

Top down at Brooks, all employees approach decisions by putting the runners at the center of everything they do. Managers stress that every job a person has ties back in some way to the runner. To enable such a holistic view, Brooks went through digitization and process configuration across departments, while never losing sight of the end goal – providing greater value for the runner. This transformation includes:

- Digitization of supply chain execution – driving high levels of partner satisfaction.
- Digital fitting – providing a digital proxy for in-store shoe fitting to try and reduce return volumes.
- Digitization and integration of customer touchpoints to enable omnichannel experience management.

Perhaps the most important facet of their transformation involves right-sizing, given the market opportunity. Brooks is looking to differentiate themselves, not only through innovative products but also through continued focus on customer centricity. After all, greater complexity often results in larger issues, like being able to successfully capitalize on consumer trends, which we discussed in the previous chapter. By focusing on simplification, the company can make sure they don't have lines of business that are competing for resources, market attention, retail partnership development, etc.

When it comes to adopting new digital processes and applications, there will always be people who resist, saying, "This is what I do." Brooks' choosing to have less organizational hierarchy, even through rapid growth, helps employees see the rationale and justification associated with transformation. Providing this line of sight to customer centricity, it becomes easier to manage change and bring people on board to serve the runner better. Departments, employees, and managers must align on the goal and a set of tasks in order to achieve a project successfully. When faced with challenges associated with disagreement on process, Brooks focuses on what they like to call "assume positive intent." In other words, even if you disagree with others, do not take it personally, and assume that they are raising a concern or issue to be constructive and that the intent was to put the runner first. As Kathlyn says, "Employees understand that they need to align on the path and set of tasks and march to the same destination." A shared and common goal of the customer's needs should be at the heart of all efforts.

Key Takeaways from Kristl and Kathlyn's Journey

- Centering on the runner and enabling the perfect run kept the focus squarely on customers and prospective customers.
- Reducing complexity and eliminating conflicts between competing lines ensured that digital transformation always reflected what matters to the customer.
- A clear customer-centric model removed ambiguity: if an initiative doesn't add value for customers, it isn't pursued.
- These core principles enable deliberate expansion and sustained growth.
- As consumers use running shoes for walking, commuting, and work, Brooks is well-positioned to develop new models and capture new audiences.

Try This: The Customer Echo Chamber

The Scatterbrain Monster thrives when teams lose sight of what truly matters. To stay anchored, bring the customer into the room every day.

Step 1: Invite the Customer

For the next 30 days, spend 10 minutes a day with your team reading raw customer verbatims out loud. No slides. No dashboards. Just voices.

Step 2: Friends and Family Filter

End each session by asking:

> "If this were our family or friend, would we be OK with this experience?"

Step 3: Transcribe Using AI

Use Gen AI to transcribe and summarize the conversation. Do the key themes align with what your customers are really saying?

Turn down the noise, tune into the customer. This daily habit helps your team stay grounded in what matters most.

Chapter 3

Know Thy Mess

"Transformation starts with a radical commitment to the truth—shared facts are the foundation of awareness, acceptance, and action."

—Steve Dennis, Author of *Remarkable Retail*

Consider that the average large-scale enterprise operation wastes at least 20–30% of its annual IT budget on complexity-related inefficiencies.[1] In addition, in a recent McKinsey study, they found that IT complexity can reduce a company's digital transformation ROI by up to 40%.[2] So, not only are companies wasting money on inefficient systems, but also they are not realizing expectations associated with transformational efforts. This is not an outlier. Gartner estimates that 80% of companies will fail to realize full digital value due to complexity in their IT landscape.[3]

To make matters worse, your employees are wasting not just money but also time trying to navigate these ancient systems. According to Forrester Research, employees lose up to 30% of their work week dealing with inefficient or outdated IT systems.[4] In a 5,000-person company, that's 60K hours/week or over 3M hours/year. It's like a tailor having to untangle a giant ball of thread every morning before they even start sewing.

The previous two chapters focused on understanding and assessing trends in transformation efforts. We discussed how to stay focused on the only driver that ultimately matters: adding customer value. For this to occur, however, companies – particularly large-scale legacy operations – need to pay equal attention to a rampant and growing problem: increasing levels of unnecessary complexity within their own systems. After all, the greater the number of organizational applications, processes, and systems, the greater the challenge when it comes to transformation. The probability of screwing something up – potentially something critical – escalates with greater levels of complexity. You might ask yourself, how did things get so out of control?

Of course, most companies didn't start as overly complex places. Over time, though, these companies often grow and add new processes and systems into their operations. They acquire competitors and divest divisions, bringing in new people while letting others go. Such actions, while natural to an organization's evolution, also tend to leave a trail of legacy components, or what amounts to a technical and resource debt. Maybe an acquired company was brought in with its own purpose-built applications and processes, but had the time and effort to deal with the old systems after the new employees were on-boarded and migrated to different systems. Such redundant systems and applications might even still be in operation, despite only a fraction of the previous user base. Often companies only think about the impact of complexity when it's absolutely required not as a continual change process. If you are addressing complexity only in a dire or urgent situation, it can be incredibly disruptive.

As this cycle continues, the technical and resource debt continues to grow, particularly if no time or energy is spent addressing the cluttered mess. Each process needs a process owner. Each application needs service and support! Each database needs to be integrated and maintained! Your once streamlined operation has been overtaken by the Hairy Monster!

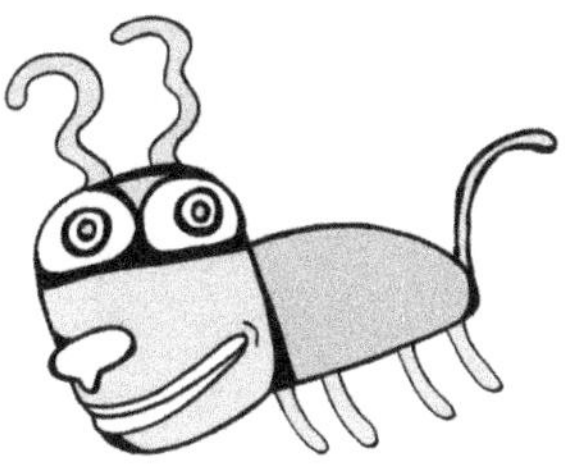

The Tangled Truth

The Hairy Monster thrives on complexity, confusion, and clutter, especially in legacy organizations. It grows and becomes more emboldened through neglect and a failure to prioritize. It's composed of the legacy applications, outdated process flows, and seldom-used infrastructure that have become intertwined and inexplicably connected.

Over time, as an organization grows, diversifies, adds on capability, and divests noncore systems, it becomes more and more difficult to tackle the Hairy Monster. The Hairy Monster thrives in environments where there is application overload – aka app fatigue – where inefficient workflows, increased security risks, and confusion among employees lead to decreased productivity.

What's more, the Hairy Monster feeds off employees' habitual or even emotional attachments to particular applications or services. Decommissioning the application might result in a sense of loss, analogous to their own place in the organization or might require employees to learn a new process or new skills.

"If it ain't broke, don't fix it" is the catchphrase of the Hairy Monster, eager to let employees live with unnecessary complexity and redundant operations. For effective transformation to begin, it's critical to understand why this happens to avoid replicating it in the future. Developing good hygiene practices will keep operations lean and mean, but also productive and secure.

The Time to Get Ready Was Yesterday

AI transformation brings on a set of challenges and is particularly tricky for companies that are still dealing with many of the monster transformations we discuss, especially the Hairy Monster. One of the reasons we are writing this book is trying to develop more transformative capacity for all organizations prior to potentially the most disruptive transformation, which is represented by the AI-enabled organization.

Why is AI transformation so tricky? Well, there are several reasons:

- Data issues include quality, availability, privacy, integration, etc.
- Technical challenges associated with legacy IT infrastructure.

- Ethical considerations associated with bias.
- Job uncertainty. Will AI agents displace workers or render them ineffective by removing the processes that they manage? It's a tough question but companies need to be transparent and authentic (see Chapter 5) associated with their response.

In the age of AI, where transformation often requires significant reorganization and systemic changes, the Hairy Monster can overwhelm even the most capable. To defeat it, two monster slayers are essential: the Investigator and the Storyteller. These folks work together to uncover and simplify the tangled mess created by outdated processes, bloated systems, and confused priorities. The Investigator reveals how and why the organization got into this state as well as how to unravel layers of complexity to identify redundancies, while the Storyteller helps employees understand the path forward, creating a vision that inspires and unites. Together, they set the foundation through observation and assessment.

The Hairy Monster Slayers

To defeat the Hairy Monster, the Investigator must first dig deep to uncover the root causes of complexity, asking hard questions, analyzing data, and revealing the nature of the issues that hold back the organization. They use critical thinking and reasoning to try to find out why a situation exists, who is impacted, and who can help to build a plan to reduce complexity. The Investigator helps the company understand the interdependencies between existing components, whether we're talking about a cloud storage service, a software program, or a large-scale tech stack, and how streamlining operations via consolidation, decommission, or migration can be a positive step in the right direction.

Observation – The Investigator is relentless in the pursuit of clarity, helping move from reactive "repair" mode to proactive "prepare" mode. The Investigator is adept at root cause analysis, utilizing the "5 Whys" technique, designed by Taiichi Ohno, the architect of the Toyota Production System, to uncover cause and effect relationships and enhance operational efficiency. Let's say the Investigator discovers multiple redundant systems. The goal now is to ask the "whys" of how the problem got there and then work toward countermeasures.

- Why do we have these redundancies? Over the course of many years, we developed largely autonomous divisions.
- Why did we develop autonomous divisions? We needed to develop greater agility.
- Why did we need more agility? We needed to compete with more nimble companies.
- Why did we have to be more competitive? Market conditions allowed new companies to enter the space and compete.
- Why did markets open up? Easing of regulations, data portability, and customer adoption created market accessibility.

The Five Whys, in other words, emphasize the importance of understanding.

In addition, the Investigator uncovers the extent of the situation. How many redundant systems exist? How many components are serving a relatively small contingent of the employee base? Can we measure the costs-to-maintain versus the benefits delivered? Why are certain teams, departments, or employees resistant to changing over to centralized processes? What is expendable versus what is critical?

When it comes to taking stock of complexity and redundancy, the Investigator must focus on:

- **Decommissioning applications:** Identifying redundant systems and processes.
- **Assessing context:** Understanding why these systems were implemented and whether they are still relevant.
- **Mitigating resistance:** Anticipating who will resist changes and developing strategies to engage them.

While the Investigator uncovers truths, the Storyteller ensures those insights are understandable, actionable, and inspiring. Storytelling is the bridge between observation and transformation – it is the process by which dry facts are woven into a compelling narrative that unites the employees and drives action. Storytellers, in other words, clarify situations and contexts so that everyone is discussing the same challenges. They need to make sure there is a common, baseline understanding of the situation.

Directives are actionable; storytelling is inspiring. Getting everyone to understand the history, challenges, and potential future for the transformed organization is not an easy task. Time and time again, we've seen that employees want to be a part of any transformation effort rather than have that transformation thrust upon them. They want to be a part of the story. Stories can be powerful communication tools that bring in characters, actions, aspirations, and results. They can use visual sources, such as infographics and images, to offer an idea of what a transformed future might look like. That's the power of the Storyteller: a keen ability to speak to a diverse audience in language and images, not just for communication, but a shared understanding and mechanism for assessment.

The Storyteller relies on many techniques to communicate, including grounding mechanisms that resonate with employees. Two of these mechanisms are objectives and key results (OKRs), which are used as a goal-setting measure, and key performance indicators (KPI), which track goal performance. The Storyteller can use OKRs to create alignment and encourage engagement but also build a bridge between quarterly goals and the overall transformation efforts. Often, information is shared within an organization but not effectively processed. Effective storytelling thus not only focuses on understanding but also on assessment and perception. Every good story has a good villain, which is our Hairy Monster. Stories can be repeated and build consistent messaging that becomes a single source of truth.

Additionally, the Storyteller has a unique capability of crafting stories in a collaborative manner. Storytelling takes information from the Investigator, including complexity and redundancy, to present a shared vision for a more agile company, adept at creating customer value and retaining at-risk customers, while also increasing market share.

What's Hiding Behind the Curtain

Before we begin, perhaps a little delineation is needed. We refer to a component as something that enables the business to function. This could be a service that is not directly visible to the user and often runs in the background. An example would be a cloud storage service allowing users to store files online. It could also refer to a process that represents a sequence of steps an employee uses to complete a task. Business processes might focus on operational, support, management, or strategies. An example is a customer support process. Lastly, it might also refer to an application that is a software program used to complete a specific task. Another term we refer to is a *tech stack*, which is a set of technologies used to develop an application, including programming languages, frameworks, databases, front-end and back-end tools, and application programming interfaces (APIs). For the purposes of this chapter, these are all part of organizational complexity and need to be addressed for transformation to succeed.

Transformations stall and fail to meet expectations when companies don't have a realistic picture of what's embedded in components used by a division or group. In addition to these data-centric components, companies are often equally burdened by a barrage of processes, including regulatory procedures and compliance that might be different from one division or group to another. Multiple instantiations of similar processes or applications might be modified for a particular group's needs. Maybe it's just that they need to comply with regional or country-based policy or that the nature of the work they do mandates an auditing process. The Investigator plays a crucial role in looking behind the curtain and identifying the different processes in use, why they are used, and the interdependencies between them – essentially, the what, why, and so what associated with process complexity.

The Investigator asks:

- What inefficiencies exist, and why?
- What's redundant and can be reduced and shared?
- What hidden costs or opportunities result from our complexity?
- How can we prevent this from happening in the future?

The Investigator also has a firm grasp on how the organization is situated when it comes to dealing with process complexity and its impact on transformation. We have found that organizational efforts generally fall into four quadrants (see Figure 3.1).

Pants on Fire is always urgent and simply scratching the surface in terms of investigation. Hero Mode is always urgent but doing a deep dive into investigating the issues. Then there is intentional change, but addressing only the visible, easy-to-fix issues (cosmetic). Efforts that are intentional or strategic and get to the root cause fall into the Always On Transformation quadrant.

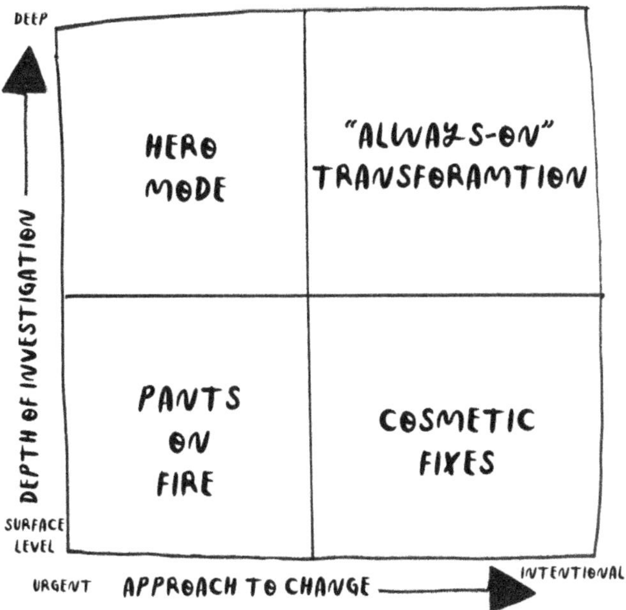

Figure 3.1 Four quadrants of organization efforts.

Developing a Complex

Of course, it's not just about spotting the complexity in your organization. It's also about understanding how it occurred in the first place and how to address it. The Investigator takes a holistic approach, considering how a variety of factors often contribute to excess complexity. Rather than linear thinking – this happened and then this happened and then this happened – the Investigator understands how interdependent and interconnected systems often produce complexity when working in an ambiguous and volatile environment. The Storyteller helps convey the story behind complexity to try to present the same patterns of behavior that led to this situation in the first place. This includes the story of how interactions of employees and components lead to new patterns of unpredictable behavior (emergence), how small changes can lead to oversized outcomes complicating unpredictability (nonlinearity), and how organizations can respond to disruption and changing conditions through self-organization.

In *The Role of Complexity Theory as a Foundation for Taking a Systems Approach in Your Organization*,[5] Jonathon Westover, author and professor of organizational leadership, explains that there are several considerations for why organizations can become complex. Typically, Westerover says, complexity relates to:

- **Size of the organization:** Large organizations with multiple layers of management, divisions, and groups often complicate communication and organizational efficiency. The larger and more diverse the company, the greater the need for effective coordination.

- **Regulatory environment:** Most companies need to comply with a myriad of different regulations, from consumer protections to privacy regulations to workplace safety. The additional demands often result in organizations applying sets of safeguards and protocols to make sure there is compliance but also adding further layers of complexity.

- **Technologies:** This is the primary factor related to increased complexity, which includes cybersecurity, integration points, access and permissions, version releases, etc.

- **Novel and dynamic situations:** This could include the impact of global events like the pandemic or new work environments (remote and hybrid work). These shifts were uncharted territory for many organizations and left them with unclear expectations and arrangements.

Clear the Clutter

One way to avoid the Hairy Monster becoming a problem is to take stock of your systems on a regular basis. In other words, do some spring cleaning. Getting rid of clutter and removing things you don't use or need that simply take up valuable space can be liberating. One interviewee referred to the clutter as "a boat anchor dragging the ship to a stop." Companies need to take the same approach, albeit carefully. Here, we are talking about backend systems, but of course, this cleaning could also apply to physical and digital workspaces. While some people can successfully operate in a cluttered environment, others find it stressful and anxiety-producing. Imagine onboarding a new employee or bringing in a new partner. They need to be introduced to a patchwork of different procedures, applications, and systems. How much time and effort will they spend to become familiar with these systems (adoption)? What are the integration issues so that you are not creating redundancies in operation? How much time will they invest in these systems, knowing that the organization is in transformation to streamline processes and evaluate applications – will they just need to learn new systems next quarter? Not only is operating in such an environment a poor experience, but it can also lead to wasted time and resource allocation as users try to navigate their way through the mess. Here, the Investigator and Storyteller can help mitigate resistance by recognizing who will be impacted by the cleaning and proactively engaging them.

Prior to removing any digital processes or services, a spring cleaning should include the following:

- **Inventory assessment:** Assess all the different applications and services in operation. Who uses them and for what purpose? Understanding a service in terms of data flows is necessary to understand upstream and downstream systems that might be impacted or affected by its removal.

- **Ownership:** Who owns a process, service, or application? How long have they had ownership? Who do they report to, and how is the component serviced and funded? Do all systems need to be serviced and maintained?
- **Updates and costs:** How often do systems need to be updated? What are the associated costs? Are they offering sufficient added value, relative to the cost?
- **Benefit and use:** What is the derived benefit from the component or system? How often is it used – daily, weekly, monthly?

Removing any components offers its own risks. Most organizations have an intricate set of relationships and dependencies. When one component goes away, what takes its place? Will decommissioning an application impact other systems or departments? As organizations grow, the challenges associated with operational inefficiencies often result in a renewed need for streamlined decision-making, innovation, and a focus on work satisfaction and employee engagement. Spring cleaning is where complexity is tackled head-on.

How Ready Are You?

Maturity models offer an effective way for companies to assess and measure their abilities in various areas. When it comes to transformation, these models use a set of predefined criteria to evaluate a company's current state of development. This can include a Capability Maturity Model (CMM), a business process maturity model (BPMM), or a digital maturity model (DMM).

As the name implies, a DMM shows the digital maturity of the organization across different dimensions. These might include leadership, innovation, employee competency, collaboration, culture, and systems integration. Most DMMs show phases from nascent to emergent to advanced. Many use numerical scales to measure the levels so that an organization can determine a current score and a goal of where they would like to be. This allows multiple groups from across the organization to participate, giving management an aggregate "crowdsourced" score of where folks perceive the company currently is across these dimensions. In addition, the score also helps illustrate what areas still need work and what kinds of resources will be necessary to get there.

A maturity model can also show how a company might compare to the competition. The Investigator gathers insights from different divisions on:

- **Capabilities:** What can the organization do now?
- **Timelines:** How long will transformation realistically take?
- **Resources:** What tools, funding, and personnel are required?
- **Competencies:** Where do skill gaps exist, especially for AI integration?
- **Peer group assessment:** How does the organization stack up against industry benchmarks?

Most consulting companies have maturity assessments and frameworks. While they are fine, the problem is that maturity models are often not specific to your organization or industry. They do not take into consideration your history, struggles, or ongoing projects, as they need to be used as a tool but have to be customized for your unique experience and journey. The Investigator and Storyteller can develop and adapt maturity models specific to your organization. This helps create a shared vision for what needs to be done to achieve your transformation goal.

Key Takeaways

1. Slaying the Hairy Monster requires cutting through complexity and confusion to create clarity and focus.
2. The Investigator reveals the truth, while the Storyteller simplifies it into a motivating narrative.
3. Practice storytelling that is not only immersive and engaging but also helps with consensus around a shared vision of what should be done.
4. By observing and assessing before acting, organizations can move confidently into transformation, ready for the reconfiguration that AI demands.

Case Story: JELD-WEN

A Door to the Future, a Window to the Past

Founded by Richard Wendt in 1960, JELD-WEN began as a small millwork plant with 15 employees in Klamath Falls, Oregon. Wendt took an opportunity in the post-WWII housing boom, making quality windows and doors. Over the next few decades, the company grew through strategic acquisitions and expansion outside the United States, including new operations in Canada and Europe, along with a consistent dedication to innovative practices.

In 2011, during the housing downturn, JELD-WEN underwent recapitalization and became a publicly traded company in 2017. In the subsequent 10-year period, the company went through a series of leadership changes for a variety of reasons including cultural and structural shifts and changes in business strategy. The current CEO, Bill Christensen, came on in 2022 and is focused on rebuilding their strategy focusing on the right balance between growth and operational efficiency with the goal to recapture market share.

Today, the building products manufacturer for the residential and commercial sectors has moved its global headquarters to North Carolina and operates in 14 countries with more than 16,000 employees. JELD-WEN's focus on global distribution, diversity in their product line, innovative design and construction, and a broad price point range (from entry level to premium luxury) allows them the ability to compete against well-known manufacturers, as well as regional players. In addition, their commitment to innovation and sustainability has garnered them both consumer and construction industry appeal, emphasizing sustainable products and manufacturing processes.

Growth Through Acquisition

Companies typically make acquisitions for a variety of reasons: Sometimes, it's about entry into a new market. Often acquiring a company is a cheaper and faster way to bring in talent and add competencies rather than by trying to grow those internally. An acquisition might even be about taking a potential competitor out of the market.

From 2015–2020, JELD-WEN made a series of strategic acquisitions including LaCantina Doors in 2015 and Domoferm and American Building Supply in 2018. They folded much of the acquired structure and operations into the parent company; however, digital infrastructure remained largely intact. On the plus side, this allowed the acquired company to retain existing systems avoiding the burden associated with integration, replacement, training, and transference of maintenance and support contracts. This provided efficiency and speed of integration; however, because of redundant systems, it led to unused capacity and challenges associated with scale. In addition, customers had direct relationships with plants, which created significant inefficiencies in the supply chain.

The other challenge is that this practice made driving consensus around a unified strategy vastly more difficult. That's problematic when it comes to issues associated with transformation, where the underlying task at hand is often to unify a broad range of systems, processes, and data flows. JELD-WEN facilitated exercises with the outcome being an optimized technology stack, which is essentially the tools, databases, and applications needed to create digital products and services. In taming the Hairy Monster, around process complexity, several issues emerged including:

- Internal fears on what was proposed; "why would we try that?"
- Oversimplification of what was required in a manufacturing environment with high variability and configuration needed.
- Vendor templates that did not work.
- IT-led initiatives that became a recipe for disaster; right stakeholders were not involved and not aligned.
- Wide disparity in data definitions; fragmentation from data both operationally and commercially.

During this time, JELD-WEN was expanding into new markets, meeting demand, and innovating in sustainable manufacturing. However, process complexity made it challenging for the organization to look at capacity planning and organizational efficiency holistically. To accelerate transformation and scale new digital processes and systems, JELD-WEN would need to take a deep dive into system redundancy and utilization.

Matt Meier started at JELD-WEN in 2024 to help navigate a transformation impacting the culture, commercial sales, and operations of the organization. One of the first things Matt needed to do was assess any previous efforts to right-size the organization when it came to technology infrastructure. He took a surgical approach to understand what was available, what capability JELD-WEN was looking to deliver, what transformation initiatives align to those outcomes, and then what could be accomplished.

Based on previous experience, he understood that integrating horizontally acquired businesses takes time, effort, and a plan to successfully incorporate and align technical systems. Matt faced a daunting question: with dozens of critical systems covering manufacturing, finance, and fulfillment, how does one effectively integrate and decommission legacy systems, migrate processes, and train employees while remaining operationally efficient and keeping everyone onboard? Matt likes to say that 95% of any transformation is a people challenge rather than a technical one. To start, Matt needed to build consensus on the process and strategy and drive results using previous organization's playbooks, dusting them off and modifying them to make them applicable to JELD-WEN's transformation.

Looking Through the Window

With a background in manufacturing, IT, and digital delivery, Matt has experience working at GM, Rolls-Royce, and Whirlpool to Driven Brands, an auto services conglomerate. Matt was drawn to the challenge of helping this respected manufacturer assess, deploy, and scale new digital processes and systems to transform, enabling new levels of operational efficiency, delivering unique capabilities, and providing innovative digital experiences.

JELD-WEN's model of "acquire and leave in place" accelerated value but resulted in infrastructure complexity complicating strategic planning and execution. Every acquired entity was essentially running as its own business. Matt had a sense of the issue coming into the role but was unaware of the extent until he started interviewing folks across the extended organization. "People can tell you how cold the water is," he recalls, "but you will never fully know until you jump in." According to Matt, legacy infrastructure is something to be investigated, understood, and assessed. What he found wasn't necessarily unexpected, but it helped him and his management team form a game plan of how to move forward strategically. Not having a specific background in building materials in fact helped Matt see opportunities to apply best practices from the other industries where he worked at JELD-WEN.

What Matt had seen as commonplace in other industries would feel like superpowers in the building products market, which was highly fragmented and lacked technical sophistication. There was a tremendous opportunity to develop digital enablement in the commercial go-to-market plans and operational strategies. How do you get the organization aligned on a digital vision for the company? Matt quickly understood that leadership wanted the right things – to align the company horizontally – but how that related to the company's digital transformation meant different things to different folks across the organization.

When Matt arrived in 2024, there was already an array of manufacturing automation happening across the company. Matt's focus was on how to integrate and standardize these efforts to assess productivity and efficiency. Matt understood it was more important to focus on outcomes and value rather than simply applying technology like AI for the sake of it. What's more, gathering data and analytics across the supply and distribution chain would offer multiple payoffs: greater insight in production issues and how to solve them, greater insight to consumers and suppliers on where their products were in the delivery cycle, and better mechanisms to look at cost capture.

Matt saw four major challenges associated with his efforts:

Challenge 1: How to align leadership and management?
Challenge 2: How to align across data informed decision-making?
Challenge 3: How to integrate data across divisions and functions?
Challenge 4: How to effectively develop new capabilities?

Spring Cleaning

For Matt to address the Hairy Monster meant he would need to thoroughly understand and assess the legacy landscape of applications, systems, and even platforms including an enterprise resource planning (ERP) instantiation that needed to be right-sized. Without slaying that monster, Matt would not be able to do anything at scale. He found at JELD-WEN a leadership team that understood the vision and trusted Matt to execute. Matt's focus was to lead at the strategy levels and then work it down to the functional and product levels.

After engaging employees across the organization, Matt recognized that there had been previous efforts at JELD-WEN focused on using digital processes and applications to align the company across business units. The traditional approach had been to rip out legacy systems and organize processes across a centralized platform or, in JELD-WEN's case, its ERP system. A clear and unified strategy on how to effectively and efficiently use this platform needed to be developed to accelerate transformation. Innovation had succeeded at a local level; however, to scale, a common framework was required for global transformation. So, Matt's first charge was to right-size that system and contracts and get to work in developing a common operating system and framework.

Matt needed the right IT leadership team in place. He wanted to make sure there were folks that aligned on clear accountability on corporate and regional strategy, assessment of transformational priorities, and a collaborative mindset across the different business units. As Matt mentioned, he was more interested in hiring someone for the how and not the what – in a sense, how they go about work and their cultural fit and not so much their deep domain expertise.

The next task was to assess the relative capabilities and needs (both unique and common) across the extended ecosystem. Every entity was running as a separate business including manufacturing processes, operations, and finance. Matt tends to shy away from buzzwords like composable architecture and focus on what business values systems are providing. Matt began to channel his Storytelling competency by getting out to talk to other business leaders across the organization to get alignment on what they were not able to do because of what they have in place – getting clarity on that narrative first. Then determining what is the best of the best in terms of capabilities across the business lines – should they reuse and scale or rip and replace? Right-sizing was also critical. What network would be required to deliver on commercial aspirations? Matt needed to work within JELD-WEN's network to understand the impact of proposed changes holistically. In a sense, Matt needed to understand the impact of optimizing a process to make sure it would not erode value somewhere else.

At JELD-WEN what they had built was a monolithic technology stack: a set of multi-use platforms to manage everything but consisting of redundancies. Matt's focus was in assessing what might remain after ripping them out and then layering in new purpose-built transformational and commercial capabilities. These include digital go-to-market capabilities, product information management, and content management that support customer experiences. Matt's process:

- Understand the how and why of system complexity.
- Scrutinize the legacy environment.
- Align everyone around critical expectation.
- Decouple complex systems and processes to simplify.
- Think about the timeline (nice to have versus need to have).
- Identifying what's left and make build/buy decisions.
- Remove and replace.

Matt's view is everything starts with a firm understanding of the customer and their needs: customer intelligence (CI). From there, you can then map out the most effective processes and systems to add value for the consumers: business intelligence (BI). Once you have understood those, then you start to add layers of automation: artificial intelligence (AI).

$$CI \longrightarrow BI \longrightarrow AI$$

Walking Through the Door

For Matt, transformation at JELD-WEN didn't start with a massive system overhaul. Rather, it began first by taking the time to understand where people wanted to take the company. It started, in other words, not by addressing the technology but rather the perceived outcomes they hoped for as a result of the technology. Matt mentioned the replacement fallacy for IT systems, for example, technology requests versus business requests. Matt recalls a request to replace an ERP system; however, the proposed business objectives could be achieved through optimizing controls and utilization. He needed to unpack the issues to determine the best way forward with transformation efforts. This is especially true with AI. Does it solve a unique business objective that could be met with existing systems and process modification?

At the same time, Matt was keenly aware that the story he would have to tell would need to consider different audiences. Leadership would want to hear about the entire narrative of capacity and capability after their digital transformation journey. Plant management would want to discuss what current systems can and cannot do. These different focal points meant different perspectives and opinions. Matt had to walk a delicate balance between discussing what they could achieve with current legacy systems while also discussing the benefits replacing any legacy system would offer.

Matt said to different stakeholders, "Let's think about that asset (process, system, application) that we have in place and get consensus around what we believe might be outcomes." What might we be able to do now that we couldn't do before if we replaced, modified, or integrated systems? What might be the impact to people or processes if a system was replaced or modified? How can we think of things in an incremental but also pragmatic fashion? A mix of experiments and very scrappy work in parallel? Large waterfall-type programs are hard since the script changes along the way, and you might not be getting what you thought you were doing a couple of years ago.

How did Matt deal with issues associated with people having different opinions associated with data? How do you deal with pushback? There is a science and art in understanding different perspectives in the business. Hyper transparency is critical. Matt needed to try to forecast potential friction points:

- Look for high alignment at the top of the house (leadership).
- Look for commonality – what different groups are doing together.
- Drive business strategy and context rather than technical implementation.
- Bring in issues associated with compliance early on in the discussion.

Matt put in place an enterprise data environment with hyper focus on data definition and clean-up strategies. The goal is to create AI solutions to help with categorization and de-duplication. This is already leading to the development of digital tools to support continuous operational improvement efforts. From a commercial side, it's providing for the development of new digital customer experiences and efficiencies in managing prospective opportunity analysis.

Another challenge is becoming more network optimization driven. It's difficult but necessary to understand the delicate balance in a system and how changes can have ripple effects across different systems like supply or distribution. Transformation is generally viewed as a positive; however, the principal challenge is the cadence of the capabilities. When the building products market is booming, everything is going well. In a depressed market, however, quality and delivery become paramount to maintain market share. Process complexity is a challenge in all organizations, and Matt understands that there are people and history behind these systems and processes. You need to understand and recognize who developed, who maintains, what value was provided, and even what the rationale was for implementation. As a change agent, it's important to recognize this as you look to integrate, revamp, or even decommission these systems. Matt is now focused on AI and automation to ensure the right products get to the right places efficiently through network optimization and analysis. Once that foundation is in place, they can meet the demands associated with new customer experiences.

Because Matt took time and effort to address the Hairy Monster, he and his team are already garnering some transformational wins. For the first time in the company's history, JELD-WEN is operating globally from a back-office infrastructure including centralizing finance across all the brands and a shared HR services platform to handle all HR tasks in one place along with a virtual agent to address questions.

Key Takeaways from Matt's Journey

- Be prepared for the work.
- Scrutinize the legacy systems on what you can and cannot do with a plan associated with layering in new capabilities; it might involve upgrading or replacing systems.
  - Investigate not just what's in place but why.
  - Right-sizing current platform implementations.
- Develop a vision and an operational plan to get there; build a story that caters to the needs and concerns of different audiences.
- Balance between simplifying and layering in new capabilities, anchoring on new capabilities.
- Tie things together at both the board, leadership, and management levels.

Try This: Dot the Clutter

The Hairy Monster creeps in when tools pile up and clarity breaks down. This simple exercise helps your team spot the chaos and cut through it, together.

Step 1: What's the Issue?

Pick one messy part of your business – a process, journey, or workflow.

List every tool, app, or system involved on a whiteboard or wall. Give everyone three colored dots:

- Green = I use it all the time.
- Yellow = I use it sometimes.
- Gray = I never use it.

Let your team place their dots. Step back and look for overlaps and clutter. Circle the mess.

Next, describe the problem in a sentence a fifth grader could understand.

Example: "We have too many tools, and no one knows which one to use."

Step 2: What Are We Going to Do About It?

Write one sentence explaining your plan, like you're talking to your grandma.

Example: "We're going to clean this up and pick one tool everyone uses."

Step 3: What Does Success Look Like?

In one sentence, describe the outcome you are aiming for.

Example: "Everyone knows what to use, and we don't waste time switching between tools."

Now stitch your three sentences together. That's your elevator pitch – clear, simple, and fluff–free.

See the mess. Say the mess. Solve the mess. This is your team's first step toward clarity, speed, and sanity.

Chapter 4

My Way or the Highway

"Transformation isn't about technology; it's about starting where your people are and pushing forward with grit and savvy."
—**Chris Baldwin, former chairman and CEO of BJ's Wholesale Club**

Sometimes, the challenges to transformation aren't technical but the result of human nature. Take the example of a startup we recently heard about, run by an overbearing CEO. He didn't trust his people and tried to muscle his way through every decision. He got his hands in every facet of operations, whether it was sales, product development, or marketing. As a result, he over-engineered processes, taxed relationships, and demoralized employees. The company culture, in turn, was toxic, and people began jumping ship. Those who stuck around felt defeated, disengaged, and unsatisfied.

Leaders and decision-makers in these kinds of organizations often demand blind loyalty, something that is hardly congruent with efficient and sustainable transformation. Instead of a collaborative environment, they created an overbearing and monolithic culture, which leaves employees demoralized and deflated. They attempt to centralize and codify culture through norms of behavior. They reinforce and display their culture through artifacts that they put on their walls, in the clothes that they wear, and even in how they design and set up their workspaces. The danger is when the culture of specific divisions and departments becomes a reflection of those leading and not the organization as a whole. When culture goes rogue, transformation efforts often stall or fall apart. Consensus building and collaboration, as we have discussed in this book, are essential aspects of effective transformation. They demand that management consider this essential question: how do you ensure that employees feel a part of the transformation and not feel like transformation is something that is being done to them?

Hubris Is the Path to the Dark Side

In *Star Wars: A New Hope*, an overconfident Grand Moff Tarkin declared, "Evacuate? In our moment of triumph? I think you overestimate their chances." His hubris got the better of him, and he failed to assess the security risks of a small X-wing fighter piloted by a young Luke Skywalker guided by the Force (did you really think we would not add in a Star Wars reference?). As a C-level executive or someone simply running a department, ask yourself: Do you need to be liked, do you need to be right, or do you simply need to be effective? There is a difference between being popular, influential, persuasive, and motivational. Popularity is a measure of who you are connected to, while influence is largely a measure of how you can spur those around you into action. Persuasion and motivation speak to your ability to be effective, not just in winning hearts and minds but also in providing the right incentives to evoke a favorable action.

The moment a desire to be right overtakes the need for collaboration, it's a sure sign that the Hubris Monster has reared its ugly head. The Hubris Monster turns away from diversity of thought. The Hubris Monster thrives within organizations where ego overshadows collaboration, where leaders cling to power without listening, and where teams avoid accountability. It appears when leaders separate or distance themselves from those who are impacted by their decisions. The Hubris Monster often appears when culture focuses more on individual benefit than team-based orientation. It comes when decision-makers are more interested in benefits and implications to themselves than to the larger organization. Left unchecked, this monster derails transformation efforts, particularly in the high-stakes, fast-moving world of AI.

Conquering the Hubris Monster requires the assistance of two powerful monster slayers: the Politician and the Barrier Buster. Together, they build bridges between disenfranchised parties while also bringing alignment, shared understanding, and trust back into organizational culture.

The Hubris Monster Slayers

THE POLITICIAN

These days, politicians are often controversial figures, swayed by special interests and not always representative of the constituents who elected them to office. Within our organization, the Politician can maneuver through organizational politics and build trust. They understand and represent different employee groups (aka the constituents) and advocate on their behalf. Their role is to broker arrangements that benefit a majority of employees and codify a set of practices to make decisions more equitable. The Politician is just what is needed to reduce the impact of the Hubris Monster by fostering humility and understanding. Their role is in helping leadership understand that it's not about knowing everything but rather making personal connections to make sure decision-makers understand and assess employee needs. In addition, the Politician:

- Advocates for impacted communities.
- Offers representation at the decision-making process.
- Brokers change.

The Politician can operate within a group, division, or department (inter . . .) but also across them (intra . . .). Transformation may start locally, but it scales only when it is connected to a broader strategy. The Politician's gift is stitching efforts together, making sure change doesn't stall at the edges of a department or dissolve in the white space between teams. But what makes the Politician truly effective isn't just influence or relationship-building. It's their ability to create direction, generate momentum, and bring people along for the ride. We call this the PPT formula: Purpose, Pace, Togetherness.

- *Purpose* is where it starts. People need to know where they are going and why it matters. Without that shared sense of purpose, energy fizzles and trust erodes. The Politician brings clarity to the mission turning vague ambitions into a clear and compelling direction.
- *Pace* is about commitment. It's not just how fast you move; it's the signals you send that this transformation is real. The Politician keeps things moving with steady follow-through, visible progress, and a bias toward action. When people see momentum, they believe. When they see commitment, they commit.
- *Togetherness* is the glue. Transformation doesn't stick unless people feel part of something bigger than their immediate surroundings. The Politician creates alignment by forging shared ownership bonding people to each other and to a common cause. They translate isolated wins into collective progress.

Even with a clear destination, change stalls when leaders ignore where people are starting from. The Politician knows transformation isn't about bulldozing over history; it's about building on it. People don't change just because they're told to; they change when their experiences shift, and those new experiences reshape their beliefs. The savvy Politician meets teams where they are, acknowledges what's come before, and shows how the future connects and does not replace the past.

That's how you earn trust. That's how you move from polite agreement to real progress.

Of course, affecting organizational change is a challenge, requiring help from folks skilled at removing obstacles. Say hello to the Barrier Buster.

BARRIER BUSTER

Legendary coach Vince Lombardi once said, "Football is two things. It's blocking and tackling. I don't care about formations, new offenses, or tricks on defense. You block and tackle better than the team you're playing; you win."

The same applies to transformation. Well-designed strategies often fall apart because of poor execution. Decision-makers fail to adapt or dismantle legacy thinking and systems. Most of all, transformation fails because those in charge fail to move obstacles to success out of the way. While the Politician's job is to build trust and alignment, the Barrier Buster's task is to help remove organizational distractions, allowing leadership to maximize its efficiency and empower its employees.

The Barrier Buster, in other words, establishes a culture of:

- **Adaptability over intractability:** Everyone owns their piece of the transformation. Barriers are proactively addressed.
- **A focus on action over excuses:** Instead of dwelling on obstacles, this slayer asks, "How can we solve this?"
- **Clearing the path:** Teams are empowered to act decisively, removing excuses and silos that block progress.

The Barrier Buster is essential in transformation efforts because the Hubris Monster thrives on leaders who shift blame or avoid difficult decisions. The Barrier Buster ensures there's no room for ego or avoidance, just relentless forward momentum. Together, the Politician and Barrier Buster work to establish:

- **Trust before action:** The Politician ensures there's trust and alignment before moving forward. Without this, action can feel disconnected and chaotic.
- **Action with empathy:** The Barrier Buster ensures that trust and alignment don't stagnate. They drive the team to act while respecting the relational groundwork laid by the Politician.
- **Recalibration along the way:** AI transformations are iterative. Design is improved through multiple cycles of design and testing. The Politician recalibrates alignment when challenges arise, while the Barrier Buster clears new obstacles to maintain progress.

The Politician fosters alignment, while the Barrier Buster drives action. Together, they balance alignment, strategy, and decisiveness, ensuring that organizations broker arrangements that work for different constituencies without disenfranchising large groups.

Who Do You Trust?

Ultimately, developing and sustaining trust across an organization is at the heart of what the Politician and Barrier Buster are working to accomplish. Ask yourself: Do people trust each other in your organization? What do you do to build and maintain that trust? Is it likely that someone will reciprocate trust within your organization? When someone feels betrayed, how do you win back their trust?

When it comes to transformation, organizational trust turns out to be not just a nice idea but a necessity for defeating the Hubris Monster. While the Hubris Monster thrives on cynicism, avoidance, withholding, and skepticism, the Politician and Barrier Buster persuade through acceptance, collaboration, curiosity, and inclusion. Commitment, integrity, and compassion are equally vital to a healthy trust environment. The different pillars of trust include:

- **Care:** Degree of positive intentionality.
- **Reliability:** Showing up consistently.
- **Sincerity:** Say what you mean and do what you say.
- **Competence:** Knowing your abilities and shortcomings.

Compassion is predicated on Trust and the different pillars it's built upon. Sincerity requires intentionality, in other words, communication and acting with your true beliefs and actions. Failing to fulfill expectations, not being consistent in interacting with different communities, and not being transparent about competency all erode Trust. When it comes to competency, many leaders and employees, in an effort to show value, do not adequately represent their capabilities. Being honest and reflective – "I know I can do that; I'm not sure if I can do that." This might also hamper their inclination to ask for help. In some cases, misalignment on standards for assessment can also lead to a disconnect and erosion of trust from the employee assigned to a task and the person managing the development of the task.

Have a Little Compassion

In the example we provided at the beginning of the chapter, there was no compassion or caring within the leadership of that start-up. In companies where compassion prevails, there is reduced stress and higher job satisfaction. When people perceive they are valued and cared for, they feel positive about their work commitment and voluntarily offer support and care for others.[1] You get improved interpersonal relationships, enhanced customer satisfaction, and a high-functioning work environment. This provides the underpinnings to succeed during times of transformational change. In her book *Compassionate Leadership*,[2] Kirstie Drummond Papworth noted that compassion has a reputation problem. It has been described over the years as immoral, fatiguing, and weak and is particularly absent from much of organizational life. Yet, research shows that compassion in leadership has many benefits including social connectedness, improved accountability and psychological safety, and improved conflict resolution. Compassion has three different elements associated with it.

- **The cognitive aspect:** "I understand your problems."
- **The affective component:** "I feel what you feel."
- **The drive or motivational component:** "I want to help you out of this."[3]

In some situations, work seems like a drudgery. Employees move from one endless meeting to another. They don't feel supported or motivated, and the discussion of transformation seems like just another corporate-led initiative to give them more work to do or potentially outsource them from their position. It's hard to think about compassion when you don't feel supported, engaged, or empowered. We can discuss streamlining processes, providing autonomy, and developing systems for recognition and support, but nothing changes without a focus on compassion. Organizations that focus on compassion in the workplace understand and foster employee well-being. Compassionate leaders and managers build this aptitude by organizing weekly meetups or feedback sessions, or allocating more collaborative group projects, providing motivation to help and support each other, and contributing to the common goal of the company. Empathic conversation encourages open dialogue within meetings where people treat each other with respect, irrespective of their title.

Trust Fuels Transformation

Global communications firm Edelman measures society's attitude toward trust through its annual Trust Barometer survey.[4] The results are hardly surprising and echo what we often see within companies: trust declines when innovation fails to deliver its expected outcome. Trust falters when information feels biased or unreliable. Trust drops when transformation creates gaps or inequalities between different groups. Trust fails when the transformation efforts feel more focused on making sure things happen quickly rather than effectively.

The reality is that trust is a belief . . . a *belief* that someone or something is honest, reliable, or effective but also a *risk* that someone is willing to take in engaging with another person or organization. How do you spur belief and mitigate risk? In some cases, what we might think builds trust actually does the opposite. Poorly designed or thought-through recognition and incentives used to reward employees might damage trust by appearing arbitrary or insincere. Continuous praise to one group while dismissing the contribution of others develops resentment. Siloed structures exacerbate this and might create wariness toward others.

In *The Trust Premium: How to Attract Loyal Customers Who Want to Pay More*, Yoram Solomon argues that trust can be a financial multiplier. Externally, trust results in:

- **Higher revenue:** Trust brings in more customers.
- **Increased pricing power:** Trust allows you to charge more without increasing costs.
- **Reduced costs:** Trust lowers marketing and sales expenses, increasing your profit margins.

Internally, trust adds multiple benefits to productivity and employee retention, reducing stress and burnout as well as building stronger relationships with suppliers, partners, and clients. Professor John Whitney of Columbia Business School once said that "Distrust doubles the cost of doing business".[5]

One way to understand the value of organizational trust is to think of it along a spectrum, from low trust to high trust, that directly correlates to the quality of employee performance. Identifying where your organization falls in the trust–performance spectrum is an essential step. This often involves taking a hard look in the mirror. You may not always like what you see, but avoiding reality does no one any favors. Cordial hypocrisy happens when there is a semblance of trust for the sake of appearances but actual lack of trust (mistrust) to avoid conflict. This might result from a sense of loyalty, fear of judgment, or capitulation to maintain social harmony. The only way to break this cycle is to engage in open communications where employees feel "safe" to express themselves, sharing their honest opinions.

When it comes to performance and trust, understanding where your company might reside is an important first step in assessing what processes, resources, measures, and people need to be put in place. In Figure 4.1, we list different zones of performance and trust and what companies might practice depending on which zone they find themselves in.

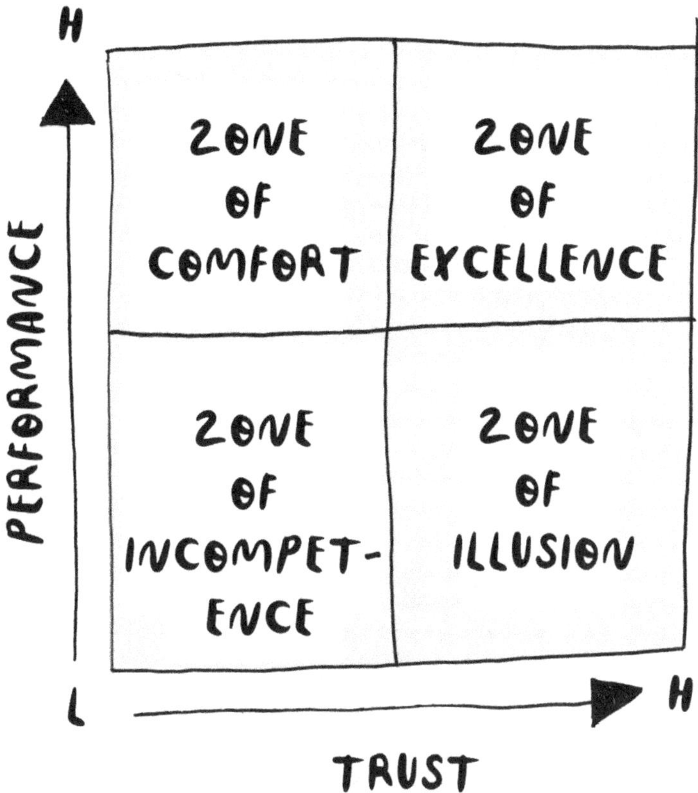

Figure 4.1 From incompetence to excellence.

- **Low performance, low trust – the zone of chaos:** This organization is in a tough spot. Here, the focus should be on small wins to build trust. There is a need for greater transparency in communication. In addition, more team members need to be involved in decision-making to feel like part of the process. The key is to find common ground where all can feel included.

- **High performance, low trust – the zone of illusion:** Performance is good, but there's something off between the employees. People don't feel comfortable reaching across the aisle or working collaboratively. The key here is to provide recognition, build trust, and include skeptical high performers in leadership roles.

- **Low performance, high trust – the zone of comfort:** People feel confident in one another, but the bottom line isn't seeing the benefits. The key here is to identify any performance bottlenecks. Often, a greater investment in training and development can optimize inefficient processes, which then drive performance improvements.
- **High performance, high trust – the zone of excellence:** The focus is on continuing to scale this success. Management should encourage risk-taking and foster an environment where doing better is an integral component of the organizational culture.

Measure Twice, Cut Once

How do you assess trustworthiness? Can trust be measured? Is trust limited or conditional, where trust needs to be negotiated before each transaction? What are the criteria used to trust someone you know nothing about? How do employees rate the trustworthiness of co-workers or management? In programs we have developed, we have had executives work on assessing and building trust in their organization. These participants work through a mental model of assessing the different phases of trust including:

- **Building:** Establishing a foundation and building trustworthiness.
- **Promoting:** Leading with honesty and transparency.

- **Facilitating:** Encouraging matching and transparency.
- **Sustaining loyalty:** Developing reputational scores to reinforce trust.

One trust equation looks at the sum of measures of credibility, reliability, and intimacy (relationship measure) over self-interest. Some degree of intimacy is critical, in terms of the care component of trust, in other words, listening to what's important and engaging with folks on their level. By sharing expectations, concerns, and hopes, decision-makers can build trust with their teams. Self-interest is in the common denominator to address the Hubris Monster. The more the relationship revolves around self-interest, the less likely trust is freely given. Questions, our Politician understands, opens minds, while statements close them. Lead with curiosity, not certainty.

In her study "How Can Trust be Created," business scholar Mari Sako[6] shows how a low-trust environment leads to less communication, which in turn results in misunderstandings and tighter controls put in place. By contrast, employees at high-trust firms typically outperform those in low-trust ones on almost every measure of productivity and success. People treat each other better. They stay at the organizations longer. They report better work–life balance. They have less stress, more energy, fewer sick days, and less burnout.

Stay Flexible, My Friends

Edgar Schein was a highly regarded social psychologist and a Sloan Fellows professor of management emeritus at MIT. Schein took a pragmatic approach to organizational culture with a focus on group dynamics and interpersonal interactions. His three-tiered model of organizational culture is still used today to offer a framework on how organizations assess culture, or, in our case, how they might recognize the inevitable connection between culture and transformational capacity. He explains that culture can be understood by evaluating three organizational facets:

- **Artifacts:** Visible and audible behavior patterns, including workplace and orientation materials.
- **Values:** Reasons or rationalizations for behavior.
- **Assumptions:** Unconscious patterns that determine how group members perceive, think, and feel.

The Politician and Barrier Buster can remind leadership that culture needs to be continually assessed and understood. Culture often changes as an organization goes through leadership transitions, acquisitions, divestitures, market trends, and movement in the employee base. Globally, we are witnessing the development of one of the most diverse multigenerational workforces we have ever seen. Such diversity provides different perspectives and opinions, which spur innovation as well as unique opportunities for learning and development. At the same time, this creates a variety of challenges, including managing different expectations associated with work style, arrangements, and interactions. This complexity reinforces the need for leadership to be flexible and adaptive rather than rigid and intractable. It also illustrates the need for leaders to understand how to be persuasive to diverse groups. Leaders focusing on building trust:

- Connect with their teams before giving marching orders.
- Own their decisions and challenges instead of deflecting them.
- Empower others to act while staying accountable to the organization's shared vision.

Companies with persuasive leaders with high levels of flexibility can meet the needs associated with a shifting transformation landscape. On the other hand, those with authoritative leadership who demonstrate little flexibility can become stuck and targets for disruption. The two quadrants that companies often fall into are with persuasive leaders but a nonadaptive culture, and they become passive followers. Teams are stuck in operational mode with little understanding of the bigger picture and the rationale associated with the importance of their efforts. On the other hand, a highly flexible culture but authoritative leadership leads to chaos. Chaos ensues from employees who all have a different version of what needs to be done.

Thoughtful transformation occurs when leaders are persuasive in winning the hearts and minds of teams. At the same time, management recognizes the need for flexibility to adapt to changing work styles and expectations, as well as shocks (external and internal) that might occur during transformation efforts. Even though hubris is something we see as a hindrance to transformation, we still need decision-making to occur. In this book, we continually discuss the need for balance. We will be discussing consensus-building later in the book, but it's crucial to understand that the culture needs to be inclusive, transparent, and trusting. Part of that trust begins by establishing a belief that leaders will make decisions that benefit the team and the organization. Sometimes leaders need to step in and be decisive, or efforts will stall in never-ending cycles of consensus-building.

Beware: Toxic Organization Ahead

In summing up the importance of culture in organizational transformation, management consultant and Harvard Business professor Peter Drucker famously said, "Culture eats strategy for breakfast." In short, if you don't have a culture aligned for transformation, then your best-laid plans will fall short. Monsters, like the Hubris Monster among others, will only grow and block your efforts. The result may be high turnover rates, decreased innovation, and a tarnished organizational reputation, which not only impacts employee experience but also business performance. How fast can leaders recover if they betray trust?

Here, the absence of psychological safety for employees gets to the heart of ineffective transformation. After all, what do employees value and expect when it comes to a safe workspace? During COVID-19, employees considered the workspace a potentially dangerous environment. Many organizations did what they could to promote a physically safe experience, often allowing for remote work. As conditions and COVID-19 restrictions eased, many organizations were left with contentious relationships between folks advocating for remote versus in-person work. Organizations, after all, were looking to bring back employees for understandable reasons, such as the investments in uninhabited workspaces and a decrease in productivity.[7] And yet, when the pandemic restrictions were lifted, it wasn't as simple as asking everyone to come back to work the next day. Thoughtful transformation (and leadership) requires new ways of thinking and redefining the status quo. If we are going to reimagine the workplace and work in the future, we need to rethink what work actually means, how it gets done, how we measure it, and how we incentivize employees. The Politician and Barrier Buster can help facilitate this enlightened understanding.

Key Takeaways

To slay the Hubris Monster, organizations need to empower both Politicians and Barrier Busters:

1. The Politician builds trust while the Barrier Buster removes obstacles to trust. Leaders must strike a balance, avoiding the trap of endless realignment while ensuring accountability doesn't erode trust.
2. Alignment is not a one-time event. The Politician calibrates alignment as teams move forward, while the Barrier Buster ensures that the team doesn't become complacent.
3. Look at what you can do versus what others can do. The Barrier Buster removes hurdles to bringing in the right competencies, recognizing there will always be challenges to transformation impacting the organization, where adaptation is vital.
4. AI transformations bring unique challenges, including ethical concerns, cross-disciplinary collaboration, and automation anxiety. Leaders must apply the Politician's relational skills and the Barrier Buster's decisiveness to navigate these complexities.

Case Story: Croma

What Will You Do If It Does Not Work Out?

In 2018, Croma, a subsidiary of Tata Digital, was riding high as India's most admired electronics retailer. A year before, Tata Digital's Group Chairman had outlined their ambition to win the consumer market in India, and Croma was a critical piece of the strategy. To do so, it required an organizational transformation to adapt to a changing marketplace. Stores were exceeding targets, and the company was expanding its presence across India. However, at that time, e-commerce penetration remained relatively limited. Croma's approach leaned heavily on its expansive network of stores as the heart of its engagement model.

COVID-19 changed this dynamic completely. Store closures forced customers online. Omni-channel capability went from a long-term aspiration to an immediate requirement. To meet surging demand for online commerce, Croma launched a revamped website in 2020 and started on their journey. Early indicators were encouraging, with traffic climbing and digital sales growing. Yet beneath the surface, gaps were widening. Customers were abandoning carts, promised deliveries were missed, and the distance between digital promise and operational reality grew steadily.

What was required was not simply a technology upgrade but a cultural and operational transformation that challenged assumptions and redefined how decisions were made and owned across the organization. To create a deeper focus on customer and digital transformation, the management decided to implement a comprehensive change management strategy starting with leadership alignment. Part of this change was Shibashish Roy (the current CEO & Managing Director), who joined the company in 2021 to lead marketing and e-commerce. With 20 years of experience working across Tata group companies and exposure to digital transformations, Shibashish understood how technology development, process efficiency, and customer experience needed to exist in a balance. He worked closely with the leadership team to catalyze the pace of the transformation.

The Foundation Years

The first Croma store, a large 20,000 square foot space featuring more than 6,000 products opened in Mumbai in October 2006. By 2010, the company expanded its private label offerings to include everything from earphones to televisions to water purifiers. Over the last 10 years, Croma has continued to grow, with stores rolling out across India in major metro areas and mid-tier cities. Currently Croma operates 580 physical stores in more than 200 cities across India.

Physical retail has been an anchor of the customer experience at Croma for several reasons including store associates acting as an education channel to help the customer make the right choices for their needs, role of the physical store in selling major appliances (White Goods) by letting the customers experience them, and providing a complement not competitor to the online channel.

Selling Electronics in India

The Indian retail market is expected to reach US$1.1 trillion by 2027. India's retail sector is on track to exceed $1.6 trillion by 2030 with organized retailers projected to capture more than

35% of the total retail market, exceeding \$600 billion in value.[8] In comparison to other retail sectors like grocery and luxury goods, consumer electronics is better organized and offers higher margins with more aspirational shopping patterns.

And yet, retailers face significant barriers, covered next.

A Fragmented Market

The majority of the Indian retail market is unorganized and dominated by hyper-regional small shops. Large retail chains confront challenges trying to integrate into hyper-local ecosystems as well as compete with the likes of horizontal commerce platforms like Flipkart and Amazon. Adding to the complex landscape is the rapid rise of quick commerce platforms (delivery in 10 minutes) like Blinkit and Zepto.

Infrastructure Gaps

Warehousing and last mile delivery are challenging, particularly in midsize cities. In addition, traffic congestion and infrastructure challenges make logistics expensive.

Price Sensitivity and Shifting Consumer Aspirations

Consumers are very price sensitive with a low level of retail brand loyalty. Online deal-seekers typically focus on commoditized categories. They expect differentiated customer service but are also reluctant to pay for it.

Diversity in Consumer Behavior

Regional, linguistic, and cultural disparities make it hard to scale from one city/region to another. Regional players understand local consumer preferences and behaviors. For a national brand such as Croma, success lies in winning the many Indias that coexist. To do this, retailers need mature data capabilities and analytics to be able to drive localized range, relevant offers, and regional communications.

The Retail Revolution: External Pressures

The retail market in India has exploded over the last 50 years. From small corner shops and department stores to superstores carrying thousands of items, there's a store for whatever the consumer desires, whether its pet supplies, home improvement tools, books, or clothing. Consumer electronics is big business in the retail world, with customers seeking everything from parts to peripherals and everything from computing to home entertainment systems. In this space, customer service is critical, as consumers need to understand compatibility between components, know how to set up systems, or differentiate between the myriad choices of tech.

In just the last three to four years alone, global events and macro-economic developments have brought about manifold shifts in markets, consumer behavior, evolution of retail channels, and operating models across organizations. Electronics retail is facing shrinking margins and price wars, fueled by pure play e-commerce giants like Amazon driving race-to-the-bottom and direct-to-consumer pricing. The pandemic exposed weaknesses within the supply chain, while geopolitical issues resulted in shortages in critical electronic components and materials. Rapid technology changes make obsolescence an ever-present risk.

Customers also demand more than ever, including Buy Online Pick-Up In Store (BOPIS) options, refurbished products, and personalized services, with online and in-person spaces available to purchase, take possession, return, and get help with whatever they buy. This is driving data collection and integration of predictive analytic platforms. Such demands are a challenge for all retailers, but certainly for large, diversified brand names where the distribution methods, selection of products, and wide variety of partners in both supply and distribution become considerations that impact growth, productivity, and competitiveness.

Add to this emerging technology trends enabling unique customer experiences, such as in-store sensors providing navigation assistance or alerts for customers to receive real-time special offers or promotions, virtual-based shopping using augmented or virtual reality, AI-enabled personalized shopping, and social commerce, and you have an ever-evolving tech landscape that retailers can't simply ignore or they risk becoming the latest Circuit City.

The Wake-Up Call: Crisis and Recognition

In 2017, the Tata Group deepened its focus on winning the Indian consumer market. In an interview, N Chandrasekaran, chairman of the Tata Group, observed that "no other market would grow faster than India in the next 10–20 years." He urged Tata companies, including Croma, to leverage this opportunity for investments and growth. To achieve this, digital advances and AI-enabled processes would need to be a key part of their transformation.

Croma's early digital approach was guided by a belief that investment in technology alone could deliver a seamless customer experience. But as demand surged, it became clear that the biggest opportunity was not the capability of the systems but the mindset and processes surrounding them. Over-reliance on physical retail meant any experience gap became expensive. Inventory mismatches, fulfilment gaps, and missed expectations hampered customer experience. These challenges weren't entirely unexpected; what stood out was the need to respond to them with greater urgency. The reality was that the rapid growth of online players completely changed customer expectations with regard to delivery timelines, range, and pricing. The legacy confidence due to a largely offline business and customer satisfaction had created blind spots. Too many teams assumed everything was working well enough. The organization recognized the Hubris

Monster that what got them here is not going to get them to where they wanted to go.

Within the company, many teams continued to rely on practices that had delivered success in the past. This created a subtle sense of certainty that customer loyalty would remain intact. Challenges like fulfillment failures and data inconsistencies were acknowledged but rarely prioritized with urgency. The mindset was that performance would course-correct on its own. The company recognized that superficial modifications would be insufficient; instead, fundamental restructuring was necessary to realize the full potential of transformation. It became apparent that solving these issues would require more than new tools. It would require a shared willingness to question assumptions, align around customer outcomes, and adopt new ways of working shifting organizational hubris into institutional humility and innovation.

Shibashish along with the Croma leadership helped recognize that this quiet complacency was a risk. Conversations revealed that each department had its own version of priorities and its own definition of success.

Diagnosing Root Causes

Erosion of customer trust can be correlated with operational failures. When a customer sees a product online, pays for it, and schedules a delivery, the expectation is clear. The promise is made. But when that promise breaks down due to system lags, outdated data, or misaligned teams, the damage goes far beyond a failed transaction. It fractures trust.

Leadership at Croma confronted three interrelated challenges as transformation became essential for its future success.

First was the pace of innovation and how data-informed decisions were made. Despite investments in analytics, discussions often centered on whether data was accurate, rather than how to act on insights decisively. There was a need for a single source of truth that could help teams shift from verification to accountability.

Second was the belief that technology could overcome structural inefficiencies without changes to processes or behaviors. While there was conviction about the power of digitization, there was less focus on how roles, incentives, and governance needed to evolve to support it.

Third was a pattern of project approvals built on best-case scenarios. Plans often assumed ideal conditions for adoption and impact, leaving little room for course correction when challenges emerged. For example, project approvals leaned on optimistic projections assuming aspects like timelines, approach, and adoption would move forward as designed. The lack of "plan B" and risk mitigation approaches by the business team resulted in lack of adaptability.

These were not just operational gaps. They reflected a cultural need to strengthen accountability and reinforce customer promises as the organizing principle of decision-making. Any transformation would require the dismantling of a culture where departments operated with independent roadmaps and separate priority lists and where requests to enhance customer experiences were often met with polite agreement followed by quiet deprioritization. All this revealed structural rather than individual accountability gaps.

Building Alignment and Clarity

To address this, Croma learned from impactful community leaders who broker change and advocate for impacted people. They begin shifting the conversation away from technology as the main solution. Instead, teams were encouraged to frame problems in terms of customer impact. A failed delivery was no longer just a logistics issue. It became a broken promise that risked eroding brand trust. Data was presented in clear, relatable terms, connecting operational decisions to human consequences.

One example was the way the idea of pilots was reimagined. Pilots had historically been seen as ways to test new ideas in isolation. Over time, they evolved into mechanisms for delaying decisions. Proposals were frequently met with questions about business cases and ROI that often slowed momentum. Leadership reframed this process, focusing on how teams would manage risks and scale ideas rather than requiring complete certainty up front. This shift helped create a more enabling environment where incomplete ideas were welcomed and treated as opportunities for learning.

The changes were supported by a new operating model that replaced the traditional analyst-plus-business structure with a product-focused approach. This reorganization centered decisions around customer experience rather than functional silos. The approach also included bringing in experienced talent from digital and e-commerce backgrounds. Their role was not just to introduce new practices but to help connect teams to broader possibilities and encourage experimentation without fear of failure.

Removing Barriers to Progress

Alongside mindset shifts, Croma incorporated barrier busters to focus on hurdles that were slowing progress. One of the most persistent was the way incentives were fragmented across teams. Store teams were measured on footfall and conversion. Digital teams prioritized app engagement. Supply chain leaders focused on throughput and efficiency. Each group was optimizing for its own targets rather than aligning around a shared outcome.

To tackle this, leadership repositioned operational priorities in a way that spoke to each team's values. Fixing inventory visibility was not framed only as an IT initiative. It was presented as a way to improve conversion rates, reduce returns, and protect the customer experience. When different functions understood how the same improvements advanced their goals, momentum increased without the need for directives.

This period also saw the launch of express delivery for appliances. The idea had been discussed many times but was considered too complex and expensive. When it was reframed as a promise to the customer and a signal of respect for their time, it unlocked the commitment required to bring it to market. The results exceeded expectations. Conversion rates improved significantly, and the service became a differentiator for both digital and in-store customers.

Enabling Transformation

As the transformation progressed, the ownership of ideas shifted. Instead of relying on central committees to approve every concept, teams began to self-correct weak proposals and defend promising ones with confidence. The work became less about getting permission and more about demonstrating impact.

The change was also visible in how data was used and measured. For example, store teams were rewarded for store traffic and in-store conversions, digital teams prioritized online engagement, and supply chain leaders prioritized throughput. Alignment around customer value led to inventory visibility reframed as a way to reduce returns, improve conversions, and improve customer satisfaction.

Merchandising teams began relying on analytics to design hyper-local assortments that reflected regional preferences. The concept of the Net Promoter Score evolved from a quarterly metric to a dynamic tool for continuous improvement. In-store experience improvements were informed by customer feedback and tracked against clear accountability measures.

A Catalyst for Change

Throughout this transition the role of leaders was to act as an enabler rather than gatekeeper. One element of this was creating space for what teams called culture carriers similar to our Politician, individuals across functions who could connect silos, frame issues in accessible language, and guide others through uncertainty. These culture carriers helped sustain momentum by translating strategic shifts into everyday practices. They also provided a balancing voice when change risked moving faster than teams could absorb.

Shibashish played an important role as a catalyst, helping set expectations and encouraging teams to think differently. His approach balanced pragmatism and optimism, creating an environment where questioning assumptions became a sign of strength rather than dissent. The Hubris monster was defeated through a realization that lasting transformation was not about any single individual. It was about the organization learning to see itself with a different perspective and act with renewed urgency.

Building Confidence and Capacity

The impact of these efforts became visible in both customer metrics, technology deployment and cultural signals. The number of approved concepts rose sharply. Teams began tackling operational challenges with greater speed and clarity. Express delivery became a symbol of what was possible when teams aligned around shared promises rather than functional goals. AI became an enabling technology not an obscure concept via endless discussions.

For example, OmniStore, the company's AI-powered commerce platform from Tata Consultancy Services, operates across all the retailer's outlets, enabling a unified experience across multiple shopping modalities. Croma's vision is to be number one in customer experience and satisfaction among its competitors.

Another key example of this was the manner in which the HR team leveraged AI to hire at scale. Having to recruit across 200 cities, they faced critical hiring inefficiencies that included prolonged time-to-hire cycles, inconsistent candidate quality, limited visibility into recruitment metrics due to inadequate reporting capabilities, and significant HR resource drain from manual, dependency-heavy processes.

Perhaps the most important shift was in mindset. Employees became more comfortable challenging their own assumptions. The question "What will you do if it does not work out?" evolved from a rhetorical concern into an invitation to plan, iterate, and improve.

Croma's experience demonstrates that true transformation is rarely about technology alone. It is about building the capacity to reflect honestly, adapt quickly, and stay anchored to what matters most for customers.

Key Takeaways from Croma's Journey

Defeating the Hubris Monster requires collective effort, not just individual leadership. Having everyone feels a part of transformation rather than transformation being imparted onto them was a key element in Croma's success. Several key elements were critical including:

- Question assumptions, even when success feels secure.
- Reframe challenges in human terms relatable to everyone.
- Align incentives so that progress feels shared, not imposed.
- Make space for ideas to grow without fear of rejection.
- Enable people across levels to act as bridges between teams.

Try This: Be the COO (Chief Obstacle Obliterator)

You don't need a fancy title to lead change. You just need to clear the stuff in the way.

Step 1: Throw It Down

Gather your team. Hand out slips of paper. Ask: "What's one thing that's slowing us down but no one's really talking about?" Write it anonymously. No names, no blame.

Step 2: Lottery It

Put the papers into a bowl like a lottery and everyone picks one piece out.[9] What surprised you? What's new? What themes arose?

Step 3: Clear It Out

As a team, spot the biggest roadblocks. Choose one. Now – channel your inner COO. Not Chief Operating Officer, but Chief Obstacle Obliterator. What's one real move you can make together this month to bust it.

Chapter 5

Transparency Is the New Currency

"When you align the organization, set clear goals, and keep everyone informed of progress—even small wins—it builds excitement and drives the transformation forward."
—Darren Herman, Bain Capital

There is a moment in any transformation effort when everything seems to slow down. Teams hesitate. People ask for more meetings, more alignment, more clarity. And yet, the more you meet and discuss, the less progress you make. It's as if you're trapped in some kind of fog, where everyone nods in agreement, but nothing moves forward.

Careful: you may have entered the lair of the Cagey Monster.

The Cagey Monster thrives in environments where transparency is unstructured or selective, where updates about transformation efforts are inconsistent, ambiguous, or downright chaotic.

The Cagey Monster doesn't scream for a return to the status quo or resist new ideas outright. No, this monster is much more subtle and, as a result, much more dangerous. The Cagey Monster thrives in situations where the excuses sound perfectly reasonable:

- "Let's align internally before sharing this too broadly."
- "We don't have all the answers yet, so maybe it's best to wait."
- "They don't need to know all the details."

Such thinking might at first seem like responsible leadership but over time creates the perfect conditions for confusion, mistrust, and inertia. Boards receive reports that look promising but lack real visibility into execution. Executives believe various teams are aligned, only to discover that different groups are moving in completely different directions. And middle managers, the very people responsible for making transformation happen, become paralyzed by indecisiveness. Without clear guidance, they hesitate to act, waiting for a level of certainty that never arrives. The cost of such inaction? Wasted time, lost momentum, and missed opportunities.

Companies that look to develop a culture of transparency begin by making sure their efforts are supported by the four pillars of effective communication and interaction, including:

- **Clarity:** Are you clear in communication? Clarity looks to cut through the noise and get to direct messaging. What's the ask? What's my role? Why is the company engaging in transformation?
- **Capacity:** Do you have the means to engage in effective and regular communication across a large, diverse organization? Do you have the capacity to engage in active listening and empathic reasoning?
- **Confidence:** Do you have the measures in place to ensure that communication has the expected impact? Do you have the conviction that over time, transparency will lead to more engaged and resilient employees?
- **Continuous learning:** Is there an iterative feedback loop where you can assess the impact of your messaging? Can you refine your messaging to deliver more personalized communication?

But transparency alone isn't the answer. Studies have shown the benefits associated with transparency. In an HBR report on the impact of employee engagement on performance, 70% of employees reported higher levels of engagement when leadership regularly updated them on organizational strategy.[1] If transparency is chaotic, unstructured, or poorly timed, it can create just as many problems as it solves. It's more than surveying employees regularly and sharing results to illustrate how the company is addressing concerns and responding to issues. True transparency has to be mastered. It's meeting them where they are. Without transparency in communication, the rumor mill starts running out of time. To truly defeat the Cagey Monster, organizations need to practice structured, purposeful transparency, the kind that doesn't just inform people but accelerates execution. And to do that, you're going to need some help.

The Cagey Monster Slayers

The Demystifier understands that transparency without clarity is just noise. And noise doesn't drive action. Most leaders assume that once they have explained the strategy, people understand it. That's a mistake. The truth is that understanding doesn't happen in a single meeting. It happens through availability, repetition, simplification, and assessment. Without those, even the best strategies get lost in translation. The Demystifier's job is to make sure that never happens.

You can think of a Demystifier like a pilot flying in turbulence — they don't flood passengers with unnecessary details, but they always keep them informed of the essential information and what's coming next. They cut through jargon and consultant-speak, breaking complex ideas into simple and repeatable messages. In other words, they don't just communicate; they provide a sense of clarity by understanding their audience. They help their audience assess and make decisions based on a nuanced understanding of available information.

If the Demystifier provides clarity, the Empath provides the support structure to address concerns and provide flexibility and resiliency when it comes to managing transformation. Poorly timed transparency can create panic. Oversharing without context leads to chaos. A great Empath knows that transparency is a delicate tool that must be wielded with intention and discretion.

The Empath knows how to modify communication in terms of tone, addressing issues, beliefs, and tasks to resonate with different groups across an organization.

The Empath works on three dimensions:

- **Cognitive:** The ability to understand another's thoughts, emotions, and perspectives. How would you respond in a similar situation? Does your understanding of another's experience accurately reflect how it resonates with that person?
- **Emotional:** The willingness to share another's emotional state and acknowledge their feelings. It may involve feeling a sense of care, connection, and appreciation for another person's emotions.
- **Behavioral:** An aptitude for demonstrating a sense of empathy for others, such as communicating concern and understanding and matching body language. Empathic behaviors at work include caring communication, behavioral mirroring of nonverbals, being curious about and eliciting other people's perspectives, inclusive collaboration and teamwork, and active listening (giving someone your full attention and trying to understand what they are saying).[2]

"Your Lips Move But I Can't Hear What Your Sayin'"

Take the case of organizations that struggle with a consistent understanding of a transformation's purpose across all levels. A typical company launches a transformation initiative with a grand announcement, followed by a few leadership updates and a cascade of meetings. Within a few weeks, confusion sets in. Consistency of messaging erode over time? Different teams begin to interpret the same message in different ways. Priorities shift. Execution stalls. The transformation effort that once seemed so promising dissolves into a series of disconnected projects.

The Demystifier prevents this by repeatedly connecting and reconnecting employees with the rationale and goals of the transformation. They become the conduit for employees to understand the most common questions – "What's my role?" and "What's in it for me?" Instead of vague strategic goals, they help to create foundational tasks associated with successful execution. Instead of one-off updates, they establish rituals of transparency that prevent ambiguity from creeping in.

In one of our interviews, an executive explained that the Demystifiers in their organization implemented structured execution reviews where each team owned four measurable outcomes per quarter, with clearly defined ways to achieve them. Instead of having endless status meetings where teams struggled to explain progress, the Demystifier created structured engagement reviews to keep all folks involved – "in the loop." Instead of assuming alignment after a single presentation from leadership, the Demystifier reinforces clarity through weekly standups, where execution risks are regularly identified and addressed.

Celebrate Victories and Build Belief

Poorly sequenced transparency leads to distrust and disengagement. Teams either feel blindsided by sudden shifts or grow cynical when they hear about bold new initiatives that never seem to materialize. The Empath ensures that transparency builds momentum, not confusion. They create structured communication rituals that keep the various groups within an organization informed without overwhelming them. They know that people don't believe in change because of one big announcement; they believe in it because of a series of smaller, visible wins.

This is why some of the best transformations create rallying cries – memorable, unifying missions that turn strategy into action. Organizations that do this well don't just launch a transformation; they brand it. They give people a reason to connect to the change emotionally and intellectually. Andy Grove, former CEO of Intel, famously said, "Business success contains the seeds of its own destruction. Success breeds complacency. Complacency breeds failure. Only the paranoid survive." In a sense, he was making sure everyone in the company understood to stay vigilant, embrace change, and never get too comfortable. The Empath's ultimate skill is sequencing – knowing what to share, when to share it, and how to make it resonate. Without them, transparency becomes a liability instead of an asset.

Radical Transparency

Are you an effective and open communicator? How do you know? How do you take into consideration your audience's attention span and ability to retain and process the information you provide? If you purposely withhold specific information, what assumptions do people make in the absence of complete information transparency? If the Demystifier and Empath can help facilitate basic transparency in a company's transformation efforts, then radical transparency represents a next-level approach. This philosophy, championed by high-growth companies like Netflix, Bridgewater Associates, and Tesla, encourages transparency throughout the organization and even with their customer base, sharing information normally kept private like salaries, performance feedback, and internal challenges. Just like any competency, radical transparency needs to be practiced to make sure it ultimately achieves its goals without causing any undue misfires. The core philosophy revolves around five basic principles:

1. **Open communications:** Everyone has **access** to all company information, even traditionally sensitive topics.
2. **Trust and collaboration:** Culture of **shared** responsibility.
3. **Accountability:** Mistakes and failed expectations are discussed **openly** to improve decision-making.
4. **Timely and honest feedback:** Employees are encouraged to give direct and **unfiltered** feedback in a timely manner.
5. **Data-informed decision-making:** Decisions are made with **data** using objective metrics rather than internal politics.

The bolder words in the list represent typical "friction points" that radical transparency tries to address head-on. In open communications, access is an operative word where companies need to think about equal access, meaning that information should be available via different channels in formats that employees can absorb and understand. A good example is the privacy policy information provided to consumers (access), which is often difficult to interpret and understand and nearly impossible to read and assess. A study from the Consumer Policy Research Center (CPRC) in Australia found that consumers would have to carve out an average of 14 hours just to read the privacy policies of the sites and apps used in one day. Some of the longest privacy policies were in excess of 300,000 words (three times the length of the book you are now reading!).

Supporters of radical transparency often discuss the benefits, including faster and better decision-making, greater levels of trust, improved speed, and increases in innovation capacity. That said, there are significant challenges, not only in making sure the organization is ready for this level of transparency but also with the issue of oversharing.

TMI, TMI!

What happens when you share too much information? Is this a TL/DR (too long, didn't read) situation? Often, communication will go out based on what leaders think employees should know, but not what they actually have time to consider. What people pay attention to and spend time assessing and understanding is shrinking as a result of information overload, competition for our attention, too little trust in what we read, and little practice in sharing and interacting. Companies need to effectively communicate to multiple stakeholders to create solidarity with transformations. This transparency provides the glue between all departments and roles to enable an understanding of what it will take and everyone's roles and address concerns/issues. The question remains: how do you make sure people assess and process information as effectively as possible?

We already mentioned a pilot talking with passengers, but what about a physician engaging with patients? Can you imagine if the pilot or physician spoke in a stressed, anxious voice? For the physician providing difficult news to patients, they need to be aware of the information their patient is processing. In stressful situations, people tend to rely on faster, more intuitive processing methods rather than engaging in slower, more deliberate analysis. This shift can lead to biases in decision-making and affect memory retrieval.[3] The same is true for transformation. Successful change management requires effective, frequent, and accessible communication. It also means having an understanding of how tone impacts communication. In a time of crisis, you need to be aware of how information could be perceived. Leaders need to be cognizant of transparency and how audiences might make assertions based on different factors, including the absence of complete information, potential competing information and stress-induced circumstances.

In addition to the volume of information, other secondary issues with transparency include widening the pool of decision-makers or the pitfalls of social comparison. Widening the pool of decision-makers is good practice in that it involves more people in the process (they feel part of it) but also potentially slows down the decision-making process by asking for everyone's input. In addition, some folks might not be in a position to offer insightful feedback for weighing in on the decision-making process. Social comparison occurs when people have a need to compare themselves to others. In the workplace, employees are often driven to compare the equity of contributions (inputs) and rewards (outcomes) relative to others. Perceiving the ratio of rewards to contributions as worse than other people's creates mental dissonance that can spiral into envy, distraction, stealing, withdrawing effort, or quitting.[4] Engaging is different from communicating; it's setting up a dialogue that involves active participation, which is predicated on empathy.

I "Get" You

To truly understand their own organizational work environment, companies need the ability to recognize the role of emotions in personal effectiveness, relationship building, and strong leadership. They need to assess emotional intelligence (EQ).

In Figure 5.1, companies with low EQ and closed transparency find themselves in the insular quadrant. Here, there is little trust and engagement. Everyone is suspicious of what is going on in other departments. With a higher EQ but still closed-off transparency, employees might feel manipulated. *What would that look like?* If we have a high level of transparency but low EQ, that is when we get into oversharing. Organizations strive to achieve both high EQ, through empowering empaths, and greater levels of openness, through empowering Demystifiers.

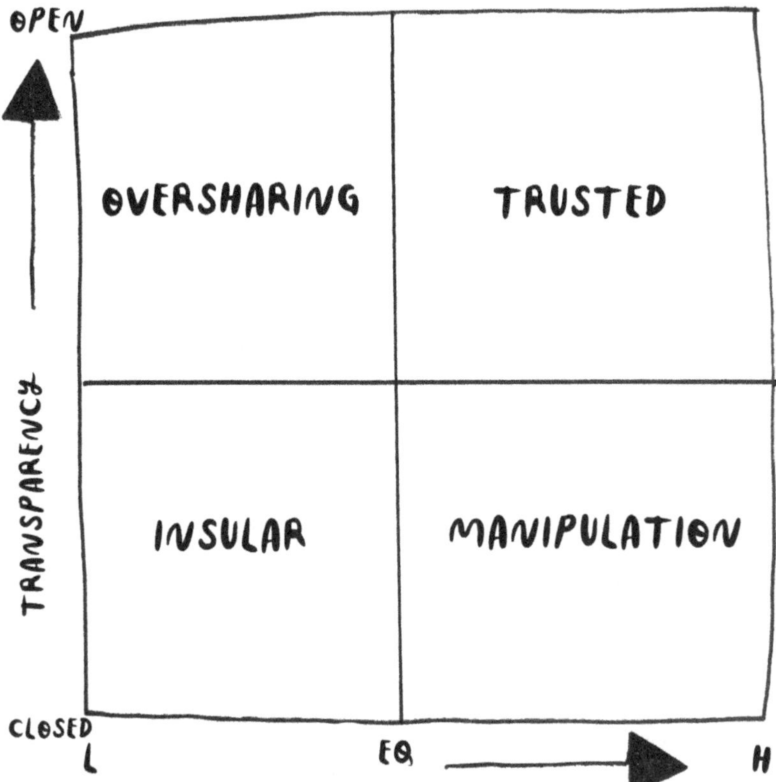

Figure 5.1 From insular to trusted.

Honesty Is the Best Policy

Are you truthful with your limitations and capabilities? Do you take responsibility for your actions and admit when you are wrong? Do you ask for help when you are out of your depth or simply over-committed?

Honesty is different from transparency or authenticity. Honesty refers to the quality of being truthful, sincere, and straightforward. It involves telling the truth, even if it is difficult or uncomfortable. As we have discussed in this chapter, transparency is about being open about actions, decisions, and intentions. It is critical for accountability.

Authenticity is about being as real as possible to your values and beliefs. Authenticity is associated with your personal (or even brand) identity and is critical in building and developing relationships. You cannot be authentic without being both transparent and honest. You need both. Leaders who promote transparency but are not completely honest with themselves, employees, and partners miss the boat. If you succumb to the Cagey Monster, you come across as inauthentic and, as a result, trust erodes.

Healthy workplaces require honesty to function effectively. Honesty involves volunteering as much information as possible so that others can assess validity and make appropriate decisions based on the completeness of information. And yet, being honest and transparent is challenging and can strain relationships. Without a full understanding of issues, people will often come to their own conclusions and have different beliefs across the organization. As AI accelerates the incidence of deep fakes and misinformation, erosion of trust is making society skeptical of any information that they encounter. Companies, departments, leaders, and employees need to work to develop cultures focused on transparency and honest interactions. This extends to being honest and transparent about themselves, beliefs, and organizational values.

Key Takeaways

The Cagey Monster, as we've discussed, thrives in an environment of unstructured transparency where updates are inconsistent, ambiguous, or chaotic. Organizations that

(Continued)

defeat it don't just talk about transparency, they practice it. That means:

- Understand that authenticity is built on transparency and honesty. This fundamental assessment will directly impact trust in your transformational initiatives.
- Know your audience. Be aware of tone, amount of information, frequency, and level of understanding.
- Establish execution rituals to prevent ambiguity, such as structured check-ins and leadership forums.
- Build systems where progress is visible in real time, through dashboards, scorecards, and objective tracking mechanisms.
- Use AI to amplify transparency rather than replace it, monitoring alignment gaps, surfacing risks, and enabling data-driven course corrections.

Ultimately, this isn't just about sharing more information, it's about making transparency a force multiplier for execution. Because the Cagey Monster fears nothing more than clarity with purpose.

Case Story: Patagonia

The Brand Behind the Brand. . .

While the outdoor apparel market is crowded with competition, Patagonia has long solidified its reputation as a company where values of sustainability, transparency, and conservation are as central to the company as the products they sell. Founded in 1973 by American rock climber Yvon Chouinard, the legendary outdoor apparel brand immediately embraced an anti-corporate appeal, preaching that "profit happens when you do everything else right." The company is committed to environmental activism and embraces unconventional workplace practices that encourage employees to balance work with their passions. Prioritizing profit shouldn't be the primary goal, as founder Chouinard had espoused, but rather a byproduct of doing business the right way. Translation: if the surf is good or the powder fresh, folks are free to hit the waves or mountains.

By the mid-2010s, the Ventura, California, company had grown into a successful Benefit Corporation (BCorp) with a devoted workforce and a reputation for integrity and sustainability. They donate 1% of top-line revenue, regardless of profit, to grassroots environmental efforts. They took ownership of the idea that happy, purpose-driven employees would produce great work.

Battling the Elements

As sales have grown and consumers have embraced the idea of sportswear and outdoor apparel as everyday wear – "athleisure" – competition has increased. Many well-known brands – North Face, Marmot, REI, among others – compete in the same lane with Patagonia. What's more, several trends in corporate social responsibility (CSR) have become fundamental for all brands competing in the space:

- **Sustainable and transparent manufacturing:** As more information has become available to consumers, products are increasingly scrutinized to make sure they are not only ethically sourced but the manufacturing facilities comply with CSR. Programs like Patagonia's Footprint Chronicles give consumers a unique view into where and how their products are manufactured. Their Worn Wear program started as a clothing swap, diverting apparel and gear that might be designated for the landfill to give them a second life.

- **Ecofriendly materials:** Greater scrutiny on materials and the impact on the environment led to waterproofing without PFCs (fluorocarbons). PFCs, also known as forever plastics, can leach into the water system during manufacturing and build up in the food chain, becoming toxic to humans and wildlife. Outdoor enthusiasts aren't particularly keen on having gear sprayed with a chemical that is destroying the environment.

- **Performance and technical innovations:** This includes a broad area of smart textiles that might include temperature regulating or moisture wicking, athleisure, and multifunctional apparel to transition from outdoor wear to casual wear and breathable, weather-resistant fabrics like GORE-TEX.

- **Inclusivity and representation:** A greater focus on product development and marketing to traditionally underrepresented communities in the outdoor gear market (disabled, women), as well as branching into different outdoor activities.

Save or Repair the Planet/Company

After Dean Carter joined Patagonia as head of people and culture in 2015, the company was at an inflection point in 2018. While sustainability and transparency were still the fundamental principles of the brand, Dean recognized that the company's human resources policies didn't completely reflect those ideals. This wasn't simply corporate "virtue signaling" on his part but in fact about a desire to make a transformational change in employee culture and internal processes to better reflect the brand's larger values. Dean recognized that the company's HR policies and programs should do the same — reflect the new mission statement. Patagonia's founder and leadership team changed their mission statement from a concept of "doing no unnecessary harm" to "We're in business to save our home planet." This entailed shifting deeper into products that would restore the planet, like food grown through regenerative organic agricultural practices. It also prompted the question, "Who are we saving it for?" This honest consideration of the company's new purpose led to an increased focus on inclusivity to incorporate communities most impacted by the climate crisis.

This meant that Dean and his team needed to evaluate all policies, procedures, and applications with a central question: how does it extract or add value for employees? This led to a complete revamping of policies and processes. In a sense, Dean was making sure Patagonia didn't just talk the talk but walked the walk as well.

Rethink Everything

For Dean, the Cagey Monster wasn't apparent in the way that leadership engaged with employees or how they interacted with the public; it was more associated with whether Patagonia was being honest with itself. Repairing the planet meant that they would have to review everything from the products they sold to the internal practices they fostered. It took a huge amount of courage to rethink why the company exists, who they were serving, and the totality of their impact. It would take an even larger effort to assess everything using this lens. For one, they would need to transition from products that might harm the planet and move toward services and products that are regenerative (saving the planet). This would not be like using carbon offsets, which is paying for the ability to do harm to the planet. It meant making tough decisions around specific products that don't align with the company's mission. Patagonia's number-one product is fleece. However, microplastics slough off in the washing machine, leeching out into the water supply. Patagonia had a very transparent stance about poisoning the ocean. While Patagonia engineered fleece to be less sloughy, there were still microplastics released into the ocean, not just by Patagonia but by everyone's fleece. To build a solution that would not only benefit Patagonia but also impact all products, Patagonia collaborated to bring about a solution by working with appliance manufacturers to ensure washing machines came with micro-fiber filters. Other efforts entailed:

- Promoting sustainable farming through regenerative ecofriendly agriculture, Patagonia Provisions. The food industry impacts biodiversity, climate change, and soil health through a focus on regenerative farming. Patagonia is leaning into its ethos by improving soil health, reducing carbon emissions, and restoring ecosystems.

- Re-evaluating every product and ranking it from net negative to net positive impact, asking essential questions like is the product not only functional and durable, but can it be used for more than one purpose?

- Being completely transparent about controversies. In 2015, PETA uncovered footage of sheep being horribly mistreated in a wool supplier in Argentina. Patagonia immediately cut ties with the manufacturer, but the incident revealed more than just animal cruelty; the industry was not sustainable, contributing to land degradation, carbon emissions, and water wastage. Patagonia paused wool sales, developed responsible wool standards, switched to certified suppliers, and increased transparency to track their entire wool supply chain.

As the company focused on honesty and transparency associated with initiatives to promote their vision, Dean worked on making sure internal processes associated with HR reflected the cultural shift the company was making. Dean focused on building trust, inclusivity, transparency, and psychological safety. "It's incredibly important for companies to leverage systemic, unconventional, and regenerative practices to drive a more sustainable and thriving future . . . purpose-centric leaders and cultures can accomplish good on a previously unimaginable scale." Dean fostered open communication, regularly sharing the why behind changes, and even engaging employees in co-creating solutions. This helped develop trust, allowing employees to embrace transformation rather than fear it.

Walk the Walk

Internally, Dean infused the culture of repairing the planet and being net positive to transform the workplace to reflect brand values. Taking the concept of a regenerative mindset and applying it to HR processes by asking how the company could give back more to employees' lives than it takes. One of his first moves was to overhaul performance management. He realized that traditional annual reviews and ratings were extractive, often draining morale and time without benefiting employees. Dean ended the formal performance ratings. Patagonia shifted toward ongoing feedback and development-focused conversations, freeing people from anxiety about numeric ratings. Dean asked managers to treat team members as if they'd be with Patagonia for 100 years. This mindset of long-term people development led to policies that favored trust over control and focused on **employees' experience**. This ensured Patagonia's mission reached employees at all levels at each phase of their tenure at Patagonia and included:

- New hires and immersive outdoor experiences associated with orientation. This helps to reinforce the mission.
- Environmental Internship program. This gave employees up to two months of paid leave to work for an environmental nonprofit.
- Internal discussion and activities that helped employees acknowledge the privilege in its traditional market and focus on initiatives benefiting frontline communities suffering from climate change.
- Focused on working parents and covering child care. Dean leaned into Patagonia's already generous parental leave policies and encouraged a culture that "normalizes" parenting needs. One hundred percent of new mothers at Patagonia returned to work after maternity leave in recent years, far above national averages.
- Changed the work week to a half-day on Friday while closing the office every other Friday. This meant employees were able

to take three consecutive days off every other week, which led to a significant improvement in questions like "I have a better relationship with my spouse" and "I have more time to get outside and do the things I love" – with no change in productivity.

Dean's commitment to transparency, honesty, and authenticity completely slayed the Cagey Monster. By focusing on what the company stands for and taking those concepts internally, Dean embraced Patagonia as a pioneer in responsible business practices. Patagonia's experiment became a showcase for how rethinking work can improve life. By focusing on putting more value to employees than extracting, Patagonia built a culture of trust and purpose. Employee satisfaction increased, engagement rose, and the company was able to be agile and transform while meeting financial goals.

Dean points out that revenue does not need to be sacrificed to do the right things for your employees and the planet. Key considerations were:

- Leading with purpose and value. Does this action reflect what we stand for as an organization?
- Authenticity and transparency build trust.
- Being honest with yourself and challenging the status quo: do your processes, products, and strategies reflect what your values?
- Focusing on the employee experience and treating them as whole people. Investing in people and supporting their personal lives leads to greater performance and loyalty.
- Infusing a purpose-driven culture into the workforce.

Try This: Does This Make Sense?

The Cagey Monster hides in complexity, thriving on jargon, ambiguity, and insider speak. If your transformation sounds smart but no one actually gets it, it's time to simplify.

Step 1: Demystify

List three outcomes your team is driving this quarter.
    Under each, add up to three key inputs.
    Keep it human. Ditch the jargon, acronyms, and buzzwords.

Step 2: Connect

Share your list with a colleague outside your team.
    Ask: "Does this make sense to you?"
    If not, revise. If yes, you're on the right track.

Step 3: Repeat and Reflect

Try it with two more colleagues from different departments.
    What landed? What didn't? Keep refining until the message is clear across the org.

Bonus Move:

Ask GenAI: "Would a 10-year-old understand this?"
    If not, simplify further.
    Clarity kills confusion. The simpler your message, the faster your team can move.

Chapter 6

Enter the Test Kitchen

Transformation is filled with unknowns. Known unknowns and unknown unknowns. How will different work models impact corporate culture, productivity, and worker satisfaction? What happens if we develop the wrong product? What happens if we develop the right product for the wrong market? Or the right product and market, but our customers don't know how to use it properly? Every company is in a continuous state of transformation, some purposeful, some unintentional. Even going out of business is a kind of transformation. There are large-scale transformations that impact the entire organization and others that impact only a group, division, or process. In this book, we have identified several monsters (barriers) that hinder successful transformation efforts.

The Lackadaisical Monster is clearly present when companies become complacent and set in their ways. Transformation occurs when needed and usually never at scale. Organizational learning might be done to check off a box to meet an industry standard or requirement or provide training to enable a new application, process, or tool, but it's not systematic across the organization. There is no time for holistic collaborative learning, let alone assessment and reflection. These companies lie in wait for transformation to happen to them rather than experimenting with continuous change and addressing what the future might hold.

Companies looking to shake off the Lackadaisical Monster need help by enabling what we refer to as **LEAR – Learning, Experimentation, Assessment, and Reflection**. This way of thinking can spark a cultural shift across the organization, enabling adaptation and learning. To get there, we need some help. We need folks who have skills in gathering and organizing information, uncovering dormant issues that can be tested, developing experimental models to address issues, collaborating with diverse stakeholders on interpreting results, iterating, and helping to develop prototypes to test. Experiments might be focused on internal workforce productivity, collaboration, and adoption patterns, or externally focused on customer needs, product development, and feature assessment. Sometimes they can be doing many things at once – developing applications, processes, and tools that serve internal stakeholders and can be commercialized for customer use. Here, you need the help of the Mad Scientist and the Analyst.

The Lackadaisical Monster Slayers

We use the term "Mad" figuratively here. They are not angry or insane but simply think differently. They believe that most anything – process efficiency, customer value, employee engagement – can be measured and assessed. Experiments on changes in the status quo can be understood to determine their potential benefit but also used to assess limitations and potential negative ramifications. They know how to take employees questions about the world around them and turn them into testable hypotheses. Experimentation, in the Mad Scientist's view, is a collaborative applied view of learning.

They would be right. Their view is that running experiments is the only way to identify the best possible approach to product development, website changes, and especially organizational transformation. They understand that fear of the unknown slows down innovation, creates risk aversion, and stifles forward progress.

The Mad Scientist understands that the Lackadaisical Monster is not rooted in laziness but rather in complacency and accepting the status quo because of an uncertain or complex future. They understand that finding the optimal path forward is way more efficient than spending endless development cycles to address uncertainties. The Mad Scientist is an educator helping departments and groups across the organization to understand the phases, components, and benefits of experimental design and implementation. From developing product teams to assessing operations, the Mad Scientist can facilitate experiments to help address the optimal way to move forward given a set of constraints.

THE
ANALYST

Experimentation can be simple, but often never is, largely because so much is happening at the same time. Complexity occurs when we consider all the different variables required for experimentation. We need to have independent (what you change) versus dependent (what you observe) versus control (what stays fixed) variables. Perhaps we want to experiment with the impact of a process change, considering factors like day of the week, time of day, frequency of utilization, and number of people impacted. Or perhaps we have an experiment on new customer product development and need to take into consideration market segmentation, competition, regulation, value assessment, services consideration, and support analysis. Experimentation can become complex data projects, which is where the Analyst goes to work.

The Analyst is responsible for collecting and interpreting operational data, analyzing patterns and trends, and making suggestions for data-informed decisions. In any organization, there are different types of analysts – business, financial, marketing, data, etc. Our monster-slaying Analyst is both an "organizational" analyst *and* a market analyst. They analyze patterns across the organization, integrate with other analysts to make sure the Mad Scientist has the data needed to successfully run experiments, measure them effectively, and iterate over a set time frame.

The Analyst provides research on market conditions to find needs, gaps, and opportunities. This is critical to increase transformative capacity and efficiency. For example, they might identify that certain employees are slow to adopt certain digital processes. Is this the result of needing more time to learn a new process? Or is there information that employees don't understand? Maybe there's another, unanticipated factor that is inhibiting adoption. The Analyst works with a team to gather data, develop testable hypotheses, run experiments, and report the results. They can also help in weeding out bias – that is, what you think versus what you know. Perhaps there needs to be a modification to the design. The Analyst ultimately works with the Mad Scientist to develop methods and standards to successfully scale experimentation across the organization.

Know More, Do More

Organizational learning is the process by which organizations acquire, interpret, and apply knowledge to develop new products and services (innovation); adapt to changing market conditions; and develop internal process efficiencies. But how do we develop and accelerate organizational learning? First, the Mad Scientist can help management see that there are various different types. Education studies have long revealed that there are three predominant modes of learning:

- **Rote-based learning:** Memorizing information through repetition. Most learners will forget a large quantity of this knowledge over time.
- **Simulated learning:** Learning by doing in a simulated environment, like a case study or simulation application, to practice skills and procedures.
- **Experiential learning:** Acquiring knowledge in a completely immersive environment, which reinforces the importance of context and organizational challenges.

Organizations that focus on learning understand the role mentorship can play in not only transferring practical knowledge but also creating a sense of connection. They also understand that it builds confidence for the mentee and also the mentor associated with providing useful, practical, and actionable advice. Organizations that focus on mentorship make sure that they recognize the value add, allocate sufficient time and space for mentoring, and most importantly compensate accordingly. There are folks that are naturally inclined to mentor or be mentored, but if there is no thought put into connecting the right folks or incentivization patterns, the organization will have a difficult time growing, scaling, and creating an effective mentorship program. Organizations focused on learning also understand that much like sports teams need a variety of different coaches to help them succeed, organizational teams need advisors that can provide a sounding board for ideas, challenge conventional thinking, and suggest resources for them to have the best possible chance for success.

The Analyst/Mad Scientist helps you recognize the different types of learners and ways of learning within an organization. In addition, embedded within an organization is knowledge, facts, information, and skills that we need to bring forward to develop organizational learning. These include tacit, explicit, and implicit knowledge. Tacit is knowledge we possess from personal experience, such as knowing how to motivate teams. Explicit is documented (company handbook, policies, etc.) that can be easily shared with a wide and diverse audience. Imagine tacit knowledge as a vast reservoir of precious material to extract, codify, and share.

Adapt or Die

Adaptation is at the heart of any effort to defeat the Lackadaisical Monster. Many organizations try to put in place mechanisms in the hopes of being adaptive. Unfortunately, policies, procedures, uncertainties, risk avoidance culture, and information silos stifle adaptability, often limiting an organization's ability to transform.

The Analyst and Mad Scientist develop processes to expand organizational learning, not just in bringing diverse groups and interests together but in creating a blueprint for adaptation, and consequently transformation. Because transformational challenges are complicated by many factors, the Analyst uses systems thinking or understanding how systems within an organization are connected to each other rather than isolated in their own domain. There are some that say thinking is simply thinking, but we can help folks learn how to think outside of their own domain to appreciate the intricacies of how systems are connected to each other. This shift from observing events or data to viewing things holistically with cause and effect assessment can help identify patterns of behavior and surface what promotes those events and patterns. The Analyst helps employees observe the world around them while engaging empathically with others providing a more comprehensive view. They force folks to think about the interrelatedness and connectivity associated with problem-solving.

Experts in learning describe a mental model, which is a set of beliefs on how you make sense of the world and consequently make decisions. After all, if employees all have different mental models, how can you achieve consensus? How can an organization get on the same page?

This idea of creating a shared mental model is, in fact, a big part of organizational learning. This is not a shared belief in everything, but rather it is being on the same page about the most important things for transformation. This is much different and more challenging than just simply "Thou shall do this or else." It's easy to have a top-level executive declare, "Here's what we will be doing and why we are doing it." It's much more challenging to persuade folks that the proposed direction is in the best interest of everyone involved.

Our shared belief in talking with people across different organizations is that creating a shared mental model can be done only via experimentation, with the caveat that everyone must agree on what constitutes "ground truth" and how to agree on interpretability. Without continuous learning and experimentation, transformation efforts suffer from half-hearted efforts or a lack of focus. It becomes an exercise in checking a box and giving in when things get complex or messy. It becomes territorial with decision-makers arguing that they have taken into consideration everyone's best interests without actually having done so. Discussion on direction leads to conflict and tension. Making a new, combined, effective mental model involves thinking critically, asking questions, and offering a safe space to challenge the status quo, which the Mad Scientist and Analyst help to orchestrate.

How can we obtain common ground on the most reliable or accurate interpretation or make a new combined mental model? Think critically, ask questions, and have a safe space to challenge the status quo.

Experiment Like You Mean It

Does the thought of experimentation conjure up images of lab coats and test tubes? When you hear the term Mad Scientist do you think of Dr. Frankenstein putting together discarded human parts to develop a monster? Experimentation is continually done at an individual and department/group level. For experimentation to help management make better decisions, there needs to be a process of standardization so experiments can be replicated and expanded. Our Mad Scientist is an expert in putting together the design of the experiment so that it can run effectively, efficiently, and consistently across the organization. This includes setting up the following elements:

- **Assumption** is an underlying belief about the validity of your idea.
- **Evidence** is required to validate or refute a given assumption. It could be something you observe and measure.
- **Hypothesis** is a proposed explanation for a given phenomenon (what you want to test).
- **Benchmarking** is establishing thresholds for a given measurement.
- **Aspirational markers** are what you think is reasonable to achieve given the product/service becomes operational.

Genchi Genbutsu is a Japanese principle often associated with the Toyota Production System. Literally translated as "actual place, actual thing," it's a phrase connected to the management idea that quality insight comes from direct observation, or "Go see for yourself." In doing so, a manager can observe an actual issue on the manufacturing floor and assess it in a holistic perspective. They can talk to employees, observe the process, and examine the actual equipment firsthand.

By observing the world around them, employees can develop ideas on how to make products, services, and processes more beneficial, efficient, and even innovative. These "What might happen if" statements resonate deeper with firsthand knowledge. Our Mad Scientist helps with the experimental design by developing more specificity associated with the hypothesis. This is critical since experimentation takes up resources, so you want to be judicious in understanding the value, potential, and time risk.

If we look at the matrix in Figure 6.1, some experimentation might be designed simply to build a better model and framework. Quick and easy experiments can build competency and trust. They can be deployed to test new processes and understand adoption patterns. High-effort and low-impact experiments should be avoided since they drain energy and waste time for little payoff. In this case, we might want to revise the hypothesis selection and assessment phase. What we are interested in moving to is the Experimental Olympics quadrant, where we can run simultaneous tests to identify new digital tools and processes for employees or customers. Companies with an experimental culture have a virtuous cycle of experimenting, iterating, and learning. In these organizations, momentum beats perfection, and "Fail Fast" is rebranded to "Learn Fast." The experimental Olympics quadrant is the pinnacle, where all your efforts and trials have paid off, and you can

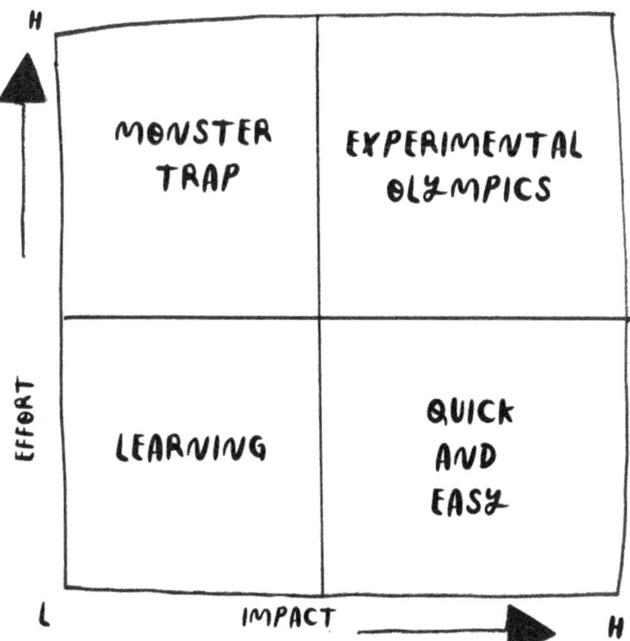

Figure 6.1 From learning to the experimental Olympics.

put forward experiments to develop the evidence needed to make substantial changes.

It is a good bet that you already have people in your organizations running their own experiments, homegrown mini Mad Scientists, trying to see what might work best for them. This might be around efficiency gains, health benefits, social connections, and so on. Let's say we have an employee, Syd who starts their workday at 8 am after going to the gym at 7 am and grabbing a smoothie. They believe they can get more done in the morning, improving efficiency, but they also worry about their ability to get into work efficiently. So, they change their schedule, getting to the gym at 6 a.m. and starting the day at 7 am. They soon realize they are getting more stuff done and feel less stressed during the day. Syd also realizes that there are more opportunities to interact on a collaborative level with a variety of folks at work prior to the rush of the workday, competing for everyone's attention.

The unknown was understanding how much more productive they would be coming in an hour earlier as well as greater potential for collaboration. In his own way, Syd developed a hypothesis and conducted their own experiment to assess benefits, potential, risks, and mitigation mechanisms. This is a relatively basic example of learning through experimentation, reflection, and assessment. If we take this experiment and apply it to organizational issues, it might fall into the learning quadrant – low impact + low effort. These distinctions are important to learn. The Mad Scientist can assist in how to set up the experimental design, scale across the organization and quickly get results.

We might have experiments that assess a function within a process that we would like to roll out across the organization. An example is the triage function within customer service calls. In the triage process, it's important to categorize and prioritize incoming complaints based on complexity, issue, and urgency so that they can be routed correctly. Experimentation can be done with routing logic by customer segment, triage method, looking at manual agent versus AI triage method, or first question script – "Tell us your issue" or "please select an option." This might be low effort but high impact associated with the benefit it could provide.

All experiments have some central components to them, including:

- **Framing a testable idea:** In our example, Syd wanted to test and see if getting in an hour early could make him more productive.
- **Defining the evidence needed to test the hypothesis:** Syd might develop a scorecard of what productivity looks like over the course of a typical workweek and come up with an assessment method.

In the experimental design, we are not looking for a solution, but instead to validate a set of assumptions. Let's say we have an idea to develop an AI-enabled product of some household item – a flower vase, coffee carafe, lamp, etc. This sounds high-tech and fancy, but it's not testable yet because the product lacks definition. If I ask multiple people to develop an AI-enabled product, they might come up with different ideas for the product. Using LLM or Generative AI, they may put in a slightly different prompt ending up with different ideas. This is why folks need to be better at framing the idea in terms of value, function, or usage. The Analyst can help by collecting market research, including what people are buying, what they value, issues with coffee consumption, etc. Good experimental design can help deal with situations that might skew results, such as low-traffic scenarios as a result of website design.

The Mad Scientist understands the impact of levers for experimentation. Levers include targeting (new versus returning users), messaging (formal versus casual tone), channels (phone versus chat-based), or timing (weekday versus weekend). Oftentimes, the end result is too small to measure statistically. This can skew results, and random variations can look like real effects. Acting on tiny sample sizes may lead you to abandon good ideas or roll out bad ones. In short, small experiments tell you something happened; they don't reliably tell you why or something you can bet on. The Mad Scientist and Analyst work together to aggregate data, assess exploratory versus "official" experimentation, and decentralize decision-making while centralizing the experimental process. This is critical in developing agreed-upon metrics and entrusting teams. Digital native companies – those founded or operating in the digital world – are familiar with this kind of experimentation. However, within legacy companies, experimentation sounds like a risk. Reframing the value of experimentation for different audiences could help internalize the value. Let's say you have multiple product teams, each looking to make changes in the code to add features, functions, etc. Every code change needs a variety of people to sign off on it. By shifting the messaging from "Let's allow teams to continually experiment with the design" to "Let's give management a way to remove code from production instantly," you develop a value proposition that a specific group can understand and sign off on. The Mad Scientist and the Analyst are central to infusing an experiential culture across the organization. By standardizing methods and procedures, organizations can slay the lackadaisical monster through avoiding developing silos of experiments, acting on bad data, building trust in the experimental method, stalling innovation, and removing systemic bias.

To Be or Not to Be

Do you have a nagging suspicion about the efficiency and optimization of your website? Or do you think a new product feature could increase customer value? An A/B test is a well-known method to test these hypotheses but also a powerful experimental method for organizational transformation. Incentive structure, work modality, training and upskilling, and communication strategies can all be turned into A/B tests to assess adoption rate, employee engagement, and productivity. The idea behind the test is to assess an independent variable while ensuring other variables are fixed. Suppose you had a pet accessory ecommerce site, and you had one large picture of a cute kitten pushing a ball on your home page. You hypothesize that by placing multiple images on your home page of a variety of cats doing different activities would boost your click-through rate (CTR). This is a measure of how many visitors to your website enter, explore content, and engage in different activities – learning about products, adding themselves to a mailing list, shopping for products, etc. You would have two condition states (A, one picture; B, multiple pictures) and a hypothesis that B would lead to a higher CTR. Through A/B testing you determine folks prefer B over A, but why? Is it a result of a greater number of pictures leading to a higher CTR or the variety of different cats and products in different contexts and want to now shop for those items? The goal is to try to disprove the null hypothesis, which is the original state. Colin Mcfarland, who was director of experimentation at Skyscanner, said "Design like you're right, test like you're wrong."[1] A variety of experiments are done over a period of time to try to invalidate the control state (null hypothesis).

Initial experimentation might provide exploratory analysis that leads to additional experimentation. The Mad Scientist and Analyst need to bring folks together to agree not only on experimental models but also on assessment and reflection. This is designed to develop a shared mental model that can lead to action and rationale. With A/B tests, there needs to be alignment on business goals. In this case, we looked at website CTR, but it could easily be ported to different business goals, like how to onboard customers effectively.

It's Alive, It's Alive!

Besides A/B testing, the Mad Scientist and Analyst might do a series of field tests, running the experiment in the real world. Why is this important? Well, research and development (R&D) can be largely defined and operationalized once we identify the features and functions. Deployment, by contrast, is another animal; it's sometimes tough to ensure things go as planned. When we deploy things, they are subject to many different variables. Think about the cultural, demographic, technical, social, and economic factors that come into play when applications become available to the public. This is one of the reasons field tests are critical. Cognitive walkthroughs are experiments where users are invited to walk through the concept in detail, providing you with feedback. Simulations, either physical or virtual, provide you with an assessment of how people are interacting with the end-user experience. Trials can be used as well on functional prototypes to get a well-rounded understanding of how control groups, like beta users, are interacting with the application.

Of course, running a trial or even a simulation may require building a prototype or minimal viable product (MVP) as a necessary stage to see the application, product, or process out in the wild. Translating an experimental setting to an organizational environment is a challenge based on challenges that need to be factored in – competing initiatives, behavior patterns, integration points, etc. Companies often have applications they have developed in the beta stage for a period of time. They do this to let the early adopter community know that it's still being tested. It's still being tested. What is it being tested for?

Usability: Do the early users understand how to access, use, and get value from the application?

Robustness: Are there software bugs in the code that might have to be addressed prior to the application going to a GA (Generally Available) release?

The Mad Scientist might have to help the group understand the parameters of the testing situation and how to reduce false positives and negatives. They might have to help develop adequate random samples.

At some point, the Mad Scientist will likely need to work with the team on how to move forward to the next phase of testing. Experimentation cannot be used to slow down development. There is always another set of experiments to be done, more data to be tested, but working toward a perfect set of experiments is expensive, time-consuming, and – if we're being honest – doesn't exist. How can the team move forward with a high degree of confidence to identify reactions, stress testing, and adoption patterns? The Mad Scientist and the Analyst provide the structure and methodology to scale experiments but also the assurance on when to move forward with conviction and confidence.

Stop, Think, Assess

There are two aspects to LEAR that are critical in building up your experimental capacity. You don't want your Mad Scientist so inundated with experimental requests that it's impossible to think clearly about what you are learning from these tests. How do you assess which experiments should be run?

The 2 × 2 matrix (Figure 6.1) of impact over effort illustrates one way to set your priorities. Let's say we are working within one of the desired quadrants and have several hypotheses that we believe are valid, testable, and generate value. Which do you pick, and how do you create consensus moving forward? We could get some help from our Analyst. After all, they are skilled at gathering, collecting, and organizing information to help us build the evidence required to make adequate decisions. Another method is a simple assessment grid (see Figure 6.2). This compares different hypotheses against each other over a number of different attributes that the group believes are important in assessment – level of effort, impact, risk, etc. These are easy to create and basically have different people and groups involved in the experimentation scoring attributes for the different hypotheses proposed. In doing so, you can create a visual means of assessing the benefit/risk trade-off associated with all the different hypotheses under consideration.

Assessment scoring methods are a means to achieve some form of consensus between groups who have a vested interest and who

	IMPACT SCORE (1-10)	TIMING	LEVEL OF EFFORT	ALIGNED TO STRATEGY?	RISK SCORE (1-10)
HYPOTHESIS #1	7	MID TERM	●	YES	6
HYPOTHESIS #2	5	INTERMEDIATE	◑	NO	3
HYPOTHESIS #3	8	LONG	◢	YES	6

Figure 6.2　Rank and scoring matrix.

may stand to benefit from the experimentation process. Ultimately, as an organization grows its capacity to efficiently run experiments, it becomes easier to find data and make data-informed decisions. In addition, experimentation can be replicated, assessed, criteria noted, and trust in the process developed. Our Mad Scientist takes on the task of training others within the organization on how to make impactful experiments, while the Analyst helps narrow down testable hypotheses and ensure the market and organizational research is in place to assess the benefits and drive consensus.

Look in the Mirror, Not Out the Window

All of our work on hypothesis selection and experimentation will be quickly forgotten if we don't take time and effort to reflect on what occurred and why. The Analyst and Mad Scientist help with facilitation, transforming experiences into meaning. Reflecting is the "what," while experimenting is the "how." Reflection is critical and needs to be allotted for in an employee's task allocation and incentives. The US military, for instance, uses an after-action review to facilitate learning and improvement, analyzing the expected outcome of an event to revise future approaches, decide on incon-clusive results, strengthen and address weaknesses, and reduce the risk of misaligned actions. Once the experiment has been com-pleted, our Analyst helps to gather information from all those who took part in the experimental model. Actions help to reflect and understand how to:

- Extracting meaningful insights.
- Enhancing adaptability and continuous improvement.
- Avoiding repeated mistakes.
- Strengthen decision-making and strategy.

In the reflection toolkit from the University of Edinburgh, Dr. Roger Geenway[2] introduced the four F's framework for the active review process, highlighting the key elements to consider:

- **Facts:** An objective account of what happened.
  - What, who, where, when?
  - What was expected versus what actually happened?
  - What was the turning point or critical moment?
  - In what order did the events happen?
- **Feelings:** The emotional reactions to what occurred.
  - At what point did you feel least or most involved?
  - How did the situation make you feel?
- **Findings:** The concrete learnings that you can take away from the situation.
  - Why . . . did or didn't it work?
  - What would you have done differently/more of/less of?
  - What did you learn?
  - Do you wish you had done anything differently?
- **Future:** Structuring your learning so that you can use them in the future.
  - How will you implement your findings?
  - What has already changed?
  - What can you plan for the future?

Reflection needs to be done quickly once the experiment is concluded. If too much time passes, conditions change, invalidating the experiment and a need to start from the beginning again.

Reflection also involves understanding how to sell the vision to decision-makers, whether you are working on an internal process change or a new innovative product development. You may discover a need for further investigation through experimentation to determine support mechanisms, workflow development, user interface/experience assessment, or other instruments to make sure it's ready to go from the lab or a controlled environment to the public. In highlighting the organizational value of better experiments and thoughtful reflection, we can keep the Lackadaisical Monster at bay and shift thinking from "Fail Fast" to "Learn Fast."

Key Takeaways

The Mad Scientist and the Analyst are two central monster slayers critical to accelerating organizational transformation. Some of the important elements to consider from this chapter include:

- Organizations are always going through some transformation. "Always on" transformation means LEAR needs to be systematic and operationalized. Those organizations not investing in LEAR are at the whims of the Lackadaisical Monster.
- Experiments elaborate processes but can be done quickly and with high impact to reduce risk and build consensus.

(Continued)

> - LEAR is fundamentally a collaborative activity, from deciding on hypotheses to test to assessing what was learned and how to act on it.
> - LEAR helps organizations identify three key things to address: capacity, velocity, and assessment. What do we have? How fast can we move? What do we need?

Case Story: Ferrari

Changing Lanes

When Benedetto Vigna took the wheel as CEO of legendary sports car company Ferrari in 2021, it marked a radical shift. It was the first time in the company's 80-year history that a leader came not from the automotive tradition but from the world of semiconductors and sensors. Benedetto certainly had the know-how and pedigree to navigate an increasingly tech-driven world. A physicist by training and tech exec by experience, he had spent more than two decades in the microelectronics industry and was credited with innovations that changed the way smartphones and gaming devices interact with users.

Still, Benedetto's appointment was something of a surprise. Ferrari, after all, is one of the world's most prestigious luxury brands, with a reputation built on performance, design, and a storied history. The lore of the company's identity as a racing brand as well legendary founder Enzo Ferrari's personal history has long captured the public imagination with movies like *Ford versus Ferrari*, a film highlighting the company's dominance at the prestigious Le Mans race, as well as *Ferrari*, a biopic focused on Mille Miglia's race across Italy. (And let's not forget Tom Selleck's Ferrari 308 GTS in *Magnum PI* or the 1961 250 GT California Spider featured in *Ferris Bueller's Day Off*.)

Shifting into a Different Gear

The organizational culture of Ferrari was steeped in aspects of precision, performance, pride, and passion. Lessons from racing were embedded in their DNA including fast feedback loops, innovation under pressure, and redefining the limits of possible. In racing, negligence errors are analyzed and assessed but not tolerated. At Ferrari, there was a reverence for legacy and tradition with deep loyalty to the company's history. There was also an element of secrecy and control associated with carefully managing information flow and maintaining a tight grip on brand, image, and internal development. This led to a hierarchical structure in the organization focused on mastery and control. This was the opposite to the Silicon Valley culture focused on experimentation and disruption that can be seen in several high-tech companies.

For Ferrari's board, bringing Benedetto on as CEO was strategic. The company had achieved great success on paper: strong profits, limited model releases, and a deeply loyal customer base. Yet under the surface, there was a risk. Insufficient company's speed, uneven digital fluency, and some cultural resistance to new ways of thinking by some managers. Ferrari needed more than incremental improvement. It needed to learn differently, experiment broadly, assess deeply, and reflect faster. In short, it needed to activate the LEAR mindset – and Benedetto was the catalyst.

The Starting Line: Heritage Meets Headwinds

Before Benedetto's arrival, Ferrari's growth had been steady and its brand powerful. But change was looming fast. Rivals like Porsche were racing ahead in electrification. Tesla was redefining the relationship between software and speed. And consumer expectations were shifting – luxury no longer meant leather and horsepower alone; it also meant digital personalization, sustainability, innovation, and experience.

Decisions around tech and data were laborious and time-consuming because of poor teamwork among some managers. Electrification was treated as a future threat, not a current opportunity. The company's culture had long emphasized craftsmanship and tradition, but this attention to past ways of doing things made learning loops and experimentation feel foreign, scary, even counterproductive for career paths. Benedetto entered this environment not as a disruptor, but as a disciplined builder of capacity. From the outset, he signaled a new way forward, more open and direct.

Learning: Rewiring Ferrari's Thinking

"Our roots are deep, but we must have the courage to evolve the company using our unique competencies."
—Benedetto Vigna, 2022

Benedetto identified three main challenges upon joining Ferrari: teams working in isolation, hierarchical communication structures, and slow operational pace. He noted that while Ferrari was moving at a nice cruising speed compared to the rest of the auto industry, the company needed to pick up its pace in the coming years to stay competitive. One of his first initiatives was to assess the function of hierarchy. Previous leadership operated mostly in a top-down manner where communication was tightly controlled by leadership. Benedetto saw the need to honor the past but also address the future by using the hierarchical structure when it came to decision-making but making sure communications would be open to all. Hierarchy was critical for action and moving quickly but could be counterproductive for effective communication.

Benedetto began his leadership with a period of deep listening and sensemaking. Rather than launching immediate changes, he immersed himself in the company's operations – from engineering and manufacturing to customer experience and market dynamics. He asked pointed questions: What does performance mean in a world heading toward electrification? What is the Ferrari experience beyond the vehicle? How can we preserve the magic associated with the Ferrari culture while modernizing the method?

Benedetto put in place more open communication channels and encouraged scientific thinking. He personally conducted one-on-one meetings with hundreds of employees to understand the organization better. He found that the people's competency was strong and deep, but the culture needed some refinement.

Teams shared their hesitations – about breaking from legacy, about losing what made Ferrari distinct. But beneath the concerns, Benedetto also heard something else: a desire for change. People weren't unwilling – they were simply unsure of the path. From Benedetto's own words: "Ferrari was like a compressed spring, with a lot of energy to be released in the right direction."

Experimentation: Controlled Speed in a High-Performance Culture

One of Benedetto's key moves was to bring structure to experimentation. Ferrari, known for its perfectionism, had previously treated iteration as something to avoid. Benedetto reframed it as a source of strength. One of the challenges was the past and the strong connection to tradition. Engineers and designers meticulously labored over decisions at low pace since some managers were not collaborating and acting as one company, increasing development cycle times.

Benedetto has a specific example in mind: "When I joined the company, Ferrari's advanced hybrid sports car, the high-performance SF90 Stradale, had just been launched. Today, five years later, Ferrari continues to lead the way in luxury hybrid sports cars. At the time, many colleagues expressed disappointment about the supposedly poorly executed product ramp-up. In reality, the teams performed exceptionally well to bring such a complex and innovative car into production. The production has been highly successful, and our clients are very satisfied, but the political game among managers led to a poor internal perception."

He reorganized R&D, product development and industrialization departments, including quality. He also launched the e-building in Maranello, Italy a state-of-the-art facility that reflects the principle of technological neutrality, as it houses the production and development of internal combustion-engine cars, hybrids, and Ferrari's first electric model, beyond the production of electric engines, power electronics components, and batteries. This was an important milestone in the electrification journey that the Company started in Formula 1 track, in late 2009.

Rather than leap into full disruption, Benedetto emphasized progressive, structured experiments – EV internal components development, connected car features, digital interfaces – all designed to build internal confidence and capacity. Benedetto himself maintains personal involvement in laboratory visits during problem situations to demonstrate importance as well as hands-on consideration.

Assessment: Seeing the Road Ahead

To scale experimentation, Benedetto knew Ferrari had to become comfortable with measuring progress in new ways. He didn't flood teams with data-driven dashboards. Instead, he promoted tight, purposeful metrics – what's working, what's not, and where to double down.

Assessment wasn't just about finances but about learning as well. Benedetto encouraged cross-functional conversations around what experiments were teaching them – whether successful or not. One of the biggest mindset shifts was helping teams understand that failure wasn't a verdict, it was a source of insight. Benedetto recalls a particular case: "During the test drive of a hybrid Ferrari, a problem with the car highlighted a significant project mistake. This discovery allowed us to correct the issue before moving into production."

On metrics and success measures, Benedetto focused on product development time, time to market, and tracking business process changes. He also took into consideration the importance of soft indicators like employee engagement and willingness to share ideas.

As he assessed the challenges, Benedetto identified that middle management required demonstrations of successful transformations to overcome resistance. Benedetto emphasized a balance between top-down decisions and bottom-up innovation. He also went against a legacy thinking associated with time and effort to implement changes, challenging them to move more quickly. This emphasized the importance of trust in the process and with each other combined with a push to drive change. To continue to push the boundaries, he brought in expertise from outside automotive to share experimental thinking while still honoring experience from the past. Ferrari has further strengthened its open innovation approach under Benedetto's leadership. Ferrari has expanded its network of international suppliers and partners to co-develop and customize top-tier solutions.

While Ferrari continues to develop and manufacture its core components in-house, as it has always done since its foundation, it has formed more and more strategic partnerships for noncore hardware and software. These collaborations give Ferrari access to cutting-edge technologies, allowing the company to share know-how with partners and to improve design, performance, and driving thrills.

Reflection: Looking in the Rearview Mirror

Perhaps the most subtle transformation has been in Ferrari's culture of reflection. Teams began holding structured debriefs after major launches and internal initiatives. Mistakes weren't hidden – they were mined for learning. The company shifted its mindset from "do not fail" to "learn fast through failure," building a feedback loop that connected R&D, engineering, marketing, and customer experience. This reflective discipline allowed the company to course-correct quickly, improve product-market fit, and scale what worked.

AI has a future role at Ferrari but Benedetto views it as a tool that must be used wisely, advocating for a hybrid approach. He believes AI is good at summarizing past data, but he also understands that judgment remains essential for innovation. This approach honors Ferrari's history while adopting a balance between traditions (creativity and judgement) and future thinking on rapid experimentation and innovation.

Ferrari, under Benedetto, became not only a builder of beautiful machines, but a learning organization.

Around the Turn: Value, Velocity, and Vision

Under Benedetto's leadership, Ferrari hasn't just survived a period of industry upheaval – it has thrived.

- In 2024, Ferrari posted record revenues of €6.677 billion, up nearly 12% year-over-year while its stock price has more than doubled.
- Teams are on track to develop 15 new models, about one per quarter.
- Different teams are cooperating and sharing information without any bias, doubt or fears of becoming irrelevant.

Most importantly, Ferrari has revved up its internal transformation engine. Its people are learning, testing, evaluating, and reflecting faster and more fearlessly than before. The company hasn't abandoned its heritage. It's learning how to balance tradition and necessary change/evolution.

By activating the LEAR mindset, Benedetto taught an already high-performance organization how to accelerate learning – and, in doing so, future-proofed a legacy brand.

Try This: LEAR in a Flash

Lackadaisical Monster shows up when teams stop asking questions, stop trying new things, and settle into the status quo. This five-minute loop jolts your team back into motion.

Step 1: Learn (1 min)

Ask: "What's one thing we keep hearing complaints about?"
Write it down.

Step 2: Experiment (1 min)

Ask: "What's one low-risk thing we could try today to improve it?"
Jot it down.

Step 3: Assess (1 min)

Ask: "How would we know if it worked?"
Define a quick signal or metric.

Step 4: Reflect (2 min)

Ask: "What did we learn? What should we try next?"
Share insights out loud in the room.
Don't wait for a postmortem. LEAR fast, fix faster, and keep momentum alive.

Chapter 7

The C<blank><blank>O Issue

"Org charts aren't designed to get work done, they are designed so that the C-suite can cascade control through the organization."
—Chris Beale, Leading Agile

Remember the legendary hydra monster from Greek and Roman mythology? The hydra was a monstrous lake serpent with multiple heads, who Hercules was supposed to slay. According to many myths, the central head was immortal, and cutting off any of the other heads would cause two more new heads to grow. Sounds like a pretty formidable monster, also known as a Herculean task. Get it?

For us, the Hydra Monster appears when structural complexities and a love of hierarchy produce an endless creation of department heads and executives rather than actually addressing systemic problems.

Since the Industrial Revolution, industries like railroads and textile manufacturing have relied on hierarchies to create optimal efficiency and allow for functional specialization. Unfortunately, the end result was often bureaucracy. In the mid-twentieth century, we witnessed the evolution of the matrix structure, where employees reported to both a functional and a regional or product lead. This led to cross-functional coordination but also confusion and conflict.

Today, data-informed and AI-enabled organizations rely more on decentralization. Decentralization is a process by which companies enable departments, groups, and teams to engage in decision-making without the need to seek continuous approval from a centralized authority. This autonomy allows them to work in an effective and agile manner. By contrast, traditional organizations are stuck in a rut of endless cycles of reorganizations. Often, Legacy companies' reliance on outsourcing, joint ventures, and acquisitions has led to an even more fragmented ecosystem, with fewer clear lines of communication, decision-making, and accountability.

In our executive education sessions, we often joke that the solution to systemic problems these days is to take a C and an O and put another letter between them, and voila, you have just created a new chief officer. Sure, the company still has the original

Fab Five – CEO, CFO, CIO, COO, and CMO – but digitization has spawned multiple new heads, including:

- **CISO:** Chief Information Security Officer.
- **CDO:** Chief Data or Digital (take your pick) Officer.
- **CAO:** Chief Analytics Officer.
- **CDIO:** Chief Digital and Information Officer.
- **CDAIO:** Chief Digital and AI Officer.
- **COCO:** Chief Omni-Channel Officer.

Personally, we would like to see the Chief People, Place, and Policy Officer, otherwise known as the C3PO.

In some cases, we ran out of letters, so some had to be reused, like the CDO or the CEO could stand for Experience or Executive. In some cases, we see combining functions together, such as the CDIO, which covers the positions of the CDO (digital) and CIO (Information or Innovation). In other situations, we have the Chief Digital Transformation Officer (CDTO) or Chief Transformation Officer (CTO). Many of the folks we have interviewed look at the Transformation Officer as a temporary position that is established to centralize and scale transformation, but ultimately to be deleted and transfer transformation processes and skills back to different departments. However, what happens if you are in a constant state of change?

More often than not these days, creating new C-level positions becomes the solution to reduce complexity at many organizations. The rise of more officers within the organization creates more bureaucracy, spreading decision-making powers across a variety of chiefs, who then need to figure out how to drive consensus. Every new C-suite title comes with its own priorities, budget, and fiefdom. Every new leader wants their own team, roadmap, and data. Rather than being resourceful, they demand more and more resources. Before you know it, instead of solving problems faster, the company is stuck in endless meetings, competing priorities, and leadership turf wars. The typical solution these days is simple.

Add another leader – Chief Complexity Officer perhaps? – and just like that, the Hydra grows another head.

Simplicity Scales, Complexity Fails

The logic of adding a new leader makes perfect sense – on paper. The company faces a challenge, so they appoint someone to take charge of it. Data is a mess? Appoint a Chief Data Officer. Unsure of your AI strategy? Welcome, Chief AI Officer! Customer experience lacking? Sounds like a problem for the Chief Experience Officer.

And yet, with every new role, the problem isn't being fixed – it's being fragmented. Now everyone has a piece of the problem, which means no one really owns it. Marketing builds one version of the customer database. Sales builds another. Customer service builds its own. Now, instead of one system that works, the company has three broken ones that don't talk to each other and haven't solved the original issue.

Inside the organization, leadership has become a game of corporate chess, with each executive trying to secure a budget, influence, and control over the transformation agenda. After all, when you're up to your neck in alligators, it's hard to remember that your initial objective was to drain the swamp. The original intent to make the organization more efficient and agile takes a back seat to corporate Survivor, making sure you have your island or alliances protected from outsider threats.

Externally, customers don't care that you have a newly appointed Chief Data Officer. They don't care about your org chart.

They just want a seamless experience. So, instead of understanding how a potential transformation can unlock value, executives want to show the investors, board, or general public they are with the times by introducing new roles and checking the box. The result? More leaders, more meetings, more presentations, but less actual execution. Because the real issue was never about needing more leadership – it was about designing a system that works.

The fact is, the Hydra Monster isn't a leadership problem. It's a system problem. Companies keep trying to fix execution with leadership, when they should be fixing leadership with execution. If your work happens across silos, teams, and locations, then adding another executive isn't the answer. The answer is designing a system where work actually flows. To do that, companies need to move from fragmented decision-making to aligned execution. That's easier said than done. Time to call your two versions of Hercules to fight the Hydra Monster. Make room for the Corporate Gymnast and the Pirate.

The Hydra Monster Slayers

The Corporate Gymnast has a unique ability to cut through organizational complexity without getting tangled in it. They can help align teams without adding more red tape. Their unique capacity is to actually know who makes decisions, even if the organizational chart says otherwise. In short, they quickly adapt to get up to speed and add value, moving from one corporate structure to another. They can assess team culture, dynamics, and goals when joining to understand how to add value and enable forward movement. In transformation, where teams are created and dissolved, the Corporate Gymnast's competency in moving through organizational minutiae and bureaucratic red tape without missing a beat is a skill that is in short supply and needs to be elevated and shared.

Because they are adept at moving from one corporate structure to another, they have keen insight into what makes teams flourish. They add their experience and expertise to assess issues with organizational complexity, including:

- Recognizing whether there is enough diversity of thought, opinion, and representation within the team. Too many folks with shared thinking, experience, and personality lead to groupthink and less innovative ways of tackling issues or transformational processes.
- Assessing ways to reduce switching costs between teams. Switching from one team to another adds a cognitive load as well as a reduction in social capital. New team members struggle with new workflows, languages, and mental models. In addition, switching from one team to another leads to changes in building relationships, establishing trust, and navigating local politics.
- Possessing the agility to move from one team structure to another so they have oversight in terms of differences in processes and tools, cultural resistance, and lost momentum as a result of losing a team member.

THE
PIRATE

We're not talking Blackbeard, Captain Hook, or someone pushing Taylor Swift songs on the dark web. Rather, our pirate is a goal-oriented, innovative thinker willing to take on risks. This Pirate lives by the motto "Where there's a will, there's a way," understanding that determination, hard work, and a dose of out-of-the-box thinking gets things done. Pirates are natural risk takers but different from the Silicon Valley startup types who "move fast and break things." Rather, our Pirate carefully weighs and assesses their actions, understanding that trust needs to be developed and sustained. Even though Pirates take on more risk than average employees, they also comprehend the consequences of shouldering that burden. In short, Pirates can:

- Create "islands of transformation" inside the organization.
- Prove new ways of working before asking for permission.
- Move before bureaucracy can slow them down.

The symbiotic relationship of the Corporate Gymnast and the Pirate shows adeptness to help organizations execute without collapsing into chaos.

Behind the Curtain of Confusion and Chaos

Let's be honest, we all sometimes hide the real issue of why things are not working. There is a tendency to blame others or blame products or processes, a kind of finger-pointing that takes time and effort away from critical thinking and resolution building. Narratives like "The application is broken" or "Leadership is over-subscribed" take hold, distracting us from shining a light on the real issues. Initiatives like "relationship building" seem obvious and expected — no one is ever hired at the C-level to alienate themselves and become divisive. This is the curtain of chaos and confusion. Attempts are made to flatten out organizational hierarchy and increase levels of agility and flexibility, and yet things remain unnecessarily complex. Why?

Too many layers of bureaucracy and people in charge result in slower decision-making. Transformation needs agility, not bureaucracy. With many heads, decision-making and accountability get mired in the minutiae of finding "who signs off." Conway's law (named for computer scientist Melvin Conway, who introduced the idea in 1967) suggests that the technical structure of a system reflects the social boundaries of the organization that produced it. In other words, complex products, or in our case, transformational efforts, mirror the organizational structures they are designed in. It's no wonder that transformational efforts often fail to meet expectations.

The most common situations leading to confusion and chaos include:

Conflicting metrics and incentives: Sales is based on short-term wins while transformation is predicated on long-term bets. Operations are focused on stability, while disruption looks to disrupt the status quo. Key performance indicators (KPIs) are not aligned to change the goals.

Cultural inertia: Complex organizations often have strong cultures, which result in resistance to change, fear of failure, and endless cycles of setting up and running pilots. This, in turn, leads to transformational fatigue, causing employees to disengage, leading only to further cycles of failed projects.

Unhealthy competition for resources: This includes budget, people, infrastructure, and applications to support internal teams, resulting in purpose-built development of initiatives.

Misalignment of incentives: The organization has an overall strategy, but incentives and tactics are designed to fit only within a specific department or group. As a result, it becomes difficult to port these processes, applications, and work streams to another department run by a different C-level individual.

Not having a seat (or the right one) at the table: Oftentimes in hierarchical organizations, executives are placed under the current executive and have no real authority over strategy, even though the person might be accountable for implementations. There is also a cultural disparity between technology-based versus non-technology-based organizations. Some people might think of this as the Silicon Valley versus traditional organizational structure. In Silicon Valley-type technology-based organizations, tech-oriented folks may be across the entire organizational structure, whereas in traditional organizations, tech folks might be relegated to IT service and support as opposed to high-level strategy formulation.

Ultimately, these factors allow fiefdoms to develop across an organization. Sharing and collaboration may be attempted but often fail to achieve scale because of such structural and procedural issues. Obtaining a C-level title is a wonderful thing in terms of accomplishment and recognition. However, without alignment with other departments, divisions, and groups, transformation is done locally without thoughts of porting and scaling. So chaos and confusion continue.

Tribes, Fiefdoms, and Cults

The Hydra Monster thrives when organizations stop acting like systems and start acting like tribes. It's human nature. We're wired to form small, close-knit groups of trusted people, defend our own turf, and see outsiders as a threat. This is why leadership teams subconsciously build their own mini-empires inside organizations: each leader surrounds themselves with their own people, tools, and metrics.

Sometimes, companies use personality profiles to understand more about their employees. These can be very useful for creating a harmonious transformational team. At first, it feels like a smart way to move fast, but often these groups stop sharing information, stop collaborating, and start protecting their own interests. This is when corporate tribes turn into fiefdoms – and, at their worst, into cults. What's the difference?

- A tribe is bound by trust. It works toward a common mission.
- A fiefdom is bound by politics. It protects its resources.
- A cult is bound by dogma. It resists outside thinking and fights to maintain its beliefs.

In transformation, companies need strong tribes – but they must avoid falling into cult-like thinking that resists change and rejects external ideas. Cult-like leadership takes away individual autonomy, resulting in conformity trumping critical thinking, charisma replacing evidence, and rewarding loyalty over performance. Fiefdoms are also problematic and put up barriers to transformation. Everything becomes protected or hoarded, not shared. The Corporate Gymnast and Pirate have the competencies to break through siloed thinking. By working around it and pushing through it, they highlight a different path to reduce the impact of the Silo Monster. They expose the impact on speed, efficiency, and motivation of less autonomy but also bring attention to a critical need for organizations dealing with the Silo Monster: alignment.

Team Together, Team Apart

The best organizations know that real transformation isn't about control – it's about alignment. We have often heard that for transformation to be effective and sustained, organizations need to think globally and act locally. Highly aligned companies understand how to factor local transformational activities into their global strategy. Take, for example, Unilever, the British Multinational Consumer Packaged Goods company that brings you everyday items from Dove Beauty Bars to Ben & Jerry's Ice Cream. In rural India, they launched the "Help a child reach 5" campaign that focused on promoting handwashing with soap to reduce childhood disease. It was a deeply local campaign, and they partnered with local schools, tailored messages to regional languages, and used community-based education and storytelling. The behavior change model in India was so successful that it was ported to other regions like Kenya. This reinforced Unilever's sustainable living plan globally, demonstrating alignment not just between social impact and business growth but across different regional and country-based departments.

Without considering this relatively simple notion, alignment issues occur resulting in:

- Teams are getting pulled in different directions.
- Leadership is sending mixed messages.
- Key performance indicators (KPIs) don't reflect transformation.
- Incentives don't reflect enterprise transformation efforts.

Organizations we have spoken to balance the speed of change with flexible leadership to become agile at execution (see Figure 7.1). Those that slip into more structured leadership, like fiefdoms, tend to over-engineer their transformational efforts. Without collaboration and sharing, there is often duplication of effort. In addition, any future integration across siloed applications and efforts becomes a challenge.

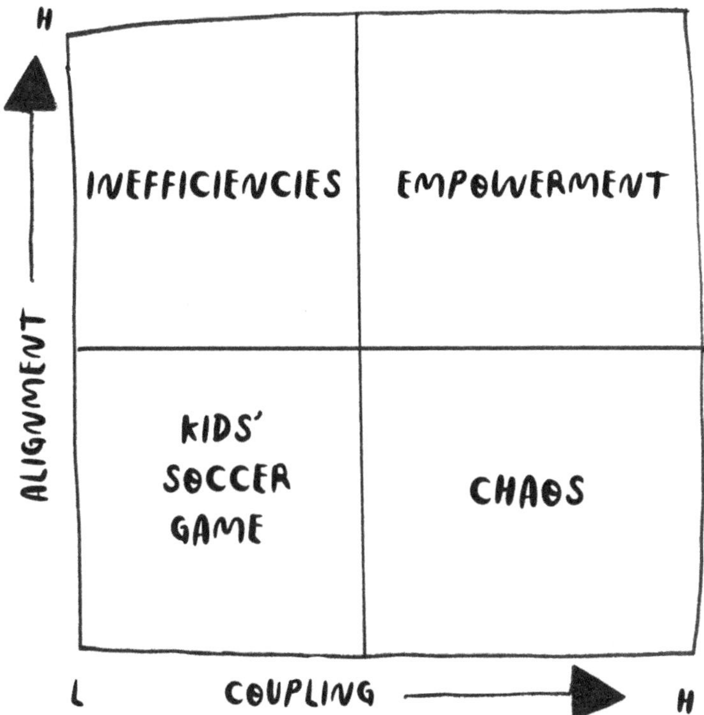

Figure 7.1   From a kid's soccer game to empowerment.

Empowerment is essential but involves a loose level of coupling and a high level of alignment. The Corporate Gymnast and Pirate are masters of empowerment. The Pirate in making sure their group executes without needing endless permissions, while the Corporate Gymnast empowers themselves through understanding how to move from one organizational structure in a fluid manner, adding a high degree of value.

In large organizations, especially those undergoing transformation, alignment is often mistaken for collaboration. When things break down, the default response is often:

"We need to collaborate more."

Collaboration, while essential, is not a strategy. Alignment not only reduces duplication of effort; it also promotes information, resource sharing, and an understanding of how individual contribution fits into the overall transformation landscape. Without alignment, transformation starts to look a lot like a children's soccer game where everybody is running after the ball and nobody is playing their position. Whether in a soccer game or in organizations, everyone is left wondering why things are not working. So, why is alignment important?

- Alignment prevents the "Collaboration Trap." Instead of blaming breakdowns on "lack of collaboration," leaders can diagnose where misalignment exists and measure accordingly.
- Alignment prevents micromanagement. Senior leaders focus on leading indicators, teams focus on execution, and everyone stays in their lane while moving toward the same goal.
- Alignment focuses on Ownership and Speed. By being loosely coupled at the execution level, teams can move fast without waiting for approvals at every step.

One of the biggest blockers to alignment isn't disagreement — it's misalignment at the wrong level. Too often, leaders dive into the weeds before getting clear on what success looks like at each level. That's what creates chaos: different layers of the organization measuring progress with different yardsticks.

Pyramid of Alignment

Think of it like a pyramid: at the top, executive leaders must align on the big-picture outcomes. Take, for example, a retail business with physical stores, a digital storefront, and multiple e-commerce sales outlets. Is the goal an increased share of wallet or a higher customer lifetime value? How can all the different groups align on customer value and try to achieve an omnichannel strategy, providing a consistent experience across all customer touchpoints? In the middle, program leaders must define what progress looks like for major initiatives – say, reducing delivery time for same-day purchases or increasing pickup conversion. At the team level, teams must be clear on execution metrics like engagement scores. Understanding how to align quickly and effectively is a skill that can be learned from the Corporate Gymnast. Pushing through minutiae and red tape to achieve alignment and making sure initiatives move forward is the realm of the Pirate.

The biggest miss in most transformations is assuming alignment is happening at the team level. We see this when organizations force people to "collaborate more" instead of aligning them to metrics that matter at their level. When each level is clear on its objective and everyone is heading toward the same outcome, the confusion starts to clear. Good leaders operate like helicopters: they hover high enough to see the whole terrain, but know exactly when to parachute in. The best ones bring others up with them, so everyone sees the full picture. They also know how to leverage the competencies of Corporate Gymnasts who can operate autonomously with high levels of alignment. Netflix popularized the idea of being highly aligned and loosely coupled, meaning teams operate with autonomy but stay connected through shared objectives. Alignment is not about getting people to collaborate more – it's about making sure every level of the organization understands what constitutes success and stays focused on the right metrics.

All for One and One for All

Historically speaking, there have been many trends focused on simplifying and/or flattening the organization. Holacracy and decentralized autonomous organizations (DAOs) were two attempts. Holacracy, a decentralized management framework, became popular in the mid-2010s after less than successful attempts to try to infuse innovation and collaboration into the enterprise (social collaborative enterprise and enterprise 2.0). Holacracy represents a form of autonomous organizational structure where leadership and decision-making are divided among all workers. Autonomy is a central tenet of Holacracy but also encourages coupling or collaboration. Holacracy tries to maintain a balance between individual needs and connectedness in the organization. Individual team members have more agency as they work on projects that achieve the team's mission. Holacracy promotes:

- Circular teams function under a set of rules, a list of goals, and detailed methods for achieving those goals.
- Dispersed authority where each member has the power and authority to contribute to decision-making. Everyone can become a Pirate.
- Role fluidity enables team members to move between roles and apply their skills to different departments at the same time in a similar fashion to our Corporate Gymnast.

Many of the issues we discussed in this book that impede transformation were addressed in Holacracy, including greater innovation (experimentation), transparency, and engagement. However, the largest downside is a lack of accountability. If these benefits are what is needed, then why don't more organizations adopt Holacracy? Well, that's one of the reasons we are writing this book to provide a greater level of transformational (not just digital) capacity. Frankly, Holacracy represented a threat to the status quo and a power imbalance between management and employees. Even with that, there are some powerful principles associated with Holacracy and flattening structures.

DAOs represent trustless coordination, allowing groups to make decisions and manage resources without centralized leadership. They became well known with the onset of blockchain implementations, with organizational decisions like voting made visible and on-chain. They allow for borderless collaboration where teams can form, operate, and disband without legal or national boundaries. This elevates the need for the Corporate Gymnast and Pirate since everyone is mostly operating in this capacity. DAOs are still used for many Web 3 projects (involving blockchain implementations and open-source initiatives). However, they experience difficulty when trying to get into the mainstream. For one, governance is hard and falls prey to a lack of expertise and apathy. Also, most jurisdictions do not recognize them as legal entities. Lastly, DAOs often lack clear role definitions, speed in decision-making, or accountability structures.

Both DAOs and Holacracy represent unique new ways to address structural complexity; however, for all the reasons we have listed we will most likely not see widespread adoption. We will still have to rely on our Corporate Gymnast and Pirate to help us slay the Hydra.

Outcomes Versus Optics

Transformation without outcomes is simply organizational cosplay. It's what happens when leaders go through the motions without really trying to move the needle, focusing on optics rather than outcomes. In our interviews, we heard about many initiatives that seemed like window dressing or leaders checking a box rather than pushing for substantive change. These included campaigns built around a flashy new slogan and not tied to any clear metrics, to cultural campaigns that did not focus on changes in incentives or behaviors. In addition, we heard about endless "pilot programs" that never scaled, leading to transformative fatigue. Why do some organizations drift toward optics rather than focus on outcomes? The three most common reasons:

- Pressure to produce short-term wins without thinking about substantive change.
- Fear of failure so that the optics provide necessary cover but don't hold up to the deeper level of scrutiny.
- Lack of alignment when leaders develop optics for personal reasons, such as promotions.

Reversing the course and developing a culture focused on outcomes rather than optics requires thoughtful design. Your Corporate Gymnast and Pirate will keep you focused on the key questions: What specific problem is being solved? What systems and incentives need to be addressed and changed in order to support this? What is the benefit/risk trade-off for all stakeholders involved? What are appropriate success metrics for each phase of the implementation? What kind of system of delivery works for continual improvement? To do this, decision-makers/management need to focus on:

- Making work visible, measurable, predictable, and improvable.
- Rewarding uncomfortable honesty. Creating a safe space for those who surface issues rather than just recognizing those who spin success.

- Tying transformation to customer value. If customers don't feel the change, does it have any real value?
- Limiting change for change's sake. Spur critical thinking to ask why before any change initiative.

Key Takeaways

The biggest mistake companies make is thinking that more leadership = more progress. Most companies get stuck in one of two traps:

- **The bureaucracy trap:** Too much process, not enough execution.
- **The over-engineering trap:** Big transformation efforts that never actually ship.

But the best companies don't add heads; they align execution.

In the age of AI and digital transformation, the organizations that win won't be the ones with the most leadership titles, they will be the ones with the clearest system of execution. If you want to stop the Hydra from growing, you need to navigate two tensions:

- Balance in leadership between structured versus fluid.
- How fast versus slow the organization adapts to change.

Case Story: PPG

Painting a New Digital Landscape

A Fixture on the Pittsburgh Skyline.   Drive east through the Fort Pitt tunnel into Pittsburgh, Pennsylvania, and you enter a space where worlds collide. On one side, the predictable sprawl of the city's industrial suburbs; on the other, downtown Pittsburgh's modern urban skyline, framed by the city's notable three rivers. It's a stark contrast, one that reflects the city's complex identity and that clashes between old and new, between a vision toward the future with lingering presence of the past.

Nestled among the skyscrapers of downtown, the headquarters of PPG – the venerable paints, coatings, and specialty materials company – reflects this tension more than most companies. With spires of reflective glass reaching into the downtown skyline like a modern-day castle, the buildings are a far cry from traditional office buildings. Instead, they are a throwback to a time long passed but forged in the materials of our modern world.

No surprise then that one of the biggest challenges of the company and the people who run it has been to adapt the business's well-established manufacturing and supply operations within an evolving digital landscape.

Adhering to Market Needs.   Founded in 1883, PPG now operates in 70 countries with more than 45,000 employees worldwide and net sales of $15.8 billion annually. This Fortune 500 company's core business is to develop and deliver paints, coatings, and specialty materials across eight different business sectors, including aerospace, industrial coatings, architectural coatings, and automotive. Consumers can find PPG coatings in insulated Yeti coolers or on aluminum Liquid Death Mountain water cans. In the industrial sector, PPG's epoxy, acrylic, and polyurethane coatings are used to protect surfaces. These coatings provide beneficial properties, including corrosion and abrasion resistance, temperature and UV resistance, and waterproofing. This market has seen significant growth because of:

- **Aging infrastructure:** Maintain protection and longevity.
- **Industrialization:** Expansion of manufacturing requires industrial coatings for machines and facilities.
- **Renewable energy:** Increasing adoption of renewable energy systems, such as wind turbines and solar panels, which boost demand for coatings designed to protect against extreme weather conditions and environmental stressors.
- **Corrosion protection:** Fluctuations in temperature and humidity lead to greater concern associated with corrosion and protecting structures from rusting.

Other trends and shifts are placing downward pressure on coating manufacturers to comply, including:

- **Shift toward sustainable coatings:** Eco-friendly and low-VOC (volatile organic compounds) coatings, including water-based and powder coatings as alternatives to solvent-based products.
- **Advancements in coating technologies:** Nanotechnology-based coatings, self-healing coatings, and high-performance polymer coatings are enhancing the durability and functionality of industrial maintenance coatings.
- **Rising automation in application processes:** The use of automated spray systems and robotics for applying industrial coatings is improving efficiency, reducing waste, and ensuring consistent quality.

- The pandemic has accelerated digital trends in paint delivery and increased expectation associated with ordering, delivery as well as service and support.

Layering in Digital Capabilities.   Much as Pittsburgh embraces the future while paying attention to the past, PPG continues to layer in digital capabilities and processes while also reflecting on its manufacturing roots. The challenges for digital transformation in manufacturing continue to build and require funding for specialized skill sets. Much like in the consumer space, industrial clients now demand the convenience of online applications, immersive experiences, and AI-enabled services for ordering, accessing purchase history, color matching and consistency, job-specific pricing, and delivery specifications. This is critical to stay relevant.

The challenge for companies like PPG is that digital applications need to be designed to match the way an applicator might specify paint in a physical environment. This requires folks with a background in human factor engineering to design systems that mirror how things are done in a physical environment and benefit end users. Paint is a nuanced material with lots of complexity (including colors, finishes and materials), so providing an easy-to-use system is critical. The caveat comes in making sure that manufacturing can deliver on expectations.

There are changes to transformation across all of PPG's sectors, but especially acute are the changes within automotive, which is broken up into automotive OEM (manufacturers) and automotive refinish (body shops). Different from consumer paint, automotive paint is focused more on durability, protection, and applicability. Acrylic paint typically lasts 10 years or less, while urethane paint can last much longer. In addition, there are differences associated with the demands of automotive paint, such as the need to mix the paint quickly to get the right consistency, color, and finish, something critical to efficient and fast processes.

These new demands are driving greater focus on digital transformation across the sector, from supply chains to manufacturing to customer service and support. The shift to digital systems is putting strains on all coating companies to adopt new technologies and digital processes, rethink the operating model, and replace or digitize equipment while upskilling employees. Auto refinishing is the process of coating or repainting a vehicle's exterior, often after damage, to restore its appearance. In auto refinishing, which has several tools used for digital color matching, by analyzing consumption patterns, PPG can become predictive associated with demand, stocking needed colors and finishes. However, this is further complicated by complexity. Some PPG businesses have 100,000 stock-keeping units (SKUs). This is partly because of customer requirements and partly because of PPG's inorganic growth (60 acquisitions in the past 20 years).

Mixing the Model for Transformation Capacity. As the global IT director for the industrial segment at PPG, Laura Harshberger understands the challenges associated with digital growth and transformation. Working at PPG for the past 15 years in a variety of roles – IT from analyst to manager – she has seen the development of the company with acquisitions and expansion into new product segments and emerging markets. Laura understands that to anchor digitization within the organization there needs to be business continuity (no disruption in current operations) and value delivery (measurable outcomes on how any change delivers customer value). As her team implements new digital initiatives from customer management to process improvement in manufacturing, she has been witness to what initiatives work and has a unique perspective on digital transformation within PPG, for example, launching a quality management system that touches sales, technical and customer service, quality assurance and control, manufacturing, EH&S (environmental, health, and safety), logistics, and procurement. In this case, the company needed a product owner team, including data quality analysts and data stewards, to have accountability for this widely used central system. The new system can't be "owned" by just one of the departments, because they may neglect the needs/goals of other departments. We need all departments to start thinking more holistically and care about the full process chain, not only their link in the chain.

Laura can attest to the difficulty in facing the hydra monster and figuring out ways to slay it. In most cases, she is using her voice at the table of business leadership teams to help them understand the complexity and silos in the system landscape. Laura is continuously asking how different parts of the organization collaborate to achieve scale at digital efforts as well as accelerate digital thinking. It's a continuous challenge, but experimentation is the only way to push boundaries with breaking down silos that cause friction for digital transformation efforts. As we discussed in the chapter, silos form due to insular thinking, isolated not shared platforms, processes and applications, and incentive patterns focused on the business department.

Breaking Down Barriers.   As the industry rapidly digitizes to meet the needs of consumers and market shifts, PPG is launching feasibility studies and transformation programs. Efforts like low-cost sensors in manufacturing (vibration, pressures, image) are providing real-time data on equipment issues to prevent safety incidents and maximize uptime. RFID sensors are tracking product quantities and location in the aerospace sector. Meanwhile, cloud computing is allowing access to data to different stakeholders. However, most of the efforts have not achieved scale. Some sectors and manufacturing centers are slower to adopt, resulting in a patchwork of digital capabilities.

Much like other manufacturing companies, PPG experiences friction with expectations and commitments pushing beyond departmental barriers to advance alignment, especially when it comes to digital processes and thinking. Is it possible for manufacturing companies to become digital leaders? Using digital processes for efficiency, scale, and innovation is highly predicated on collaborating to develop new digital processes. Understanding trends and expectations for customers and for customers of those customers is critical.

Forget B2B or B2C, everyone expects unique experiences driven by digital. Car consumers want to look at a new car color in a VR showroom with different lighting. A body shop wants the convenience of mobile ordering and online color matching using AR tools to see paints in different contexts. All these new digital processes need to be supported with a digital operations model as well as integrated service and support infrastructure.

Being able to answer questions like where my batch of paint is in the manufacturing process? When is it scheduled for delivery? Can I include instructions for where to deliver it and when? The Corporate Gymnast can help coordinate digital experiences across different departments. In the case of PPG, jointly developing coating solutions by means of virtual AR and VR digital applications can accelerate time to market as well as collaboration models, not just throughout the organization but with external stakeholders as well. These may be driven through customer-facing digital applications, which are seamless for the consumer but need to be orchestrated on the back end through end-to-end collaboration.

Holding on to Legacy Processes. One of the challenges lies in manufacturing. Manufacturing varies based on product and quantity. Some products can be manufactured in batches while others are more discrete. As Laura explains, making paint is like making beer; variations on the process and complexities of the product mixes hamper the ability to automate the process. Even though there are more challenges, the process still needs to be automated using sensing and smart manufacturing capacity. Some companies, especially specialized chemical manufacturers, have figured out how to digitize and scale this process. There is an opportunity for

PPG to learn from other industries and identify what methods and processes are transferable.

Other areas where digitization can be impactful include changing how PPG prices products. Shifting to price for performance rather than volume or weight can be tricky. For one, what does performance entail: delivery on time, on budget, predicting consumer needs or the actual performance of the coating – longevity, sustainability, weathering? What changes would need to occur? Measuring the performance of products through sensing is a first step, followed by customizing chemical products and services to improve performance. How does PPG develop value-added data services? Could we provide customers with data throughout the process, so when they are applying the coating on a vehicle/appliance/airplane, they know that each batch has the same quality parameters?

To accomplish any of these initiatives, Laura sees a process of connecting information from end to end, from supply all the way through to customer use. For example, on automotive refinish, PPG can collect data on machines within body shops to mix colors, monitor levels, and adjust formulations while assessing usage. This data can then be used for demand planning (what are supply needs?), forecasting (regional or shop-based needs), and providing more consistency in terms of customer experience and needs. Issues like formula adjustment (color + consistency) in the auto shop can be explored. Understanding why some shops do manual adjustments is key; can this be predicted, and can PPG provide enhanced value?

One of the biggest challenges is addressing the differences in paint manufacturing. Paint manufacturing is still reactive rather than predictive; manufacturers like PPG are using similar equipment like dispersers and mixers across manufacturing to benchmark, assess, and identify issues. Adding sensing and using data collection like programmable logic controllers (PLCs), recipe management systems, and maintenance management systems (MMSs) provides more automation to manufacturing, allowing centralized control and predictive maintenance, increasing uptime, and preventing safety incidents. These new systems also allow PPG to meet the consumer needs through greater digital process automation. However, they do not move the needle in terms of collaboration.

Laura focuses on alignment through process ownership, which is similar to a product manager within other industries. Take a process like quality control. Quality managers ensure that products meet specific standards through the production process but are relegated within a specific manufacturing facility. However, if you are the owner of the process, then different core cross-department functions will need to be added like governance, communications, HR, and IT. It forces cross collaboration and cuts horizontally across the organization. The process owner becomes adept at understanding the needs across different business divisions such as aerospace that might have different quality needs than other divisions.

Can production supervisors become process owners? Do they have the skills and competency to take on new responsibilities? Can you upskill or train managers to take on more responsibility?

Another issue is changing attitudes and culture to align with digital thinking. Change the philosophy of finding someone or a group to fix issues and adopt a do-it-yourself (DIY) attitude and mindset to address issues as they come up such as fewer people, more automation, and less process variability. Many people associate data/systems with IT accountability. In a digital ecosystem, other departments are responsible for the data health of the system. In some cases, a large system like an enterprise resource planning (ERP) has several modules, crossing many departments. In this case, a process owner is key to understanding how the data flows downstream, ultimately onto customer-facing documents or labels. And they need to own the data quality and the training of people putting data in the system day in and day out.

Laura continues to push for changes in process and moving to the need for process owners, quality management tools, incident reports quality, and safety. In different leadership meetings, Laura has a unique role in seeing across segments and departments from a system perspective, so conveying that knowledge is important. Laura is continuously getting in front of leaders and explaining the business justifications. There is no doubt that PPG's competition is making strides that will provide external push, associated with accelerating transformation.

Try This: Are We Playing Five-Year-Old Soccer?

The Hydra Monster grows when everyone chases the ball but no one plays their position. This simple 2 × 2 helps your team see where alignment and autonomy break down and how to fix it.

Step 1: Grab a Marker

On a whiteboard or paper, draw a 2 × 2 with:

- **X-axis:** Loosely Coupled → Tightly Coupled.
- **Y-axis:** Loosely Aligned → Highly Aligned.

Step 2: Fill In the Field

Label each quadrant and add real examples from your org:

- **Top left:** Empowered Zone (e.g., Netflix).
- **Top right:** Over-Engineered.

- **Bottom left:** Chaos Factory.
- **Bottom right:** Five-Year-Old Soccer Game.

Step 3: Move the Ball Forward

Choose two to three initiatives not in the Empowered Zone. Ask:

- What's missing – alignment or autonomy?
- What's one change that could shift it up or left?

Play your position. Pass the ball. Win as a team.

This map helps teams break free from chaos and build true cross-functional flow.

Chapter 8

A Coalition of the Winning

"Magic happens when you build trust, create resilient coalitions and stick with it through the ups and downs."
—Rafee Tarafdar, CTO Infosys

Why do silos appear in organizations? Companies espouse collaboration, communication, and cross-divisional cooperation. However, it's easier said than done. Divisional turf wars are created through competition for limited resources – budget, people, and executive-level attention. Think of it as organizational tribalism. Such division only feeds a silo-based mindset. Most companies start off as scrappy entrepreneurial ventures, developing capabilities, building processes, and learning how to operate efficiently while continuing to innovate and capture market share. If you're not collaborating and learning how to build alliances, you're done, game over. Along the way, something happens, they reach an inflection point, and develop silos. This might be any or a combination of informational, operational, procedural, or technical (we're talking data, processes, people, and systems). Why? In the previous chapter, we discussed organizational complexity that has accelerated with the introduction of greater levels of digitization. The threat here isn't technological obsolescence. It's organizational divisions. It's a lack of unity. A Silo Monster feeds on poor communication, planning, and shared vision. It makes cross-divisional collaboration difficult. As we have discussed in this book, transformation is a team sport, and sustainable transformation needs coordination and cooperation across the enterprise. The challenge isn't technology (we have plenty of that). It's the people inside.

Ask yourself: Are your employees aligned with the coming change? Do different departments and groups share a common vision of the change? Do they understand and agree on what it will take to get there? Will they listen and cooperate or cause friction and unexpected challenges? To create alignment, build consensus, and reduce friction, we need to think about how to defeat the Silo Monster and develop a more collaborative culture. To do that, we need to understand why silos occur in the first place, how they become fortified and pervasive. Then we can seek out competencies, develop action plans, and overcome barriers reducing the power of the Silo Monster within our organization.

Ch, Ch, Ch, Changes . . . .

Organizational transformation happens for a variety of different rationales, such as peer-based competition, executive buy-in, process efficiency, and increased data-focused innovation, etc. However, all transformation is about people; if you get the people equation right, you have a much better chance of getting the transformation right. Change is hard, no matter which way you look at it. Change evokes a fight-or-flight response. Change is work, and transformation means letting go of embedded practices and processes. It is unknown, so it is often met with skepticism. If change looked pretty much the same, well then, it's not change; it's status quo.

COVID-19 accelerated the urgency for transformation. Remote work, online shopping, telemedicine, remote automation, and VR/AR were all levers driving the need for transformation. These efforts involved breaking down silos to drive collaboration with different divisions and groups. Was it forced collaboration, or did it happen naturally/organically? The days when you throw in an executive in charge of transformation to disrupt the status quo (think bull in a china shop) are becoming few and far between. The urgency effect of COVID-19, forcing companies to adopt digital or suffer their fate, has diminished. This was seen when what previously felt like multiyear-long efforts began to take weeks or as little as days to be realized, including:

- Quick-service restaurants (QSR) accelerated offering online ordering with delivery or curbside pickup.

- "Non-essential" retailers, a label developed by the government, had to expose their inventory with services like buying online and either picking up in-store or offering same-day delivery.
- Healthcare providers needed to rapidly accelerate their use of telemedicine, which was underused before COVID-19. This was facilitated by reduced regulation and increased availability of appropriate billing.

Now, we have reverted to standard practice. The urgency may have lessened, but the transformation is accelerating in part due to AI. Complacency replaces urgency, and organizations need to build sustained practices for transformation.

"We Have Seen the Enemy, and He Is Us."

This quote from Walter Kelly, who created the newspaper comic "Pogo the Possum" was highlighted in a poster from 1970 designed to promote environmental awareness and introduce the inaugural Earth Day. The meaning behind the message was simple: we all share responsibility for trashing Earth, so we should all do our share in cleaning it up. This quote was based on a previous quote, "We have met the enemy, and they are ours," uttered by Commodore Oliver Hazard Perry during the War of 1812. This quote is famous in history annals as a source of hubris and military braggadocio. As discussed in Chapter 4, hubris is another organizational behavior that blocks transformational efforts. The original quote, focused on overconfidence and excessive pride, was turned into "Let's all pitch in because we're all at fault." We can take this meaning and apply it to what we are seeing in organizations. Transformation is everyone's responsibility, everyone has a stake in the transformation, and until it is seen in that vein, monsters will continue to derail efforts, especially the Silo Monster.

What's the Impact of the Silo Monster?

If not addressed in your organization's, silos will grow in power, size, and variety. There are information silos, capacity silos, and innovation silos, namely, anything that makes the organization unique is hoarded and not readily shared with other departments. This results in the following:

- **Diminished employee morale:** Employees feel isolated, lacking motivation, disengaged, and frustrated with work. Gallup, the analytics and advisory company, conducted large-scale opinion polls and found that "in 2023, employees in the United States continued to feel more detached from their employers, with less clear expectations, lower levels of satisfaction with their organization, and less connection to its mission or purpose, than they did four years ago."
- **Lack of information sharing:** Poor information sharing leads to duplication of work, and a lack of alignment exacerbates feelings of frustration. Think about the differences in finding information within your organization versus outside. This is the difference between purpose-built internal search systems compared to a variety of mechanisms to find information online,

including search, social platforms, or LLMs that have continuously aggregated information and provide an easy way to find, retrieve, and summarize data for us.

- **Inadequate decision-making:** Diversity of thought and experience are critical to consider for effective and sustainable transformation. Factors that need to be considered are, yes, technical, but even more so human-centered (behavioral) and socio-economic, as well as regulatory, accounting for privacy, security, and compliance.
- **Erosion of trust:** Echo chambers occur when groups of people reinforce their own ideology and beliefs and exclude others with different opinions. Think about a group like IT that speaks a common language (IT jargon), shares similar customs and beliefs, and engages in group-based processes that become exclusive. Trust erodes over time both inward (coming into the IT division) and outward (trust that others understand the challenges and constraints associated with IT).

Who Is Feeding the Silo Monster?

When people or divisions within companies operate independently, isolated from each other, there's limited collaboration. Collaboration can happen, but it might feel forced, not organic, and difficult to sustain. Instead of a town hall–style discussion, there's quiet chatter and sidelong glances at the water cooler. This is how the Silo Monster emerges.

What causes the Silo Monster to grow at a company? So many reasons – some structural, some procedural, and others simply cultural. In the previous chapter, we talked about how companies can often become dangerously hierarchical over time, with new departments and leadership roles popping up inexplicably. Suddenly, Bob might ultimately report to Mary. Bob directly reports to Calvin, who reports to Sandra. However, Calvin is in a completely different division from Mary. Bob doesn't even know Mary, and they work for the same company! No one is on the same page. In fact, they are reading from different playbooks. Organizational units become tiny fiefdoms. These new divisions often have their own agendas, including mandates and incentives, associated with different measures of productivity and success. Sometimes, they even have competing priorities. Suddenly, there's little communication and no information sharing. When companies have used social network analysis (SNA) to identify communication patterns, they have discovered some interesting results.

Imagine an organization of four employees each represented as a circle (node) with lines going in and/or out of the circle representing connections (edges). We can then draw a graph to see who is connected to each other and who is sharing information with each other. In Figure 8.1, employees are sharing information with employee 3, but employee 3 is sharing information only with employee 4. Why? Is it due to the nature of the relationship or physical and/or structural distance between them or have silos developed to prevent collaboration and communication?

A siloed mentality is developed in organizations for a variety of reasons. We have mentioned several in this book, but we will list a few here that we think are particularly pervasive so that we can understand how to address them. The most important include organizational structure (both physical and perceived), limited resources including competition for these limited resources, mismatched systems, and, of course, lack of trust.

The physical distance between people, groups, and divisions exacerbates a siloed culture. Having a department or group in a separate building or location creates physical barriers to getting together. For example, placing the IT department in a separate building on a corporate campus allows folks to be in one central

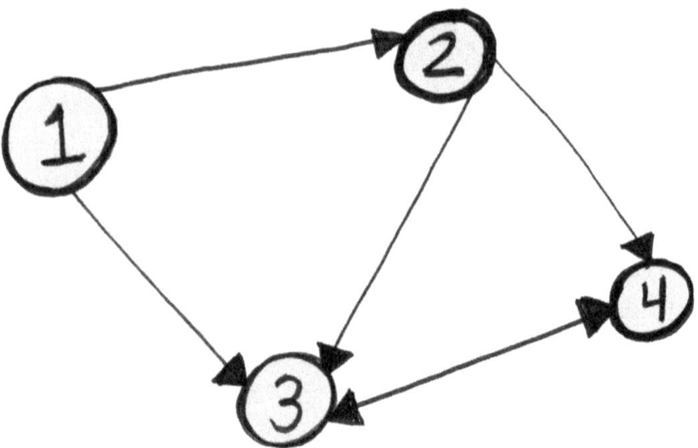

Figure 8.1   Social network graph: connected versus engaged.

location for efficiency but does little to integrate folks into the larger organization to share ideas, innovate, or focus on transformation. This is similar to a college campus, where departments or programs and schools might have their own building where they teach classes, conduct research, and have students engage in group or project-based work.

Having an interdisciplinary environment would require folks willing to walk across a street, quad, or campus to collaborate with folks in different disciplines. This is different from simply connecting with folks over a video call. *Propinquity* is a term social scientists use to describe the affinity of close interactions. People are more likely to form relationships with those they are physically or psychologically close to. That means if we want to defeat the Silo Monster, we need to find ways to build closeness, which entails thinking about removing the physical barriers. Perceived barriers that are more cultural in nature give the notion of exclusivity, not inclusivity. We have witnessed this in more traditional organizations that set up digital innovation teams, which are separated – sometimes both physically and culturally – from operations. The intent is to allow innovation freedom to explore, assess, experiment, and develop processes designed to save the company from impending disruption, or, to be less dramatic, to adequately compete in the market. However, this sets up a cultural barrier where part of the company (operating folks keeping the lights on) wonder why smaller groups of folks are getting all the attention, perks, and freedoms, or why one group's perception is that they might be subsidizing the efforts of another.

The other barrier is incentive patterns. We refer to them as "perverse" since they are not aligned with collaboration; rather, employees are incentivized by doing tasks internally and contributing to the department or group. These might be focused on growing the division, training the teams, developing greater efficiency, project completion, or, in the case of marketing and sales, increasing top-line revenue or market share. Cross-divisional collaboration, which is critical for sustainable transformation, requires incentives that align horizontally across the organization and incentivize employees to work on projects that benefit other divisions or align with strategic company initiatives requiring working with different teams and individuals. Without the right economic incentives in place, cross-departmental collaboration becomes difficult and constrained when employees are focused on how their work is aligned with their divisions only.

In any organization, everyone helps develop, grow, and feed the Silo Monster, so we should develop a collaborative and cross-divisional response to slay it (or at least tame it).

It Takes a Village

In 2003, when President George W. Bush was talking about Iraq military actions, he recognized that to succeed, the United States couldn't go it alone. It needed allies to launch and maintain a successful campaign. It needed, as the President said, a "coalition of the willing."

Coalitions are typically purpose-built – to empower a community, address an urgent situation, and deliver on a plan. In transformation efforts, creating a coalition of the willing is essential in assessing areas of strength and weakness, as well as building reinforcement loops where change can occur continuously and organically.

The key to an effective coalition is bringing together the right people to accelerate transformation and reduce barriers. You want people in your coalition to be there willfully, because they believe in the process, not because of an order or mandate. A coalition of the willing, in other words, requires not just one monster slayer, but a team of slayers committed to defeating the Silo Monster. You start building your coalition with those people at your organization with the essential competencies to drive alignment and develop communication.

All these monsters including the Silo Monster are obstacles to transformation and how companies have addressed and faced them to get prepared for their transformation journeys. Now we are ready to roll up our sleeves to do the hard work, and it starts by building coalitions.

The Silo Monster Slayers

Now that we understand the Silo Monster, we need folks who can take away its power, rendering it ineffective – slaying the Silo Monster. What are the qualities we are looking for? We want extroverts who can engage across the organizational divide, and we want active listeners who can form coalitions. In short, we need someone with diplomatic skills. History is filled with famous diplomats who bridged the gap between different factions. America declared its independence from England in 1776, but it took the finesse and skills of Ben Franklin – often considered the country's greatest diplomat – to travel to France and persuade the French to sign a treaty and recognize the independent nation in 1778. Until that coalition was formed, America had a desire for change but was still operating in its own silo across the Atlantic. You need your own Ben Franklin; you need a diplomat.

The Diplomat is that person in your organization with the necessary problem-solving skills and emotional intelligence to build the coalition of the willing function efficiently and effectively. They are skilled in the art of conflict resolution, always pushing the coalition toward a shared goal of transformation. They deploy persuasive skills to make sure there is a common understanding of what needs to be done and provide a sense of urgency to bring diverse groups together to act. They also understand that the coalition needs to develop and grow over time to build strength but also breadth of capabilities and competencies. The diplomat excels at building alliances, creating relationships, and moving cross-divisional transformation initiatives forward.

Who can complement the skills of the diplomat in building our coalition? Identifying people with the skills, background, and, most importantly, personality and willingness to make our coalition efficient and competent. Landing Apollo 11 on the moon wasn't simply about assembling a random group of astronauts in a spaceship and blasting them off. It was about putting the people with the appropriate skill sets and competencies together to ensure a successful and safe take-off, flight, and landing. This is your Team Builder.

Team Builders have an innate ability to bring people together on your team who are (1) willing, (2) complementary, and (3) can accelerate your efforts. One of the key characteristics is to understand where employees mentally sit associated with a spectrum of contributions to the fledgling effort.

What causes employees or even leaders to rally against change? Sometimes, a company is plagued by organizational memory of prior failed initiatives. It's the "We-tried-this-once-and-it-didn't-work" syndrome the old-timers often call out. It will be essential to show the naysayers how this time is different.

Maybe your coalition of the willing fails to understand what is going to motivate people. After all, a sign outside the office bathroom that says "Stay Positive, Work Hard" isn't enough. Not everyone is motivated by the same incentives. Some people focus on monetary gains, while others might look for more altruistic benefits like social capital.

Alignment Versus Empowerment

Are your teams aligned, empowered, and highly coupled? Do they have a tightly connected team culture? Or is it loosely aligned and focused on the mission? What leads to dysfunction within a team where they are not effective, perhaps lacking in trust among the different team members, looking for any way out to join some other team environment. Team members exist in a balance and a shared societal contract associated with each other's commitment to the members and the overall mission of the team. Teams out of balance will struggle and often falter in moving forward. Most of the time it will result in a difficult and challenging situation that will lead to ineffectual work, wasted resources, and lingering suspicion among the team members when joining future teams.

In our research, companies that have low levels of autonomy and collaboration are in a state of dysfunction (see Figure 8.2). No one trusts each other, and they struggle to develop collaborative efforts. If it sounds chaotic, it is. Companies that work on collaborative efforts but do not focus on driving autonomy create an estranged situation where team-based collaboration seems forced and directed, not spontaneous and natural. On the other hand, if an organization has a low level of collaboration but a high degree of autonomy, then we see the emergence of the Silo Monster. Yes,

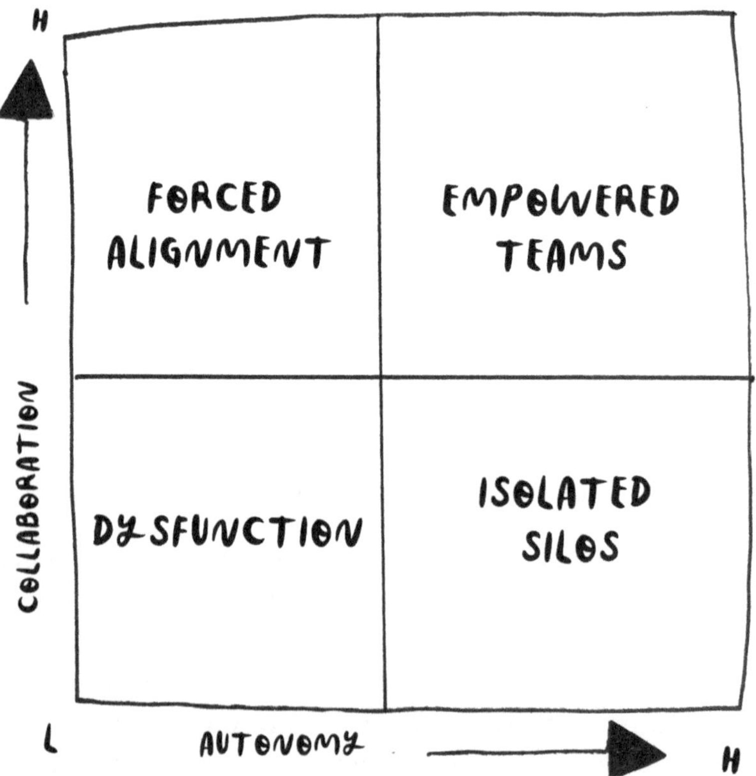

Figure 8.2   From dysfunction to empowered.

team members feel autonomous, but they operate in silos without high levels of collaboration. High levels of collaboration and autonomy are what we want for empowered teams, but how do we develop this?

Self-determination theory (SDT) is a macro theory of human behavior that argues that humans are motivated by intrinsic factors, including autonomy, competence, and relatedness. The interplay between extrinsic (e.g., incentives and rewards) and intrinsic motivators is at the heart of understanding SDT.[1] How do you drive autonomy? What does it mean to have empowered teams? Many companies focus on hard incentives to motivate team members. However, monetary incentives are often fixed in the short and midterm. Studies have shown that employees will often work to achieve their duties, not go above and beyond. There is substantial research that beyond monetary incentives, employees value autonomy, meaning, and a sense of purpose in their work.

Trust Me

Ultimately, the coalition of the willing, led by the Diplomat and the Team Builder, must always keep a keen dual focus on both outcomes (what we hope to achieve) and optics (how we plan to go about it). But here's the twist: depending on where your organization sits in the trust-performance matrix, our monster slayers need to adjust their weapons of choice.

In the Comfort Zone (high trust, low performance), your coalition needs to lean heavily into outcomes. Sure, people trust each other and communication flows freely, but that's not enough to slay the Silo Monster. The Diplomat and Team Builder need to shift focus toward driving measurable results, setting clear performance targets, and creating accountability across divisions. Think of it as turning those comfortable water cooler conversations into action plans.

Over in the Illusion Zone (low trust, high performance), it's all about optics. Your numbers look great, but the Silo Monster feeds off the underlying tensions and mistrust. Here, our monster slayers need to prioritize relationship-building and cross-functional collaboration. The Diplomat should focus on creating safe spaces for open dialogue, while the Team Builder works on developing shared wins that build bridges between high-performing but isolated teams.

Down in the Chaos Zone (low trust, low performance), our coalition needs to balance both outcomes and optics carefully. Start small – the Diplomat might focus on creating quick wins between two departments, while the Team Builder identifies and empowers those early followers who can demonstrate both trustworthy behavior and performance improvement. Think of it as monster-slaying in manageable bites.

And for those lucky enough to be in the Excellence Zone (high trust, high performance)? The monster slayers' job shifts to preservation and scale. The coalition needs to document what's working, create repeatable processes, and, most importantly, stay vigilant. After all, the Silo Monster is opportunistic – it loves nothing more than an organization that gets complacent about its success.

The thing the Silo Monster fears the most? The three Cs of an efficient work environment are cooperation, collaboration, and communication. These aren't just buzzwords – they're tactical weapons that need to be deployed differently based on your organization's trust-performance position. A high-trust environment might need more emphasis on cooperation toward specific outcomes, while a high-performing but low-trust organization might need to focus on building collaborative bridges.

Building Sustainable Momentum

The real victory over the Silo Monster isn't just in assembling your coalition – it's in sustaining it. Your Team Builder needs to continuously read the room and adjust tactics based on where you are in the trust-performance journey. As you move between zones, your approach needs to evolve. In low-trust environments, focus on building relationships before pushing for results. In low-performance situations, use small wins to build confidence before tackling bigger challenges.

Remember, the most effective coalitions are ones that continue to add members while maintaining their focus and purpose. They recognize that allies are essential but also understand that different zones require different approaches. Whether you're breaking down walls in the Chaos Zone or maintaining excellence at the top, your coalition's success depends on its ability to adapt its monster-slaying tactics to the battlefield at hand.

What strategies or tactics do companies use to try to reduce the strength of the Silo Monster? In our interviews, most companies recognize its existence and associated issues. Some take active steps to reduce its stranglehold on collaboration by purposefully exchanging team members across divisions. Imagine a cultural attaché engaging with the local constituents, learning customs, language, and behaviors. These folks gain a deeper understanding of how to engage with different divisions and build collegial ties that become a first step toward greater collaboration.

Key Takeaways

1. Slaying the Silo Monster means tackling people's problems, not just technology gaps.
2. A true "Coalition of the Willing" is built, not assigned, and requires believers, not bystanders.
3. The Diplomat bridges conflict. The Team Builder rallies complementary players around a shared goal.
4. Balance autonomy and collaboration to unlock trust, performance, and progress.
5. Use cooperation, collaboration, and communication differently based on your trust-performance zone.

Case Story: Yum! Brands

How to Build a Coalition of the Willing

Kelly Dowdy knows a thing or two about building a coalition of the willing, particularly in challenging times.

Kelly joined Yum! Brands, one of the largest restaurant franchisees in the world, in 2020. Now, you may not recognize the company name, but chances are you've grabbed a pepperoni pizza or a Chalupa Supreme or a 12-piece bucket at one of Yum!'s restaurants, which includes brands like Kentucky Fried Chicken

(KFC), Taco Bell, and Pizza Hut. With more than 60,000 restaurants worldwide operated primarily by 1,500 franchisees – and a new one opening every two hours – Yum! is #1 by unit count worldwide. By service value, they have a 5.8% market share globally as of 2023, per Euromonitor.

When Kelly came on board, the organization was in transition, particularly in terms of franchise ownership, access, and technology development between the mother Yum! brand and their fleet of franchisees. Yum!'s model was working well: they collected fees and ongoing royalties from their franchisees without sacrificing control to outsiders. The franchisees were able to leverage the size and scale of Yum!'s reputable brand, optimizing marketing, advertising, and supply chain.

Still, management at Yum! recognized that the next evolution of this core strategy was to leverage the company's size and scale to build proprietary technology that could accelerate the company's global growth. However, this was incredibly challenging to accomplish for a variety of reasons, not the least of which was the simple fact that different markets had different processes and capability needs.

What's more, at the time of Kelly's arrival, the quick-service market itself was changing, with more options competing for consumer dollars. In addition to fast casual and grab 'n' go options, consumers now have grocery-based precooked meals and in-home meal delivery subscription services available in the marketplace. There were more options than ever, and consumers were hungry for ones focused on health and nutrition.

With two degrees from Carnegie Mellon University and experience building scaled technology solutions, Kelly certainly felt comfortable leading the first wave of digital and technology development for Yum! Still, she wasn't an expert on the fast-food industry or franchise model, two areas she would need to learn to be successful in her new role. Kelly did have the distinct advantage of inherent curiosity and empathy in engaging with people of all different backgrounds, experiences, and expertise. In other words,

Kelly has long been in the business of building coalitions of the willing within organizations. She was excited to begin leading the digital transformation when she joined Yum! in January 2020, and then the world changed almost overnight.

The COVID-19 pandemic's effects on dine-in sales were devastating. By the end of 2020, more than 110,000 restaurants in the United States alone had closed, according to the National Restaurant Association. This forced quick-service chains to think innovatively about the use of technology to facilitate food delivery, online ordering, and drive-thru. There needed to be a renewed focus on consumer experience, efficiency, and loyalty, framed through the adoption of new technology and digitization.

The move to centralize digital ordering was driven by Yum! senior leadership. While some brands had first-party products (utilizing data directly from customers), others were leveraging third-party products (data collected without any direct ties to the business). Franchisees were the buyers of the technology, and Yum! was not only the franchisor but would now become a vendor of the technology to the franchisees as well. Yum had never been in this position before and had only a few brands with track records from which to build. However, the company believed that moving to a centralized digital online ordering platform would create efficiency and scale, while also capturing the ordering data across all brands globally, a foundational component that could power their AI strategy in the coming years.

It All Starts with Trust

The first major hurdle was getting the franchisees to trust that Yum! could build this technology for them better than a third party and that they should build it to serve all brands. Oftentimes, Kelly would face "organizational memory" issues. Some of the brands had attempted to build their own technology before and faced major challenges. This left franchisees asking, how would this time be any different?

Another hurdle for Kelly was convincing franchisees that this was the right effort and would benefit all stakeholders in the long run. Kelly did not own or have access to data on ordering utilization, efficiency in processing orders, or customer ordering history. That information resided with the franchisees. How would she convince franchises, some with different levels of power in the ecosystem, to join her and Yum! for this journey and persuade them that this digital transformation would bring benefits to franchisees and Yum! including efficiency gains, increased profitability, as well as a better and a consistent user experience.

Eyeball to Eyeball Conversations

For Kelly, the next step in building a coalition of the willing (COTW) was "listening," which meant meeting people where they were and engaging in face-to-face dialogue to listen (empathetically) to their concerns, challenges, and issues. This wasn't done through conference calls or on Zoom, but on the ground, through face-to-face meetings with stakeholders. She had to walk in their shoes so they knew that she not only heard them but saw them as well. She had to listen to not only their frustrations and pain points with their current technology platforms, but also what they aspired to achieve, so she knew where her products had to outperform any current competitive solution.

Kelly framed the new technology around the idea of it being "better, faster, and cheaper" for the franchisees. Better meant more reliable and scalable, with less likelihood of outages and loss of sales. "Never losing a sale" became the mantra of Kelly's organization. The team ran "failure Fridays," simulating outages that could happen and announcing the revenue lost for every minute that the platform was down, a constant reminder to the team that their mission was to never lose a sale for the franchisees. Faster meant updates and new features would go out to customers more quickly, rather than the months it often took with the current platforms. The QSR world moves speedily, and Kelly knew her products had to turn around new features and requests quickly, but never at a cost to reliability. Cheaper meant delivering a product that was affordable to franchisees, showing them that she understood the realities of the restaurant market's razor-thin margins.

For Kelly, there was no way to establish trust without meeting with the stakeholders she needed to bring on board to her nascent COTW. Kelly did two essential things to start building trust. First, rather than simply phone or Zoom calls, Kelly spent time and effort to travel and meet stakeholders on their turf, face-to-face. Second, Kelly spent most of her time listening rather than pitching, making sure she could understand the stakeholder's concerns, which ran the gamut from franchisee roles in the digital transformation effort to their fears of losing control.

The next step in building a coalition was empathy, or as Kelly refers to it, the "walking in their shoes tour." People want to know that you not just "hear" them but "see" them as well. Kelly toured restaurants to feel the problems firsthand and attended outage calls to better understand what issues were occurring on the legacy platform. In one particular case for Pizza Hut US, Kelly had her team "shadow" the Pizza Hut US team on a Super Bowl Sunday to see firsthand the traffic that their new platform would need to handle. By having a deep and intimate knowledge of these problem sets, her team was in the best place to solve them for the franchisees. Kelly, knowing that Pizza Hut US needs to scale to 3,000+ orders per minute on Super Bowl Sunday, let the franchisees know that she did her homework and knew more about their business than any other third-party provider.

More Time Together = More Trust

Kelly recognized early that a few scheduled meetings to learn wouldn't be enough; she had to create opportunities for unscheduled conversations. To do so, she moved her physical office at Yum! headquarters to be right in the middle of the franchise operation's team. This created opportunities for the leaders in technology and marketing to see her every day. It took only a couple of weeks for them to start popping into the office to have a casual chat. It was these casual chats that led to stronger trust and collaboration. Additionally, franchisees would walk by the office to see that Kelly was an integrated part of their team when they were in the office.

To measure trust, Kelly likes to use the analogy of "coins in the trust jar." Imagine you have a mason jar for each of your stakeholders. Every positive interaction you have puts a coin in the trust jar. A simple text message checking in is worth $.05. Taking time to go to a franchisee store is worth $1. However, bad interactions or major issues that arise withdraw money from the jar. A major technology outage loses $10. How you respond to the outage can actually add $3 back to the jar, but only if you show up accountable, quickly take care of the problem, and communicate plans that show confidence that it is less likely to happen in the future. These are all important in how to keep money in that jar. Often, teams think transformation is over once a technology product is implemented. The reality is that implementation is just the beginning. Constant investing in those key relationships is what sustains transformation over the long haul.

Recognizing Allies

Building a coalition of the willing involved bringing together small groups of people – in this case, the various franchisees – to help coordinate and support the DT implementation. It was also important to understand supporters (franchise owners, Yum! management, partners, etc.) who influence people directly through advocacy and indirectly with their actions and deeds.

For Kelly, the first step involved engaging the franchisee technology council. This would not only build momentum for her efforts but also give her the needed advocates to support her during the different phases of the implementation.

Kelly took a note from Michael Watkins's book, *The First 90 Days, Updated and Expanded*,[2] and broke down her constituents and stakeholders into three categories – supporters, detractors, and persuadables – helping her understand those more or less likely to join and support the coalition. This also helped her consider the level of time and effort required to enlist each type of stakeholder and question what to do with detractors, who might seek to derail her efforts. How should she deal with them? Spend time trying to move them into the persuadable category. What might be an appropriate level of effort? Who is a supporter that can help bring them along in this journey?

Selling the Vision and Mechanisms of Persuasion

When it finally came to "selling" the platform to the brands, Kelly led with authenticity, honesty, and expertise. When she was asked to pitch to a franchisee board, she remembered something the late CMU professor, Randy Pausch, would say: "When there is an elephant in the room, introduce it." Her first slide showed all the options the franchisees had for an e-commerce platform. Kelly provided an honest and transparent comparison, highlighting both the strengths and weaknesses of each system. Additionally, Kelly talked through exactly how a menu got updated, the pain points in that journey, and how Kelly's team could solve it. In the end, it was her expertise in the space, authenticity at that moment, and the amount of time spent with the franchisees, with intimate knowledge of their pain points, that won the day delivering a coalition of the willing.

Steps in building a coalition and putting the different phases of transformation into place were critical, or as Kelly describes it: "a little like playing chess." That's not to say that there were winners and losers but rather that she recognized that each of her moves had different implications. She needed to think about all possible reactions to her current and future steps. It takes the presence of mind to be able to simultaneously think tactically (what you do) and strategically (what you plan). This is something that came naturally to Kelly but also can be practiced and reinforced.

Balance of Grace and Accountability

Coming from a very engineering-oriented culture with a background in engineering herself, Kelly was keenly aware of how big a role culture, personality, engagement, and communication played in building her coalition of the willing. The process required a mix of soft skills and technical skills. For Kelly, there was an important balance of accountability and grace in the coalition. Kelly never promised perfection. She often wouldn't even guarantee dates for delivery but simply delivery windows with a confidence level attached. This was because she knew there was still uncertainty in what they were building, and she wanted to reinforce a culture of learning within the team and the coalition. She also reinforced accountability for her team in delivering on their commitments and being transparent, offering options, when they run into roadblocks.

Often, technology products fail because there is an assumption at the beginning that everything is known and dates can be guaranteed. In reality, it's a constant state of known versus unknowns, and the goal should be to drive out the uncertainty quickly, so you have more knowledge and can make the right decision to achieve the ultimate business outcomes. This decision would need to be made not by Kelly alone but in partnership with the coalition, bringing them along the journey and ensuring they agreed with the trade-offs being made.

Long-Term Coalition Building

Kelly began launching their products into the franchise organizations in 2021. After one of the biggest markets to launch in 2024, the head of the franchisee board saw her in the hallway and gave her a big hug. They were firmly on the same team and had mutual trust in one another. The product launch did not go perfectly, but the coalition Kelly had built had such strong alignment and trust that the franchisees gave Kelly and her team grace, largely in part because of how they showed up during the process.

> ## Key Takeaways from Kelly's Journey
>
> - Listen first – sit, learn, and listen.
> - Show empathy – walk in their shoes.
> - Spend time together – deepen trust.
> - Become an expert.
> - Have authenticity, humility, and confidence.
> - Communicate early and often.
> - Build the coalition for the long term.

Try This: Listen For What They Care About

The Silo Monster thrives when people stop listening across functions and start defending turf. Real collaboration begins when you drop the agenda and tune into what matters to others.[3]

Step 1: Get Curious

In your next conversation with a colleague from another team, pause your agenda. Ask:

"What's keeping you up at night? What's getting you out of bed in the morning?"

Step 2: Listen for a Full Minute

Don't interrupt. Don't prepare your reply. Just listen and silently ask yourself:

"What do they really care about?"

Step 3: Reflect Back

Instead of shifting the conversation to your world or offering a quick fix, say:

"Here's what I think you care about . . ."

Name what you're hearing underneath their words like fairness, impact, momentum, or clarity. Even if you guess wrong, you have shown you are paying attention.

Connection kills silos. When people feel heard, they start leaning in and working together.

Chapter 9

Back to the Future

"Transformation is about managing the present while preparing for the future. You can't pause one to do the other."

—Pratik Pal, Tata Group

Most people understand the value of studying the past. It doesn't matter if we're talking about wars, scientific achievements and failures, or the evolution of a Silicon Valley start-up — studying the past can offer a road map of choices made or avoided and the results of those decisions. We've all heard the classic warnings about not paying attention to history — "Those who do not remember the past are condemned to repeat it" or "History repeats itself" — but the legendary historian David McCullough may have said it best when he wrote, "History is who we are and why we are the way we are."

Understanding the future is a little more challenging. It's completely unknown and difficult — if not impossible — to assess. It's not fixed and is subject to interpretation, as well as a variety of "what if" scenarios. It's also harder to achieve consensus on what might occur and, more importantly, how to prepare for an uncertain future. Maybe Yogi Berra was right when he said, "The future ain't what it used to be."

The fact is that most organizations settle in rather than try to leap forward. When Einstein described the laws of physics, he noted that objects at rest tend to stay at rest. He could just have just as easily been talking about your organizational transformation. Welcome to the domain of the Inertia Monster, a threat that doesn't announce itself, doesn't attack, doesn't even move. And that's precisely the problem.

While the FOMO Monster pushes organizations to chase every shiny object and the Hydra Monster spawns endless complexity in the form of new leadership roles and bureaucratic layers, the Inertia Monster does something more insidious: it ensures nothing changes at all. The Inertia Monster feeds on sacred cows, those ideas that are above reproach or criticism. As a result, no one challenges modes of operation, conventional thought, or changing consumer perception and needs. The company is at the whim of shift changes in expectation, whether they are consumer, employee, or regulatory.

The Inertia Monster, in other words, isn't loud. It isn't violent. It doesn't throw up roadblocks. The Inertia Monster just sits there. Unmoving. Unbothered. Watching your transformation plans with the dispassion of a centuries-old statue. The Inertia Monster lurks in boardrooms, whispering phrases like, "Let's create a committee to study this further." It nods thoughtfully in meetings, shaking its head, thinking, "This will never work here." It rewards risk-averse behavior and makes the way we've always done things seem like the safest, most rational choice, even when that way is leading straight to irrelevance.

You won't find "resistance to change" on a project risk register. There's no budget line item for organizational inertia (despite how much it may cost an organization). Yet, this unseen force has killed more transformation efforts than any technological challenge ever could.

- For boards, the Inertia Monster creates a mirage of stability, preserving short-term results while sacrificing long-term viability.
- For executives, the Inertia Monster provides the illusion of control, convincing them they're dutifully sailing forward when, in reality, the ship anchored to the ocean floor.
- For middle managers and frontline employees – aka the ones who actually see the need for change – the Inertia Monster breeds frustration. Year after year, they watch problems remain unsolved and eventually give up trying to find a solution.

This monster's presence is no accident. It is the natural byproduct of past success mixed with complacency associated with market position. The Inertia Monster exists because management assumes what worked before will still work now. In the age of AI-driven transformation, that assumption could be a death sentence.

To slay this monster, you need two powerful allies: the Visionary and the Path Maker.

The Inertia Monster Slayers

The Visionary sees what others cannot – not just the world as it is but the world as it can be. While others are bound by today's constraints, the Visionary slices through them, painting a compelling picture of why the future often demands change now. They are known to reframe and question everything, with important questions such as: "Why does our organization exist?" "Who do we serve?" and "What value do we provide?" They use these foundational questions to ask the most important one: "What should/can we do if our customers no longer see value in us in the future?"

This line of questioning isn't just about optimism. The Visionary connects societal and technical trends, challenges ideas once seen as above criticism, and translates abstract possibilities into tangible business outcomes. They rethink the status quo by helping organizations build resilience and adaptability into operations to stay relevant and compete in an unknown future.

Amazon's Jeff Bezos famously once said, "I very frequently get the question: 'What's going to change in the next 10 years?' And that is a very interesting question; it's a very common one. I almost never get the question: 'What's not going to change in the next 10 years?' And I submit to you that that second question is actually the more important of the two."

The visionary understands that both questions merit consideration when it comes to digital transformation. In an age where AI is transforming industries; what isn't going to change? Customers will always expect convenience. Employees will always want meaningful work. Businesses will always need speed and adaptability.

The Visionary doesn't just react to disruption; they create clarity around the future before disruption arrives.

If the Visionary is the dreamer, the Path Maker is the enabler. The Path Maker focuses on preparing the organization to be ready for different states of existence. Much like the Organizational Pragmatist, they assess what needs to be put into place in terms of people, resources, and capabilities to be able to adapt and be ready for a possible future scenario. Along with the Barrier Buster, they team up to find the optimal path and remove barriers to transformation.

The Path Maker isn't seduced by every flashy prediction. Instead, they deal with concepts realistically and sensibly to ensure folks understand organizational capacity for an unknown future state. This involves being clear and practical in laying out paths to build resiliency and create opportunities for adaptation.

Unlike the Inertia Monster, which thrives in organizations that cling to old patterns, the Path Maker translates capacity planning and resource building, creating organizational readiness to make sure the Visionary's future state prediction can be realized, bridging the gap between today's reality and tomorrow's opportunity.

Eyes on the Prize

A true Visionary doesn't chase every shiny object. Rather, they frame the future through a broad vision of what's in front of them. McKinsey's Three Horizons model suggests that great leaders balance the Now (core initiatives driving today's value), Next (emerging opportunities taking shape), and Beyond (longer-term bets still crystallizing). This means organizations need to be willing to discuss what is coming in the future as much as they discuss the world right in front of them. This means they need to change their way of thinking because the near- and long-term involve different types of thinking and assessment.

The Visionary looks at different possible future states, but skillfully explains these in ways everyone can understand. Strategic foresight is a discipline where planners use data, forecasts, alternative predictions of the future, and analysis to develop or alter organizational planning. Strategic foresight looks at many different future outcomes, but groups them into three general categories:

Possible future: Anything could happen regardless of likelihood. Such thinking pushes the boundary of conventional thinking and can feel uncomfortable for folks but is necessary. What happens if AI achieves general intelligence and can run an organization better than the C<blank><blank>Os or can become better and more efficient and scalable at teaching than instructors or professors? It might also look at events where there is a mass macroeconomic shock to the system, such as a global pandemic.

Probable future: What is likely to happen based on current trends and data? This prediction might be a direct result of signals the organization or analysts are tracking. The reality is, for example, that an aging population and people seeking to stay in the workforce longer (some voluntarily, some with no other choice) have led to a multigenerational workforce. Organizations need to plan and adapt to having groups of employees with different values, communication patterns, and rates of technology adoption.

Preferable or potential future: This category of thinking asks a fundamental question: What future do we want to create? Is it one based on shared values, goals, or beliefs? This version considers deliberate actions and intent, which is why we need the Path Maker to help us understand, assess, and chart the future. Let's say, for example, that our organization wants to achieve net-zero carbon emissions. Whatever the reason – regulatory compliance, cost containment, consumer and employee perception, etc. – the Visionary can help frame the discussion in terms of mission alignment and innovation strategy.

There is, of course, one final state that certainly needs to be considered in the process of transformation – what is actually plausible? It's critical to consider what is realistically feasible given the current capacity, competency, and other competing initiatives. This is a state that weighs the possible and probable and might benefit from the wisdom of a monster slayer from a previous chapter. Remember the Organizational Pragmatist (Chapter 1)? This is a critical slayer to bring into the conversation, not to shut down ideas, but to inject a sense of realism and understanding to achieve a plausible future state.

This is where the Visionary and the Path Maker complement each other without overwhelming leaders who have a tendency to shut down when trying to assess different states of the future and how they should adapt to them. Simplifying a complex state is critical to understand probability, capacity, and planning. These two slayers don't just help organizations escape inertia – they transform hesitation into momentum. But where do thoughts on the possible future come from, and how do we interpret them?

The Science of "Futurology"

Mark Twain once famously said, "Prediction is difficult – especially when it involves the future." Many people turn to conferences focused on the future of technical innovation as a way to try to understand the future. Conferences like the Consumer Electronics Show (CES) brings together some of the most well-known thought leaders in the technology space to highlight trends, applications, and innovation across a variety of industries. Other conferences like SXSW look at technology trends and infuse them with cultural shifts in film, design, art, and music. These places help Visionaries think about the future and how their organization might play a role. The Path Maker finds the steps to develop adaptive infrastructure to be ready to meet a future state rather than being blindsided by it.

These shows are thought-provoking and provide insights into the future of retail, healthcare, education, etc., but they are speculative and generally avoid all the challenges associated with actual implementation. After all, who wants to attend a conference called "All the Reasons Your Transformation Might Fail (ARTF)"? No one wants to spend money, time, and effort to travel to a place like Las Vegas to attend a conference of professionals complaining about process complexity, risk avoidance, or how mid-level management can be blockers to innovation.

Instead, many successful companies wait on shifts in consumer expectations until they become entrenched and mainstream. These are known as late movers, followers, or second adopters. Sometimes, this is a smart strategy because the organization has the benefit of watching market reaction to innovators. Google did this by launching its search engine into a crowded space. Their advantage was a unique page ranking algorithm and the simplicity of their user interface, which won over the market and established them as the preeminent leader in online search.

Pick your futurists carefully, whether they are in business, design, cultural, or technology. Many of these trends are intertwined, and it's difficult to predict timing. All organizations face challenges in implementing strategic foresight practices regularly. After all, it challenges long-term thinking in a world dominated by short-term pressures, a great deal of uncertainty, and cognitive biases. Most businesses are wired for quarterly results, not 5–10 year transformation efforts. There is no shortage of folks to help with this. Futurists speak at different conferences and write books about the future. Strategy consultants, by contrast, could be considered applied futurists. These folks are experts at collecting, incorporating, and interpreting data about future shifts. Their strength is that they look at multiple future scenarios and offer a variety of forecasts. They are comfortable dealing with complexity and theories of social change, while also incorporating a strong understanding of historical trends.

Interestingly, the 1998 World Futures Society meeting in Chicago tried to develop a code of ethics for Futurists. Their assertion was that "Futurists should be guided by a deep conviction of the worth and dignity of current and future generations and recognize the special responsibility they carry as professional futurists." Whether you read a newsletter from an academic futurist, attended a conference where they presented their future views, or hire strategy consultants to help assess trends; this capability needs to be developed internally with your Visionary and Path Maker. Why then do some organizations still fall into a state of stagnation?

Stagnation Trap: "Good Enough" Becomes the Enemy of Great

The Inertia Monster thrives in keeping the organization in a state of stagnation. Innovation might be relegated to a lab or outsourced to a university without any mechanisms to execute on it. Intricate compliance processes and heavy-handed governance protocols contain risk at all costs, resulting in defensive posturing to defend market share. This isn't failure by explosion; it's failure by erosion.

Take GM, once the world's largest automaker, with brands such as Buick, Cadillac, Chevrolet, and GMC under its hood. In the mid-twentieth century, they controlled almost 50% of the US auto market. However, the company's over-reliance on gas-guzzling SUVs and trucks left it vulnerable to the rising consumer demand for more fuel-efficient vehicles. Think of it as a race to empty with a full tank of gas between a Hummer and a Prius. Japanese automakers like Toyota and Honda were capturing the market for fuel-efficient and compact cars, while GM was experiencing issues with too many brands and overlapping models. In addition, a complex network of dealers and legacy costs hindered agility. The reality was that GM was slow to invest in hybrid technology and struggled to adapt during the financial crisis of 2008 that led to plummeting car sales and liquidity issues. So what happened? GM filed for Chapter 11 bankruptcy in 2009 and received a \$50B+ bailout from the US government under the Troubled Asset Relief Program (TARP).

To understand how organizations battle or succumb to the Inertia Monster, we can map issues across two critical dimensions: pace of innovation, which is how quickly they implement change, and risk approach, which shows how willing they are to embrace uncertainty (see Figure 9.1).

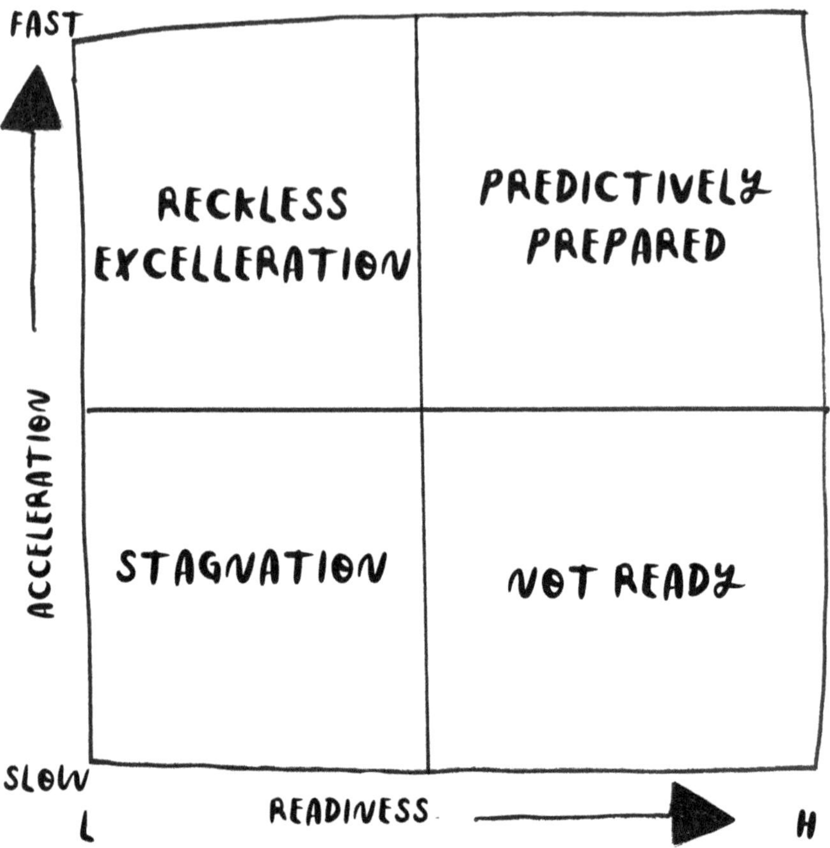

Figure 9.1   From stagnation to preparation.

This breakdown reveals four common results:

- **Underprepared:** Cautious but lacking capability for change.
- **Stagnation:** Aware of change, but immobilized by fear of risk, aka stuck in endless planning.
- **Reckless acceleration:** Moving fast, but without direction. Mistaking motion for progress.
- **Smart scaling:** The ideal state, deliberate experimentation with rapid learning cycles.

The challenge isn't just moving from one quadrant to another. It's finding the optimal balance between thoughtful foresight and decisive action.

The Exploration–Exploitation Dilemma

Most organizations clearly don't set out to get stuck. They just get really good at what they already do. And that's precisely the problem.

In behavioral science and business strategy, this is known as the explore versus exploit dilemma. Every company faces a fundamental tension:

- Exploit what you already know; optimize, refine, and extract maximum efficiency from existing markets, processes, and technologies.
- Explore what's new; invest in innovation, experiment with emerging business models, and take strategic risks on unproven ideas.

For stable, mature companies, exploitation feels safe. It's predictable, it's measurable, and it delivers consistent returns. Exploration, on the other hand, introduces uncertainty. It demands trial and error, risk-taking, and long-term thinking over short-term gains, which is exactly why the Inertia Monster thrives in organizations obsessed with quarterly results.

The problem? Exploitation alone can be a slow death sentence. Market shifts, technological breakthroughs, and customer expectations change too quickly to keep up. Companies that fail to balance exploitation with exploration become victims of their own past success.

Nokia is a great cautionary tale. The Finnish telecom giant dominated the mobile phone market in the early 2000s. At their peak, they controlled about 40% of the market share. However, when Apple released the iPhone in 2007, the game completely changed. Nokia thought that smartphones were a niche and didn't pay attention to the signals with the introduction of devices like the BlackBerry and Palm Treo. The company also failed to recognize that the shift in the business wasn't simply about designing better phones, but a fundamental change in understanding about what a phone could do and how people interact with it. Internally, the culture had become risk-averse, stagnant, and overly political. Leadership focused on retaining its power base rather than on innovation and taking big bets. Nokia completely missed the shift that was happening, thinking of phones as devices, not platforms, and ignoring the growing ecosystem of applications for phones that had become more important than the hardware found within the phones themselves.

Great companies learn to explore *while* they exploit. They de-risk innovation by testing new models while still extracting value from their core business. The ability to innovate without abandoning the foundation that made you successful is critical for being adaptive.

Beware the West Coast Lab Trap

When the Inertia Monster feels threatened, organizations often create "innovation labs" far from HQ, in either distance or accessibility, hoping that separation alone will spark transformation. These labs often start with fanfare, TED Talks, conferences, and glossy innovation decks. But without tight loops back to the core business, these labs become isolated islands out of sight, out of mind, and eventually out of budget. When not addressed, they begin to create a division in the culture. One set of folks is given free rein to innovate and ensure the "survival" of the organization, while most employees working on current operations are "keeping the lights on." Resentment can creep in, as well as the belief that folks in operations are subsidizing the folks who are tasked with innovation.

True exploration requires integration. Smart organizations don't outsource innovation to a shiny lab. They embed the mindset of the Visionary and the assessment of the Path Maker into the core fabric of their business, every team, every leader, every quarter.

This brings us to another critical distinction: the "What You Think vs. What You Know" dilemma. The greatest trick the Inertia Monster can pull off is convincing leaders that their assumptions are facts. In organizations struggling with inertia, leaders often default to their gut instincts, industry experience, and internal wisdom rather than real-world evidence. They believe they know their customers, their markets, and the competitive landscape, but in reality, they're operating on outdated mental models.

This is the "What You Think vs. What You Know" dilemma, often defined by a few common beliefs:

1. What You Think:
    (a) "Our customers value price above all."
    (b) "AI won't impact our industry for another five years."
    (c) "We can't operate remotely – our culture requires in-person collaboration."

2. What You Know (Looking at the Data):
   (a) Customer sentiment surveys show experience matters more than price.
   (b) AI adoption in the industry is accelerating exponentially, not linearly.
   (c) Companies with hybrid work models are outperforming fully in-office competitors.

The Inertia Monster thrives when organizations treat beliefs as knowledge. It persuades leaders to double down on existing playbooks instead of interrogating assumptions with data and constructive disagreement. The result is a widening gap between how they think the world works and how it actually works.

This is where the Visionary and Path Maker really shine. The Visionary helps organizations challenge assumptions by painting a compelling, evidence-backed picture of the future. The Path Maker understands capacity and capabilities, providing a holistic assessment of what needs to be done to realize adaptation, thereby shrugging off the Inertia Monster.

Organizations that successfully transition from Stagnation to Smart Scaling don't just guess at the future. They explore it systematically, validate assumptions continuously, and act decisively on real insights.

So, how do you escape this trap?

Momentum Matters More Than Mass

In physics, momentum = mass × velocity. In organizations, it's the same formula, but most companies obsess over scale (budgets, team size, scope) and neglect speed (decision velocity, learning cycles, adaptation rate).

The companies that succeed aren't the ones that start in a grandiose fashion; they are the ones that move the fastest.

A healthcare company we studied launched its AI transformation with a modest pilot, redesigning just one patient touchpoint. Rather than waiting for perfect conditions, the company created a rapid learning cycle that delivered tangible improvements in just 45 days. This small win changed the entire conversation. It shifted debates from theoretical concerns to practical results. That's how momentum gets built. Transformation doesn't reward the organization that moves perfectly; it rewards the one that moves first, learns fastest, and adapts ruthlessly. When the Inertia Monster whispers, "Let's wait until we're ready," the Visionary and Path Maker are already testing, learning, and adjusting.

Small bets beat no bets. Strategic thinking beats crisis reactions. Continuously rethinking the status quo beats waiting to become irrelevant.

Welcome to the Matrix

The best antidote to inertia isn't more debate. It's more simulation.

Instead of arguing about what might happen, Visionaries look at different states of the future. As we mentioned earlier in the chapter, these states might be ones that are possible, preferable, probable, and/or plausible. Breaking these states out this way allows small testable situations to assess organizational impact (remember LEAR?) or look at erosion of market share, regulatory violations, or inability to compete. Simulations break mental inertia by making the future feel real today. They're not predictions; they're practice runs for what's coming. Inertia isn't always about doing nothing. Sometimes, inertia hides behind frantic bursts of effort that quickly burn out. Remember, true transformation is a marathon, not a sprint.

The reality is that in a world of AI and digital transformation, perfect conditions never arrive or never exist.

The Visionary creates comfort with ambiguity, while the Path Maker reduces uncertainty by identifying what's needed. Together, they empower organizations to act even when the future isn't completely clear. The biggest myth about transformation is that people resist change. They don't. They resist change, they don't believe in.

Great Visionaries and Path Makers understand that consistency beats intensity every time. Progress happens when you resist the urge for flashy one-off wins and instead build muscle through relentless, steady motion, week after week, quarter after quarter. It's not the wild sprint that wins. It's the team that shows up, day after day, adapting, learning, and moving forward.

Become a Simulation Machine

The most dangerous thing about organizational inertia isn't that it stops progress. It's that it creates the illusion of progress. Meetings happen. Reports are written. Committees are formed. And yet nothing actually changes. The Visionary and Path Mapper slice through that illusion. They don't wait for perfect clarity. They create motion, progress, and momentum.

As the future becomes more complex with the introduction of more technology, more regulations, and greater employee/customer expectations, the nature of work is changing. Work, working, and the workplace 2.0 suggest that organizations are rethinking how work gets done, where it gets done, and what exactly constitutes "work." This is not something new; the signals have been there for a while. Freelance, crowdsourced, and gig work have been growing in popularity for several reasons, including flexibility for both the workers and the employers and a reduction in cost to employers. After all, bringing on folks full-time, providing benefits, and renting a workplace can be expensive.

The onset of COVID-19 and the pandemic resulted in a massive shift in thinking about work, and especially where it gets done. Work went online, and employees, managers, and executives had to figure out how to be productive in a remote work environment. Online collaboration platforms like Zoom, Google Meet, and MS Teams shifted from niche platforms to essential work settings. Initially, we saw a productivity boost resulting from the time savings and flexibility associated with not having the daily commute to the office. However, after a period, there was an inflection point when productivity began to decrease. Why? For one, organizations did not think about the redefinition of work to reflect the remote workforce. It was simply taking the current culture, tasks, and processes of work in the physical setting and trying to force them online and remote.

In the age of AI, the companies that win won't be the ones with the best predictions. They'll be the ones who moved first, learned fastest, and never stopped moving forward.

Key Takeaways

The Inertia Monster is stealthy and silent and creeps up on organizations. It breeds complacency and risk aversion. To slay the Inertia Monster, organizations need to (1) practice rethinking everything, (2) simulate future scenarios to understand what is likely versus what they would like to have happen, and (3) consider ways to build toward a desired future. It is important to remember:

- Momentum matters more than mass. Small wins create unstoppable movement.
- Remember the Scout motto: "Be prepared." Understand and map trends (see Chapter 1), but develop a vision for how the organization should operate in the future.
- Develop a path that understands contingencies, in other words, those scenarios that might require the organization to deviate from the path. This leads to resiliency in the face of adversity. Practice the idea that "anything and everything can happen"; you just have to understand its probability.

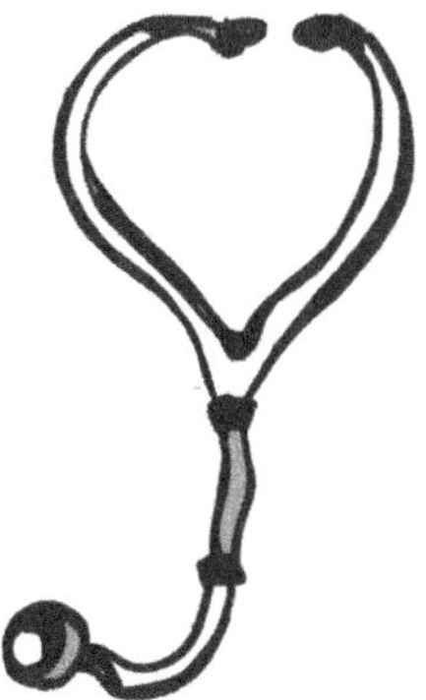

Case Story: Fairview Health Services

Simulating a Healthier Future

Healthcare is going through a profound transformation in delivery, access, capabilities, and patient expectations. Patients, their care providers, and everyone across the healthcare landscape is impacted, but perhaps the most significant are the folks on the front lines — care delivery teams and the healthcare delivery systems.

Founded in 1905 in Minneapolis, Minnesota, Fairview Health Services has expanded into a major nonprofit integrated system, operating hospitals, clinics, pharmacies, and senior-care services across Minnesota and western Wisconsin. Today, Fairview offers comprehensive services, including primary, long-term, and specialty care and home health and rehabilitation services. In addition, their health equity initiatives make sure adequate coverage is available across their service area. With more than 34,000 employees across 10 hospitals, 60 clinics, dozens of pharmacies, and an integrated network including university academic hospitals, it is one of the largest health systems in the Twin Cities. They provide world-class care for more than 1.2 million patients across various communities. Like many healthcare institutions, they grew through partnerships, siloed service lines, and culturally distinct physician groups. Their reach extended and services provided increased, but along with that so did issues with process and system complexity. Despite a growing system and impressive array of capabilities, like every healthcare system across the nation, Fairview was facing needs for cost containment, innovative care models, workforce adjustments, and competitive differentiation, while continuing to earn trust across their extended ecosystem.

Much like other regional health systems, in 2019 Fairview was confronted by shifting expectations from the community. Patients were behaving more like consumers, expecting experiences like that in retail, hospitality, and travel. The traditional mechanisms of seeking care — finding a primary care provider (PCP), getting a referral for a specialist, visiting your physician's office for regular checkups and the hospital for procedures or treatments, and relying solely on the health systems for questions and concerns as it relates to health and wellness — were all drastically and rapidly evolving. Digital platforms for receiving care, digital communication channels, and patient portals provided new ways to meet patients where they were with understandable information to manage their care were becoming more pervasive. Concurrently, patients were increasingly going online using available resources like search engines and patient communities and today are increasingly relying on LLM/Gen AI to ask questions about their health, "diagnose" potential symptoms and empower themselves. However, in many cases, they were being exposed to mis- and disinformation.

The Weight of What Was

The question wasn't whether Fairview could innovate. The question was whether it could move fast enough to meet a future that was evolving even more quickly.

When Dr. Sameer Badlani arrived as chief digital officer in 2019 (role expanded to include customer experience in 2022 and enterprise strategy in 2024), he inherited more than a portfolio. He inherited a paradox: a system full of smart people with noble intent but stymied by a risk-adverse environment and an uncertain future. Everyone agreed that change was needed. Few could agree on what it meant, what direction it should take, or who owned it.

Sameer was no stranger to this situation. He had a long career as a healthcare change maker and Inertia Monster slayer, serving previous roles as the chief health informatics officer at Sutter Health and Intermountain and, before that, as the chief medical information officer at UChicago Medicine. Although Sameer began his career as a practicing and teaching physician, he brought together business acumen, innovative thinking, and a pragmatic approach, all grounded in a deep understanding of care delivery from the patient and provider's perspective. In addition to his professional roles, as an educator working with Carnegie Mellon University, Sameer continues to contribute to both executive education programs and their master's in medical management program.

Sameer works with executives to apply critical thinking and strategic foresight along with human-centered design (HCD) to deeply understand the patient experience. HCD principles place the needs, behavior, and experience of people at the center of the design process. Like the experimental approach, it emphasizes empathy, definition setting, ideation, prototyping, and testing. Sameer's unique blend of connecting and inspiring, critical thinking, and long-term strategic decision-making is a powerful combination of traits to assess future trends and needs with a pragmatic understanding of transformative capabilities.

Transformation of Health

What can the history of healthcare tell us about future needs? What can we learn from other regions about how health can be delivered equitably and sustainably? How can we sustainably innovate to serve the needs of tomorrow's patients while ensuring today's patients have sufficient care? In recent years the point of care has been shifting away from the traditional hospital setting. Sameer needed to think about the implications of new models, digital platforms, and technologies along with new reimbursement models to support remote-based care and ambulatory care (outpatient services). The pandemic accelerated customer acceptance for seeking care outside of traditional healthcare settings. In addition, healthcare systems were feeling the financial strain of the inflation in the cost-of-service delivery falling behind payment adjustments from health insurers (payors). This was compounded by the presence of intermediaries like pharmacy benefits managers (PBMs) and rising costs of pharmaceuticals, medical devices, and technology service providers.

Additionally, the healthcare landscape was becoming more challenging. Noncommunicable diseases including cancer, diabetes, and cardiovascular disease have been steadily on the rise, straining resources and changing care dynamics. Addressing health disparities in underrepresented minorities (URM) and historically disenfranchised communities became an important part of the mission. This meant care in communities, education, and outreach on preventative care, wellness programs, and greater representation of URM within the health system further straining resources and competing for priorities. However, one of the largest changes will be in the changing demographic need for care.

The *silver tsunami* is a metaphor used to describe the rapid aging of the population. According to S&P Global, by 2030, 1 in 5 Americans will be 65 or older. This is having a pronounced impact of healthcare including:

- Older populations consume more care than younger ones including chronic disease management inside the home as well as hospitals.
- Longer life spans result in a growing demand for long-term care such as nursing homes and assisted living.
- Higher costs and utilization include end-of-life care, hospital readmissions, and polypharmacy (taking five or more medications concurrently).

As patient information was increasingly digitized and made available to patients and care providers, issues of integration, data entry, and privacy and security issues started to surface. Healthcare-specific regulations like Health Insurance Portability and Accountability Act (HIPAA) and cybersecurity breaches became hurdles to greater engagement and slowed down rollout of innovative service. Meanwhile, technology innovators like Apple, Google, and Amazon that weren't encumbered continue to disrupt the space, experimenting with providing prescription delivery, wellness applications, and human-centered applications to access, integrate, and assess medical data. Unlike other countries with universal care, healthcare in the United States is still a collection of separate systems with different data standards.

Sameer didn't start by launching flashy tech pilots. He started by getting honest about trade-offs – what mattered most to patients, caregivers, and the long-term sustainability of the system. His first move wasn't a digital initiative. It was a mindset reset and was striving for clarity in defining what is value for the different health stakeholders.

Unhealthy Impacts of the Pandemic

The COVID-19 pandemic accelerated change and transformation. As the world went through lockdowns and shelter-in-place orders, providers deployed seldom-used online platforms to stay in touch with patients and provide remote care. Health systems needed to quickly assess capacity planning and reconfigure emergency departments to address the spread of healthcare-borne infections. Fairview ramped up its digital capacities out of necessity, leveraging platforms, reconfiguring operational capacity, and using sensors and apps to monitor patients remotely. There was significant social and economic impact from the pandemic; however, all health systems faced uniquely complex challenges, including:

- **System strain and compatibility challenges:** Overburdened facilities deferred procedures including preventative care, and the workforce faced intense pressures leading to burnout and attrition.

- **Accelerated innovation:** Vaccine research and development accelerated while surveillance systems and predictive models to forecast epidemiological spread became standard tools.
- **Health equity and disparities:** The pandemic shined a light on disproportionate impacts on marginalized communities while the digital divide limited telehealth access for rural and low-income populations.
- **Financial disruption:** Cancellation of profitable procedures and outpatient visits resulted in significant losses for health systems. Financial pressures resulted in closures, limitations of services, and, in some cases, mergers.

Throughout it all, Sameer has had a front-row seat to healthcare transformation – analyzing missteps, cultural and technical challenges, adoption patterns, incentive structures, and, most importantly, pragmatic methods for addressing future needs.

From Buzzwords to Boldness

Integrated care. Consumerism. Cost compression. Health inequity. Value-based care. These words showed up in every PowerPoint, but when Sameer looked under the hood, initiatives often duplicated efforts, lacked clear value and prioritization, or stalled in endless alignment loops. One of Sameer's favorite quips is that "Healthcare has more pilots than the airline industry."

"The system wasn't broken because of bad intent or lack of expertise. It was stuck because of too many truths competing at once within a razor thin margin business."

At Fairview, inertia showed up as:

- Committees with unclear charters and limited funding.
- Competing key performance indicators (KPIs) between clinical and operational units.
- Talent burnout from labor shortages and workload.

Fairview' journey until that point had bred a natural conservatism. Every system, every approval, every clinical model had been hardened by regulation and time. Moving fast wasn't just difficult; it could feel reckless.

Sameer didn't try to shake up Fairview's operating model by anticipating the future. Instead, he focused on the modernization of digital capabilities and the mindset shift in patient value and experience. Working within the existing constraints, he led the technology team to do more with less, reducing waste and redeploying the savings toward purposeful talent acquisition. Brick by brick, capabilities improved and capacity increased. In addition, his team deployed internal crowdsourcing initiatives to engage the entire organization while not being solely dependent on a few capable but overburdened engineers. Hackathons allowed all employees, irrespective of their background, to contribute to innovation and transformation. The customer experience team leveraged patient and family advisory groups to guide and better design key digital initiatives. In partnership with the human-centered design studio, they launched new digital experiences and capabilities for patients and caregivers.

In designing these systems, Sameer and his team focused on respecting what was important to patients including their valuable time. This mindset change reflected treating them as consumers and customers with choice. Traditionally, and still now, access is defined as:

- You search for a doctor,
- You see them in their clinic,
- You sit in front of them,
- You wait, you get a room, you wait,
- Then you see them for a few minutes,
- Then you wait for the lab, and
- Then you wait for radiology and so on.

How does this impact patient experience? Breaking down the experience to understand what different patients are seeking and the value provided is critical when redesigning interactions. Sameer posited an underlying theory of action: *"If we are moving to a consumer/patient focused model, then we need to think like patients/consumers of care."* Sameer did this with a pragmatic lens of Fairview's current capacity and capability. These weren't theoretical exercises. They were blueprints for action that prioritized key strategic questions:

- How to design and operationalize different care models?
- How to embrace and assess the impacts of AI on delivery and quality of care as well as operational efficiency?
- How might personalization in preventative care demand new operating and delivery models?

Sameer understood that inertia wasn't just organizational. It was emotional as well. Each new conversation of future prediction Sameer helped drive wasn't just a theoretical and technical exercise but a way of helping leaders "feel" the future more tangibly and prepare for it. Think of it as building muscles against the Inertia Monster.

Instead of pushing speed only, Sameer created psychological safety. Simulations became a rehearsal space, rather than a battlefield, and a way for teams to test bold moves without the existential fear of getting them wrong. Throughout it all, Sameer remained thoughtful and methodical. He wasn't just asking "What's the future?" He also wanted to test the question, "Are we ready for it?"

The Patient Will See You Now

As a physician, educator, and healthcare executive, Sameer cares about his community, students, employees, and patients, but the question on his mind is how to do it sustainably. Heading up enterprise strategy at Fairview, he needs to think through different future states to make sure Fairview is positioned appropriately and can be resilient to shifts both gradual and sudden. One of these future states for Sameer is the shift in power dynamics from the health systems (providers) to the patient. This can be witnessed on many fronts, including who pays for care (customers). Traditionally, there were two major sources:

- Government programs (e.g., Medicare, Medicaid).
- Private insurers (employer-sponsored or commercial).

Today, patients' direct contributions have grown to the point where they are starting to rival commercial insurers and government programs as a significant source of revenue for many providers. Why is this occurring?

Increasing interest in High-Deductible Health Plans (HDHPs)

- More than 50% of insured Americans now have HDHPs.
- Patients must often spend $2,000–$15,000 out-of-pocket before insurance coverage begins.

Cost-Shifting by Employers and Insurers

- Insurers have narrowed networks and raised costs and out-of-pocket expenses.
- Employers are passing more cost responsibility to employees.

Rising Prices for Services

- Hospitals and specialists are charging more, and negotiated rates are not always covering the annual increase in inflation.
- Patients often pay "list price" for out-of-network services.

Growth in Self-Pay and Underinsured Populations

- Even insured patients face surprise bills and gaps in coverage.
- Gig workers, freelancers, and early retirees are often in self-pay categories.

When people pay directly for care, their behavior patterns change from those of a consumer to more like a customer. For Fairview, behaving like a retailer in a competitive market rather than a traditional health service provider model represents a huge shift and opportunity. Retail care involves the provision of a myriad of healthcare services in customer accessible and frequented locations. Also, customer experience becomes paramount and leveraged as a competitive advantage. It's a reflection of the "consumerization of care" offering accessible, low-cost, walk-in services more amenable and convenient to the next generation of healthcare consumers. Retailers like Walmart have struggled in experimenting with primary, dental, and vision care. Urgent care centers with a high-quality retail-like experience are an opportunity to grow a loyal consumer base. Even pharmacies are expanding into vaccinations and related health services.

Sameer believes retail care models can provide a differentiator for systems like Fairview. How can it be done and scaled effectively? Through careful assessment of use cases, target markets, and communicating value while addressing risk, Sameer puts a lens of HCD to look at probable, possible, and potential future states, not to shoot for one over another but to develop a adaptive and scalable systems to meet demand and ensure a consistent experience. As patients behave more like consumers, experience matters, and as the variety of choices increases, experience can be the differentiator for selecting one service provider/health system over another.

Simplifying medical terminology and connecting it with service lines is another area where Sameer has deployed HCD. Fairview recreated physician web pages to focus less on physician education credentials and more on the conditions they treat in consumer-friendly terms. So now a consumer of care can see what conditions a physician treats and what services a clinic or hospital provides in a manner that makes sense.

Observing Other Markets

Sameer is a big fan of Costco and notices how the retail giant and other non- traditional health providers, like Lifetime Entertainment, are moving into health and wellness. Understanding what consumers expect and the blurring lines between medical and wellness is an important consideration when thinking about future interaction between health services and folks seeking care. When care is convenient and accessible, it creates stickiness and engagement.

Take, for example, perimenopausal care and wellness, focusing on supporting women as they transition toward and aim to thrive during menopause. This is a complicated phase impacting physical, emotional, and mental well-being concerns include hormonal fluctuations, menstrual irregularities, sleep disruptions, metabolic changes, weight management, and bone health. It's an underserved area, and medical care doesn't really address the holistic needs. In seeking better care, women have turned to a multitude of sources from gyms to social influencers on digital platforms like TikTok.

By using not just market data but consumer data including what kind of services women might value and in what mode, physical or digital, they would like to consume it, it is critical to designing effective services. Sameer and his colleagues have deployed effective and modern solutions that provide valuable care in a way that resonates and engenders trust. For future patients, health systems need to focus on holistic care, not just clinical care.

The AI Consultant Is Now Available

Sameer takes an outcome and value-based approach to AI at Fairview. He divides AI into three broad use-case categories:

- **AI for community support:** AI can think through how consumers of care seek and retrieve information using large language models. What is the validity of the information? Are they looking for providers or diagnosing symptoms? How can we engage with them on pre-conceptions associated with their care?
- **Maximizing native AI including AI diagnostic tools:** During COVID-19, Fairview used X-rays to diagnose COVID-19 and algorithmic analysis to help determine which patient to admit and which patient to discharge.

- **Using AI to increase volume, access, and reduce costs:** Bespoke applications can work within the Fairview system to improve consumer and employee experience and create new care models.

Surrounding all three of these use cases is building safe, responsible AI frameworks and making sure Fairview can monitor and handle any ethical considerations. Sameer understands that technology is just one of the critical tools. Behind every system upgrade or AI tool lies some deeper questions: How does the organization work together? What is the value, and do we all have clarity? What does success look like, and how do we measure it?

Romancing Risk: From Threat to Opportunity

Ultimately, one of Sameer's greatest contributions wasn't technical at all – it was cultural. He reframed risk, drove clarity, and increased the value of crowdsourcing inside Fairview. In a highly regulated industry, risk has long been seen as something to avoid. Sameer showed that managed risk – when exposed early through simulation – was not a threat but in fact an opportunity to adapt to the needs of a shifting population.

Of course, this mindset shift didn't happen overnight. Sameer worked cross-functionally, bringing regulatory, compliance, clinical, and operational leaders into the simulation discussions early. He didn't wait for ideas to be "perfect" – he made them visible when they were still messy, ensuring feedback loops were tight and trust was built long before high-stakes decisions were made. Crowdsourcing, brought agility, diversity of actionable ideas, and most importantly a sense of pride in achievement across teams.

Rather than confront resistance head-on, true to his roots as a physician, Sameer took a diagnostic approach. He mapped resistance patterns, identified early champions, and created "safe spaces" for dissent. Transparency and curiosity became culture-shifting tools and accelerators.

He began to focus on what he calls culture operating models – not just what gets done but how people interact when doing it. This included:

- Focusing on psychological safety.
- Making design a central tenet of digital transformation.
- Delayering meetings streamlining governance.
- Creating "alignment loops" between clinical, digital, and strategic teams.

This work wasn't glamorous, but it was foundational. To move forward, Sameer practices what some call *strategic subtraction* – focusing on fewer things done well. In an environment tempted by shiny objects and vendor hype, this discipline became essential.

Key Takeaways from Sameer's Journey

- Inertia doesn't always look like slowness. Sometimes it looks like being busy without impact.
- Clarity of value is the foundation of effective transformation.
- Human-centered design is the foundation of creating processes and systems that are intuitive, value laden, and useful.
- Resistance is human. Deploy your strategy to acknowledge emotion, not just logic.
- Digital isn't a department. It's a way to scale strategic intent.
- Experience for both the consumer and employee is everything.
- Without scale and sustainability there can be no transformation.

Try This: Future in Motion

The Inertia Monster loves a full calendar and zero momentum. To outpace it, you don't need a big bet. You need a bias for motion.

Step 1: Pick a Sacred Cow

As a team, name one long-standing process, product, or assumption that hasn't been challenged in years. Write it down without judgment, just curiosity.

Step 2: Simulate the Future

Ask: "If this didn't exist, would we invent it today?"
    Now imagine three future scenarios:

- **Possible:** What if a competitor replaces this with something smarter?
- **Plausible:** What if this fails to meet evolving customer needs?
- **Probable:** What happens if we keep it and the market shifts?

Step 3: Make a Micro-Move

Agree on one small action you can take in the next 30 days:

- Kill it, test it, or evolve it.
- Don't wait for perfect clarity. Create momentum through action.

Chapter 10

Check Yourself

"From a risk perspective, we had to shift from a castle and moat model of security to embedding our security expertise and leadership into the business. Not to be the officer of security in these emerging businesses, but to be the partner."

—Rob Duhart, CISO Oracle Cloud Infrastructure

ates or guardrails? Guardrails set up boundaries to allow autonomy. They minimize risk without introducing excessive bureaucracy. On the other hand, gates block progress until approval. As transformation scales, gates will be inevitable, so everyone should be ready for them including how to avoid them through developing guardrails. One of the most common mistakes we see organizations make is easy to avoid but is often the result of a desire to work as fast as possible. It is simply not having the right folks in the transformation conversations addressing concerns and issues at the start of the journey. We've all heard the tech industry mantra "Move fast and break things." The thinking might be right, but you still need to be realistic. Ask yourself: Have you thought through all the potential risks associated with transformation? Is compliance adequately represented in your efforts? Have you given attention to how vulnerabilities might be created through improper use of applications, processes, and services? Governance, risk, and compliance (GRC) is fundamental to all companies looking to minimize the threat of lawsuits, regulatory fines, and security breaches. And yet the complex nature of addressing GRC issues sometimes gets swept aside in lieu of rapid forward progress. That's when we start to see yet another monster rearing its ugly head. Risk and governance, after all, are the twin forces shaping every organization's ability to move forward. Get the balance right, and you create a foundation for transformation stable enough to prevent chaos and yet flexible enough to allow progress. Get it wrong and watch out – the Reckless Monster thrives.

The Reckless Monster has two extremes. On one end, there's complete recklessness – where speed rules and consequences are an afterthought. Organizations in this space chase disruption, deploying AI models before understanding their impact, launching new platforms without security measures, and expanding without guardrails. On the other side is rigidity – where transformation suffocates under layers of policy, bureaucracy, and outdated rules written for a world that no longer exists. Here's the conundrum: How much of either – recklessness or rigidity – is permissible/useful/worthwhile?

Management may have addressed all the risks, compliance protocols, and security concerns, but there is always another risk barrier to be addressed.

And then there's the worst place of all: neglect, where neither risk nor governance is actively considered, leaving the organization drifting, unprepared for both threats and opportunities. One of the most common failures in transformation is policy overreach — organizations that implement so many controls that they crush their own ability to execute. Security frameworks become so rigid that they slow down product releases; compliance teams insist on exhaustive risk assessments that delay AI initiatives; internal approval chains become convoluted that decision-making grinds to a halt. Interestingly, the Reckless Monster has now opened the door for the Inertia Monster.

Irrationality: Humanity's Default Setting

Organizations that thrive don't choose one extreme or the other. They navigate between risk-taking and risk compliance, between bold moves and strong foundations. They protect against recklessness without stagnation by developing a comprehensive understanding of the pitfalls associated with transformation.

Some risks, of course, can never be fully mitigated. Both reactive and proactive measures can be deployed, but the key takeaway is that you have thought through a plan of action. When an issue comes up – and it will, we promise – you will have a thought-through assessment, course of action, and mitigation strategies.

The reality is that transformation involves people and people will inevitably behave irrationally, especially in stressful situations. Risks, like security vulnerabilities, need to be monitored and addressed as they arise. Adaptive companies have built-in protocols providing agile processes, assessment methods, and controls to deal with issues and mitigate any damage that might occur. Black swan events – pandemics, stock market crashes, and so on – that might curtail transformation need to be assessed in terms of likelihood and severity. For this two new slayers step into the mix: the Gatekeeper and the Navigator.

The Reckless Monster Slayers

GATEKEEPER

A Gatekeeper is not a bouncer allowing only certain people into a club or a toll collector obtaining payment. Gatekeepers possess a fundamental understanding of why gates, or in particular barriers, are in place, when they come into consideration, and how to strategically plan for them.

Much like a lock on a river, these gates come in different forms, often connected to their navigability, criticality, and time to traverse. As a result, we can think of the importance of Gatekeepers in three ways: (1) they manage access to critical resources needed to ensure successful transformation efforts; (2) they understand how to navigate the approval processes needed to support change, without it transformation stalls; and (3) they influence buy-in, without which groups and departments may resist or disengage from transformation efforts. Gatekeepers, in other words, take transformation strategies and help operationalize them by filtering and validating ideas. Much like our organizational pragmatist helps in assessing what's feasible versus doable versus practical, the Gatekeeper helps provide pragmatic advice on what will be needed when it comes to resources, compliance, and risk assessment along the journey. Gatekeepers can amplify momentum when engaged rather than become silent blockers when not activated sufficiently at the beginning of the journey.

Gatekeepers are often found at different levels across the organization. They might be risk professionals or security practitioners. They might even be middle management. This slayer understands that bold ideas aren't derailed by avoidable or unknown risks. This slayer gets that when transformation efforts move too fast without guardrails, companies become vulnerable to data breaches, compliance failures, and strategic missteps that can set a company back years. But good governance isn't about saying "no"; it's about making sure that "yes" is sustainable. The best organizations understand this. Instead of endless approvals and rigid checklists, they create adaptive governance. Guardrails that allow speed without spiraling into chaos. This means embedding risk management into decision-making, not as a blocker but as a partner in innovation.

Take Microsoft in the early 2010s. At the time, the tech giant was at risk of falling behind various cloud-first competitors like Amazon with Amazon Web Services (AWS) and Google with

Google Cloud Platform (GCP). When Sathya Nadella took over Microsoft in 2014, the company did a massive pivot away from desktop computing to become a cloud-first and AI-driven company. Launching Azure (its flagship cloud computing platform), embracing open-source, and integrating AI into enterprise software were entirely new directions for the company. Making sure they understood and accounted for enterprise risk was critical, not just for the company itself but also for their clients. They invested heavily in cybersecurity adopting a zero-trust architecture into platforms and products. They built compliance management tools and developed compliance certification for all the markets in which they hoped to operate. They established a resilient cloud architecture with redundancy and compliance zones to ensure uptime and data sovereignty. They also established an office of responsible AI to make sure ethical design principles were embedded in development.

While the Gatekeeper understands gates you may encounter, the Navigator plots the best course through those gated mechanisms. The Navigator works with the Gatekeeper to interpret and operationalize the strategy, bridging vision with execution. This is not meant to avoid any of the gates set up to mitigate risk, manage resources, or make sure initiatives are compliant, but rather to accelerate through gated mechanisms.

Understanding the risks associated with different kinds of data is an important part of the Navigator's task. After all, all transformations involve data, whether it's used to measure and assess or as a fundamental layer empowering the transformation, as it is with AI. Some data is riskier than others. Consider personal identifiable information (PII). Perhaps, minimizing or stemming the collection of this data might be an option at least at the beginning stages of transformation. Perhaps, certain regions may have more stringent requirements when it comes to data privacy, reporting requirements, or auditing. The Navigator looks for paths that have the least friction, resistance, or embedded risks, thereby helping to gain momentum, develop alliances, and build trust. As we progress forward in learning risk mitigation tactics and addressing concerns across the organization from different functions and departments, we become more adept at adhering to compliance and enterprise risk management. However, there are always new policies, regulations, and gates that arise. The Navigator's ability to address and assess these new hurdles is critical for success.

If the Gatekeeper prevents disaster, the Navigator ensures the organization doesn't get stuck in policy quicksand. The Navigator understands that governance and risk management shouldn't be a tax on innovation. Instead, these policies should create momentum, helping teams move with clarity, rather than freezing them in analysis paralysis. The Navigator fights against this inertia, ensuring that governance enables transformation instead of strangling it.

Take a company like Capital One. When it transformed into a tech-driven bank, the company didn't just throw AI and cloud adoption into the mix and hope for the best. It built a compliance framework that evolved with its transformation and embedded security into agile development rather than treating it as a last-minute checklist. By aligning governance with business objectives, Capital One became one of the most forward-thinking financial institutions, moving at the speed of innovation while maintaining customer trust.

Finding the Balance: Strategic Compliance

Every company believes it's being thoughtful and strategic about risk, but the Reckless Monster lurks in extremes. Some charge ahead recklessly, hoping to deal with the consequences later. Others are trapped in policies that no longer serve them. And then there are those that are simply adrift, lacking both the courage to innovate and the discipline to govern effectively.

It's crucial to recognize how your organization operates. Management would be wise to take a good look in the mirror and understand where they fall on the risk versus governance 2 × 2 (see Figure 10.1).

- **High risk, low governance:** Reckless. Defining characteristics: Moving fast without thinking. AI projects deployed with no security controls. New products rushed out before regulatory approval. Exciting, but unsustainable.
- **Low risk, high governance:** Restrictive. Stuck in bureaucratic loops. Compliance-driven paralysis. Long approval cycles. Nothing fails, but nothing moves forward either.

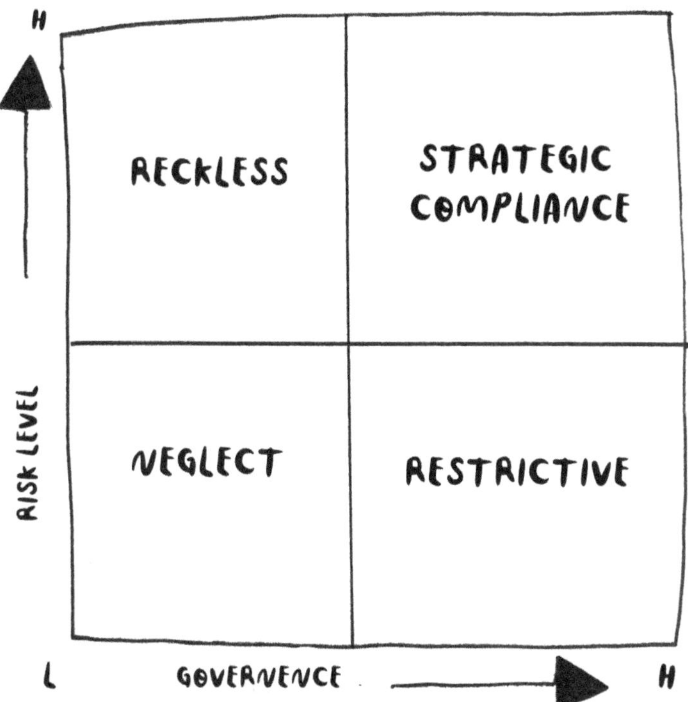

Figure 10.1   From neglect to compliant.

- **Low risk, low governance:** Neglect. No strategy, no discipline. Transformation is more of a buzzword than a real effort. This is where once-great companies become irrelevant.
- **High risk, high governance:** Strategic compliance. The sweet spot. Risk is managed, but not avoided. Governance is a launchpad, not a prison. Decisions happen fast, but with built-in safety mechanisms that ensure longevity.

Name Your Risk

Risks are everywhere. While you cannot simply remove all risks, you can be aware of them and reduce their potential impact. This is particularly true in highly regulated industries, which are more risk-averse environments with rigid controls. The Gatekeeper can help control for risk through an understanding of gated mechanisms and by putting in the guardrails to not run afoul of the GRC. The Navigator, in turn, helps pick the path of least resistance. Both help alleviate potential policy gridlock. Like our transformation monsters, risks need to be named, understood, assessed, and mitigated.

Most risks can be broken down into categories:

Strategic: These risks occur when there is no clear vision or goals, leading to misalignment between teams and fragmented efforts. Overestimating capabilities and underestimating resources and timelines resulting in derailing long-term progress.

Infrastructure: These risks reflect a lack of integration between systems and a poor understanding of what an organization might have and how it is used.

Structural: Here, risk is the result of a siloed culture and hierarchical organization not conducive for information sharing and diversity of consideration critical for sustainable transformation.

Adoption: These are human-centered risks where everything from a skills gap to resistance to change could delay and derail transformation efforts.

Execution: Risk associated with poor project management, often the result of too many pilots and not enough scale, which relegates transformation to the continual experimental stage. A lack of agility and single-mindedness of purpose results in missed learning and poor adaptation.

Governance and compliance: Here, the risk ties back to a lack of thinking through how transformation efforts come into organizational compliance. Who is overseeing and enforcing decisions? Who is responsible for making sure transformation efforts don't run afoul of specifications, policies, or laws that your organization needs to keep in adherence? All of a sudden, compliance has become everyone's job.

All of these risks need to be understood and assessed, and plans developed to mitigate various scenarios? We can evaluate each risk based on:

- **Likelihood (L):** How probable is it?
- **Impact (I):** What's the potential cost or damage?
- **Velocity (V):** How fast will it materialize?
- **Control effectiveness (C):** How well are we managing it now?

Risk scoring is often used to compare risks and sets of risks to each other. In this case, a score might look like $(L \times I \times V)/C$. The output can develop a heat map providing consensus on risk assessment. Everything we have discussed in this book is designed to reduce risks associated with transformations, but unless we think pragmatically, holistically, and with an action-based assessment, risks can become blockers for our efforts.

Permission to Proceed

As data becomes fundamental for transformation – particularly those transformation efforts related to AI – having a comprehensive understanding of data collection, storage, and permissions use is essential. Applications will be developed or modified, processes will be automated to develop efficiencies, and new digital experiences will be built for employees, customers, or partners. In many cases, applications may be hosted outside the organization. All of these involve cybersecurity risks, and those risks are growing in complexity and frequency. And as a result, threat modeling and assessment are critical parts of transformational planning. Gatekeepers understand the protocols for access and permissions and the role these play in terms of mitigating risk. Navigators help you map out the path of least resistance. Access and permissions have been put in place over years to address security, unauthorized access to confidential information, and compliance audits as well as providing traceability of user requirements. In addition, policies around data ownership provide operational efficiency, avoiding system clutter and distraction. Access might be granted based on job roles, based on the project, or based on user attributes (location or department). Remember that folks who need access might need specialized training, so you will have to figure in the time and cost associated with making sure your efforts are in compliance. It's important to make sure your efforts have the needed guardrails in place.

Threats: All Around and Closer Than You Think

A recent survey of IT professionals conducted by Spiceworks and Aberdeen Strategy and Research[1] identified the top drivers for cybersecurity budget growth in 2025. The top driver was increased security concerns. Phishing attacks, viruses, and malware – there are plenty of reasons Information Security professionals don't sleep at night, worrying about their organizations' intellectual property, trade secrets, and other sensitive information. Any transformational effort needs to include a security threat assessment to help identify potential vulnerabilities, evaluating threats both potential and accidental. The Gatekeeper can translate restrictions and procedures for employees to avoid the Reckless Monster. The Navigator knows that security risk can be mitigated by identifying a course of action that steers clear of unnecessary pitfalls.

One of the biggest considerations for any security team is the threat posed by insiders. This is not to say that there are hackers walking around your company intent on crashing systems, deploying malware, or stealing data. Rather, employees might engage in risky behaviors, that don't adhere to security protocols. Previously, we discussed the spectrum of employees on board with your transformation efforts. On one end of the spectrum, there are your ardent supporters who embrace change and support your efforts. At the polar opposite are folks who are not even remotely on board. They don't believe your efforts will succeed, let alone benefit them or the organization.

It is the same thing with insiders. Insider threats are individuals within the organization who may intentionally or unintentionally cause harm to systems, data, or operations. There are folks at one end of the spectrum who adhere to security specifications and protocols. They have been sufficiently trained to avoid at risk behavior that might potentially open themselves up to exploits or threats. On the other end of the spectrum, there are folks, much like the dissenters, who simply will not adhere to secure processes when engaging in work. Previously we discussed disengagement and how this impacted the workforce. McKinsey conducted a research study[2] showing about half of all employees surveyed expressed some level of dissatisfaction with their jobs. It is the mildly disengaged (those demonstrating below average commitment and performance) and the disruptors (those with dismal satisfaction and commitment rates) that we need to be most concerned about because they represent a source of potential insider threats. When you combine growing complexity and uncertainty with the irrationality of human behavior, you find your company heading into a perfect storm of risky behavior that must be assessed and understood, simply to have the greatest chance at transformation success.

Leverage the Gatekeeper and the Navigator to find the least riskiest option from a security perspective. Make it easy on yourself and build toward becoming regulatory aware and compliant across your journey. Start in a relatively safe place as you migrate into more uncharted and risky waters. Just as you might seek out your supporters, look as well for the detractors to avoid continued grief.

Race to Zero

Trust is central to so much of our discussion in this book: how to build it, foster it, and grow it over time. And yet there are lots of principles in the transformation world that take the opposite stance.

Namely, trust no one. Consider zero-trust architecture, zero standing privilege, and zero-party data.

- *Zero-trust architecture* is based on the "never trust, always verify" principle. Access to any resource must be subject to specific trust parameters. Any failure to meet those specifications results in denial of access.
- Zero standing privilege eliminates permanent standing privileges for users and instead grants access only for specific tasks when needed then immediately removes them.
- Zero-party data was coined by Forrester and refers to data that a customer intentionally and proactively shares with a business. Customers are becoming more concerned about how their data is being collected and used. Privacy legislation, like General Data Protection Regulations (GDPR), is becoming more common, addressing consumer protection associated with organizational data collection and use. Zero-party data is in part a call for companies to collect data for themselves but also to question third- and second-party data aggregators and collection platforms.

The Gatekeeper and Navigator can help promote trust in an environment that is more and more untrusting. Addressing GRC is critical to ensuring the success of our transformation efforts. We need to balance trust development, coalition building, and collaboration with the needs of the organization to ensure protection and risk compliance.

6S: The Framework for Moving Fast Without Breaking Things

For companies to slay the Reckless Monster, they need a guiding philosophy that ensures innovation isn't just fast but smart. You must ensure that any transformation effort is safe, scalable, and sustainable. Doing so involves some key strategic moves and needs to account for the 6S's which include:

- **Shift left:** Make sure you include governance, risk, and compliance at the start of your scoping and design. Combining the competencies of the Gatekeeper and Navigator to identify gated mechanisms and establish guardrails, not avoiding risk but rather incorporating risk mitigation strategies.
- **Share responsibility:** Make risk management everyone's responsibility, not just the work of the compliance and security team. Embed risk awareness training and develop risk registers that become living documents adjusted and assessed throughout the journey.
- **Scale through reuse:** Operationalize best practices through reusable components. Take a behavioral norm and turn it into a checklist, framework, and process. For example, how do you handle employee user interaction data when automating processes? Define the purpose: are you using the data to improve efficiency, user experience, or training? Use data minimization and anonymization to reduce risk. Then ensure transparency and ethical guardrails are included.
- **Seeing is believing:** GRC needs to be visible and traceable. Visually communicate how transformation is adhering to the organization's compliance posture and maintain audit trails of decisions and expectations.
- **Secure proactively and reactively:** All the security protocols may be in place, and yet a simple inadvertent event may still expose a large vulnerability in your infrastructure leading to a security breach. Make sure you have protocols in place for any eventuality.

- **Simplify everything:** Complex processes and systems are not only hard to understand, but they also are risky for a number of reasons (slow adoption, difficult to secure, do not adhere to risk protocols, etc.). This could be as simple as prioritizing high-impact, frequently used processes such as the ones that slow down decision-making or that frustrate employees or customers.

Of course, everything we have discussed in this book, including transparency, alignment, and experimentation, also applies to developing the right culture of GRC in transformation. These 6Ss aren't just a checklist – they are filters for every decision. Does this new AI tool meet them? Is this governance framework aligned with them? If not, it's time to rethink.

Winning the Transformation Game

In the end, slaying the Reckless Monster isn't about eliminating risk or adding more policies. It's about knowing when to push forward and when to pull back. It's about having the right governance without suffocating progress. It's also about understanding the mechanisms of risk and security controls in the organization and working to develop guardrails for transformation efforts, not roadmaps or unpassable gates.

The companies that win in transformation aren't those that move the fastest or those that play it the safest. They are the ones that balance speed with stability, innovation with security, and risk with reward.

So, the real questions are: Where does your company stand? Are you moving recklessly, hoping to deal with consequences later? Are you stuck in restrictive policies that no longer serve you? Are you drifting, unable to make a decision at all? Or are you building strategic compliance, ensuring that every move forward is not just fast, but built to last?

The Gatekeeper and Navigator aren't just nice-to-have competencies in your transformation. They are essential. Without them, you're either flying blind or stuck in the mud. With them, you're moving with purpose, slaying the Reckless Monster, and setting the stage for AI-driven transformation that is not just innovative – but unstoppable.

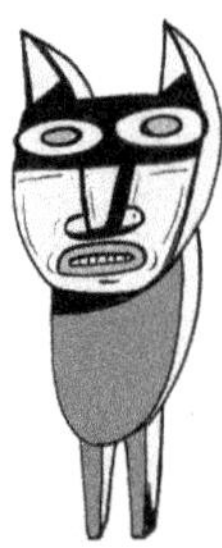

Key Takeaways

- **Speed does not have to mean recklessness:** Progress is measured in validated learning, not just velocity.
- **Learn and practice the culture of GCR:** Adapt it early to your transformation efforts.
- **Transparency beats control:** Make work visible and understandable to avoid confusion, achieve alignment, and build trust.

(Continued)

- **Get comfortable with risk:** Understand how risk occurs, assess risk in terms of likelihood, severity, and velocity, and then identify mitigation mechanisms.
- **Be adaptive:** Things change. Remember consistency in principles, flexibility in practice.

Case Story: Calm

Keep Calm and Carry On

When Tom Brandl joined mental wellness brand Calm in 2023 as chief information security officer (CISO), he was given the difficult task of making sure the company's security operations lived up to the kind of balance and peace it preached on its top-selling sleep, meditation, and relaxation app. The challenge: how to accelerate growth through development and acquisitions in an increasingly competitive market and complex industry, while maintaining safe and secure operations? In other words, how to fight off the Reckless Monster?

Since its launch in 2012, Calm – the brainchild of entrepreneurs Alex Tew and Michael Acton Smith – had been on a tear, winning Apple's app of the year award in 2017 and adding captivating "sleep stories" narrated by celebs like Matthew McConaughey and Harry Styles. With more than 100 million downloads, Calm is now the leading global name in mental wellness apps with adoption in multiple languages and a total valuation of more than $2 billion. What was born from Alex's former donothingfor2minutes.com concept website has become a booming subscription-based business, expanding into new areas, including employee well-being and enterprise-level organizations.

The digital mental health space has also become crowded, in part because of the stresses of the pandemic but also with the growing industries around mental health, mindfulness, sleep, and fitness. Several other apps, like Headspace, Simple Habit, and Aura, offer similar services as Calm. This accelerated the need for Calm to differentiate itself, partnering with established players in the health space and focusing on consumer experience, trust, and value.

Complexity and Insecurity

Tom's particular challenge came on the security side, which has become exponentially more complex in the past decade for businesses focused around mobile applications. As more consumers rely increasingly on mobile-based applications for learning, engaging, communicating, and entertaining, the number of security issues faced by app developers has only grown, reflecting the challenges developers confront in securing these applications. The numbers, after all, are staggering: analysts estimate about 250 billion apps were downloaded in 2023 alone, most of those from either Google or Apple stores to all different kinds of phones and operating systems. Studies reveal that about 32% of apps have security flaws in their first year. This figure rises to 70% within five years and can include everything from insecure data storage, outdated code, or unpatched software.

Application developers need to be aware of how different groups (partners, users, employees) interact with the application, access data, and connect with customer service and support. After all, users can store data on their phone or connect to other popular platforms like Meta or Google. And let's not forget about all the links – to external partners for commerce opportunities and to connections to allow users to share information (social sharing), as well as links that connect the companies themselves to your data to ensure you maximize the utility for the app and remain a loyal paying member. Do you see the full picture here? "Calm" is not exactly the first word that comes to mind when you think about app security.

In addition to app-based security, the other big challenge is organizational security, which covers a range of danger zones, from the development environment to operationally focused teams to back-end systems. Tom understood that it was his job as CISO to make sure that the security threat landscape at Calm was reduced, employees were sufficiently trained on security protocols and awareness, and contingencies were in place should something occur.

Secure the Base

With a master's in information technology (MSIT) and a key contributor to the Chief Information Security Officer (CISO) program from Carnegie Mellon University as well as extensive work managing risk and security at high-growth tech firms like DocuSign and Neustar, Tom brought a broad range of experience, both as practitioner and as an academic. Everywhere he's worked, Tom has embodied a unique perspective, understanding that security and risk enables business and not the other way around.

Of course, security is ultimately a job of mitigating downside risks, something that exists everywhere in today's organizations, particularly as it relates to digital transformation. This includes employees, who represent one of the largest risks to organizations. In fact, there is an entire category focused on employee security risk – insider threat detection and classification. This is not to say that each employee is a potential security threat, but the way they behave, interact, and share company-specific information or systems can create a vulnerability.

Prior to Tom's arrival at Calm, security at the company was a shared responsibility between the technical operations teams and its legal team. For the company to grow, partner, and compete in an increasingly crowded space, formalized strategies for secure operations, risk assessment, and compliance procedures needed to be established.

Tom brought our two essential slayer competencies – namely, the Gatekeeper and the Navigator – necessary to fight off the Reckless Monster. He understood that there are necessary gates required to secure access to critical infrastructure and systems but also that he and his team had to work with employees to help them navigate these gates to ensure business continuity and growth.

Navigating Insecure Waters

Ten months prior to Tom joining the company, Calm had acquired the Ripple Health group to expand its mental health offerings. Ripple, which was less than three years old, was purpose-built to be a clinical platform and included CareMemo, an app allowing patients and caregivers to communicate with care teams, and LikePaper, an app that helps users organize care, keep medical information, and set medication reminders. This acquisition involved more enterprise-type usage with well-defined processes, policies, and operational procedures, partly as a result of being compliant with federal regulations like HIPAA. While such an approach is mandated with Ripple's enterprise-focused app, this was very different from Calm's direct-to-consumer app approach, which is at the opposite end of the spectrum in terms of operational process and policy development. Tom's challenge at the time was to streamline and normalize operations from a technical, compliance, and risk perspective, but to do so in a way that combined the cultures. Calm is more akin to a Silicon Valley startup, while Ripple, at the time, was enterprise-grade and process-laden. How do you put in measurement mechanisms to track things over time? Tom had to keep this in mind when making sure that Calm remained a safe and calm environment.

Tom needed to make sure front-end systems like Google Workspace (used for everything from communication to spreadsheets development) and backend systems like Jira (a project management system used to track requirements, tasks, and issues) were integrated securely. Because many of these were part acquisitions, there were also issues of integrating different instantiations of similar systems, another hurdle in the process.

Like every other high-growth company undergoing digital transformation, Tom needed to figure out ways to integrate systems *and* people in the most secure, efficient, and seamless way possible. As Tom says, security and risk shouldn't be something that's considered a tax on the organization. Tom's focus was on how to make sure that Calm could operate in a compliant fashion with operational rigor rather than trying to fit into a mold that's required by some regulatory authority.

As Calm continues to expand beyond the consumer market to enterprise-level operations, the questions/concerns associated with data security and governance continue to grow. In the new health environment, additional training is now needed since employees will be working with personal health information (PHI) without being disruptive to the rest of the business. Tom likens the process to sailing: you don't sail in a straight line, but pick a point in the distance that you want to get to, and tack back and forth along the way. If you're always moving toward that direct goal, you can still deviate as much as you need to on the way there.

Flexibility and nimbleness are essential tools of the Gatekeeper and Navigator. Ultimately, Tom made sure employees understood the changes to how they approached security as something that enabled them to work holistically, efficiently, and collaboratively. By focusing on business drivers for compliance, risk and security, a shared understanding was developed. Development is prone to failure when security is viewed as a roadblock.

Humans Behaving Insecurely

In the process of Calm's transformation, Tom recognized that it was fundamental to make sure employees understood the rationales associated with any additional training. Humans, he knows, are often the weakest link in the chain when it comes to security. And yet, he didn't want to force something on them without explanation. As a Gatekeeper, he wanted the process to be thorough and transparent.

"It's very easy to try and solve a problem," Tom likes to say, "before you know what the problem really is." In other words, Tom wanted folks at Calm to define what they want as an outcome first and then back into the solution from there. Building something to where you want to go, not building something that will be adjacent to where you need to be.

From Tom's point of view, being intentional and thoughtful is a critical way to enable business partnerships and further strategic growth. He mentioned a recent partnership with a large healthcare payer that had experienced a security breach earlier in the year. Tom needed to provide assurances based on procedures and protocols to make sure they would see Calm as a value-added partner and not as a potential security breach waiting to happen.

Foundational Capacity to be AI Ready

Assessing vulnerabilities associated with acquisitions has become Tom's specialty over time. Tom's process was fundamental in making sure that there would be effective integration with reduced risk. These principles can then be applied to any situation where security, compliance, and risk need to be considered. These include:

- Prioritize operational procedures before integrating complexity. Layer in tools to provide additional efficiencies.
- Develop consensus. At Calm, Tom created a formal security and compliance council that defined risk tolerance levels and acknowledged areas for improvement.
- Build risk tolerance models. Be thoughtful and intentional, getting people on the same page.

Health Information Trust Alliance (HITRUST) is a certification and risk management framework helping organizations protect sensitive information and manage compliance, especially in industries handling healthcare data. As Tom states, putting a road map in place for HITRUST and having similar controls across the organization based on need, task, and access is also foundational. You need to get basic capabilities in place across the organization (foundational). "At Calm we currently have the volume turned down while meeting contractual and regulatory requirements, but we can turn it up to eight if needed based on additional requirements or standards we are required to meet in the future." Tom understands that this might happen sooner rather than later.

At the end of the day, Tom knows that technology will continue to evolve, and, ultimately, this presents a risk management problem. The question he always asks his team: "Do we have the right capabilities and mitigation structures in place?" Once you get alignment on those issues, the process becomes much easier and certainly less scary and a way, potentially, to tame the Reckless Monster.

Try This: Oversight, Insight, and Foresight

The Reckless Monster thrives when no one's watching, when teams avoid hard questions, or when the future is treated like someone else's problem. This exercise builds risk muscle without killing momentum.

Step 1: Oversight

Ask your team: "What's a risk we are already tracking but might be underestimating?"

Write it down. Be honest about whether or not it's truly under control.

Step 2: Insight

Now ask: "What's a blind spot we've been ignoring because it's inconvenient, political, or uncomfortable?"

Surface it. No blame, just awareness.

Step 3: Foresight

Ask: "What's a future risk we're not preparing for but should be?"

Think AI, regulation, talent gaps, ecosystem shifts. Don't aim for precision. Aim for preparedness.

Bonus Move:

For each risk, decide: Do we need to expand the aperture (bring in more voices)? Or narrow it (focus and decide)?

Guardrails beat guesswork. Great teams manage risk by seeing clearly before it becomes a headline.

Conclusion

"The way to get started is to quit talking and begin doing."
—Walt Disney

Wow, that was a lot. After naming 10 monsters that often lurk in the shadows, squashing your best efforts at transformation, you might be wondering: what could possibly be next? While naming our fears is powerful, Disney's straightforward advice rings especially true for transformation efforts. All the monster identification in the world means nothing without action. The question isn't just what stands in the way, but what are we going to do about it?

Consider any "overnight success" story. Dig deeper and you will usually find years of small victories, setbacks, lessons learned, and persistent efforts. Transformation is no different. While some organizations seem to change at lightning speed, it more often occurs through a series of experiments that involve capturing learning, building alliances, and addressing one monster-slaying victory at a time. Do yourself a favor and follow these tips: Be pragmatic. Start small. Get some wins in place. Bring in supporters. Address dissenters. And overcome fear of failure. Rinse, Repeat.

The path to achieving an adaptive, agile AI-enabled vision often starts with feasible short-term steps. Sure, it's good to have a grand vision of a fully transformed organization, but without a phased-in implementation addressing your monsters, elevating employee competencies, and rethinking deeply held beliefs, you just increase the chances of not meeting expectations. So, maybe it's bringing transparency to one key process or building a small coalition of the willing into your division or developing consensus across departments on customer needs and values. Each small victory builds confidence and trust. Each step forward, no matter how small, moves your organization closer to efficient, scalable, and durable transformation.

Remember what Kelly at Yum! wisely said in Chapter 8 – give yourself and others a little grace. You might stumble. You might fall. Leave room for learning and allow time for adjusting to new ways of thinking and operating. Transformation is powered by people, not processes or machines, so we need to factor in deeply held beliefs, cognition, fear and uncertainty, as well as other efforts that are competing for time and energy.

Don't forget about sharing knowledge either. The process of coaching, mentorship, and tutelage plays a fundamental role in providing a pathway to build tacit knowledge in building transformational capacity. And yet to make this happen at scale, you need to provide the right incentive structure for both the mentor and mentee. If there is any key takeaway we have learned, it's that you have to build the infrastructure and processes to transfer knowledge and training from one set of employees to another.

Each of the stories we shared with you had a specific key takeaway. Kristl and Kathlyn at Brooks started with a shared understanding of their customers, literally walking in their shoes in order to deliver value. Or Benedetto at Ferrari honored the past while innovating with rapid experimentation. These weren't grand, sweeping changes that transformed their organizations overnight, but rather deliberate and focused efforts that created momentum for bigger changes. Their "overnight successes" took years of consistent execution, relationship building, and persistent action.

Here's the real truth: it's not about being right or being liked. The people who help you execute transformation, the true monster slayers, need to be effective. Being right doesn't always get things done. Being liked won't move the needle. But being effective – relentlessly focusing on the mission, crafting a compelling story, aligning people around the right priorities, and breaking down barriers – that's what drives real change. The best transformation leaders wake up every day obsessed, not with their own ego, but with whether they are actually making progress.

Organizations that seem to get sh*t done (GSD) have built a culture of hustling but in the best possible way. Hustle culture is often associated with intense work and productivity at the expense of employee wellness. Emphasis on productivity and winning takes precedence over work–life balance, which only leads to burnout and a toxic work environment. The most effective organizations we've studied have figured out how to leverage monster slayers, like the Barrier Buster, the Path Maker, and the Organizational Gymnast, to remove monsters that put the kibosh on transformation. As we have highlighted throughout the book, these folks cannot expedite change but develop effective, value-added, whole-organization transformation. They have the skills, knowledge, and abilities to recognize these unique challenges and render these monsters ineffective.

And yet we'll keep repeating it: all the monster-naming insight in the world won't help if you're not willing to roll up your sleeves and take action. The most successful transformations we have seen share one common trait: leaders who moved from understanding to action, from planning to doing, from talking about change to making it happen.

Here's what we have learned about turning monster-slaying knowledge into action:

- **Understand your space:** Do you have the infrastructure and support to experiment, assess, and measure hypotheses that will build confidence in transformational efforts? Don't let the FOMO, Inertia, or Lackadaisical Monsters stand in your way.
- **Clean up:** Complexity creates more potential failure points, so right-sizing your infrastructure sets the stage for more efficient and effective transformation efforts. Getting a firm grasp of systems, processes, and data flows prevents unnecessary complexity in the future. Hairy Monster, anyone?
- **Develop the right conditions:** Are you enabling employees and incentivizing them accordingly? Are you ensuring authenticity in communication that focuses on consensus building and developing a shared mutual understanding? Transformation takes time and effort. Transformation needs to be thought of holistically. Don't fall prey to the Hubris or Cagey Monster.
- **Act local, think global:** Organizations need to deploy system-based thinking to understand how processes interact.

Erode silo mentality. Remember, collaboration is good, but alignment is critical. Map out and plan for risks before you become one. Steer clear of the Silo, Hydra, and Reckless Monsters.

Especially in the age of AI, where the speed of change will outpace your org chart, your budget cycles, and your legacy systems, action matters more than ever. AI doesn't wait. It exposes inefficiencies, challenges assumptions, and elevates competency as the true driver of transformation. What were once trends are now table stakes. Complexity is rising. The only way through is forward.

That's why leaders who win at transformation follow five simple but powerful principles:

- **Show up:** Be present with purpose and intention.
- **Go all in:** Commit to the people, not just the plan.
- **Learn and adapt:** Continuous learning and assessing.
- **Stick to it:** Through the ups and downs. That's where the real magic happens.
- **Celebrate progress:** Acknowledge and reward victories.

The truth is there is never a perfect time to start transformation. There will always be more monsters to name (Diva Monster, anyone?), more challenges to understand, and more stakeholders to align. The most successful transformations we have studied didn't start with some magical moment when all conditions were perfect. They started with leaders that said, "Enough talking. Let's begin." They started with small teams who decided to tackle one monster at a time. They started with organizations that understood that every marathon begins with a single step.

So whether you are facing the FOMO Monster's siren call of shiny new technology or wrestling with the Hydra Monster's multiplying complexity or staring down any of the other transformation monsters we have named, remember this: naming your monster was just the beginning. Real transformation happens when you move from naming to slaying, from understanding to action, from talking to doing.

Your monster-slaying journey doesn't end with this book. In many ways, it is just beginning. The difference is that now you have the knowledge . . . have the knowledge, the tools, and ideally the inspiration to move from insight to action.

Now, it is time to get out there and drive successful change. Let the slaying begin!

Notes

Chapter 1: WTF Just Happened

1. Gartner Hype Cycle website, https://www.gartner.com/en/research/methodologies/gartner-hype-cycle
2. Contrary Research, Instacart, 2023.
3. Feeding America, SNAP Fact Sheet.
4. Just Harvest, Action Against Hunger, March 2025.
5. Capgemini, 71% of consumers want generative AI integrated into their shopping experiences, Jan. 2025.

Chapter 2: Press 9 and Wait in Purgatory

1. https://www.hubspot.com/ (C02f11).

Chapter 3: Know Thy Mess

1. IDC, Accepting The Reality of IT Inflation and Ways to Cope, Nov. 2022

2. McKinsey, StudyUnlocking success in digital transformations. Oct. 2018

3. Gartner Study

4. Forrester and Airtable, Software is fracturing your organization

5. The Role of Complexity Theory as a Foundation for Taking a Systems Approach in Your Organization, Human Capital Leadership Review, Oct. 31, 2024

Chapter 4: My Way or the Highway

1. Fowler, J. H., & Christakis, N. A. Cooperative behavior cascades in human social networks. *Proceedings of the National Academy of Sciences*, 2010. https://doi.org/10.1073/pnas.0913149107

2. Drummond Papworth, Kirstie, *Compassionate Leadership: For Individuals and Organisational Change*, De Grutyer, 2023.

3. Tan, C. M. *Search inside yourself: The unexpected path to achieving success, happiness (and world peace)*. HarperOne, 2012

4. Edelman Trust Barometer, https://www.edelman.com/trust/trust-barometer

5. Whitney, John O, The Economics of Trust: Liberating Profits and Restoring Corporate Vitality, Sept. 1995.

6. Sako, Mari, 'Does Trust Improve Business Performance?★', in Roderick M Kramer (ed.), *Organizational Trust: A Reader* (Oxford, 2006; online edn, Oxford Academic, 31 Oct. 2023), https://doi.org/10.1093/oso/9780199288496.003.0010, accessed 11 Jan. 2025.

7. McPhail, R., Chan, X. W. (Carys), May, R., & Wilkinson, A. (2023). Post-COVID remote working and its impact on people, productivity, and the planet: an exploratory scoping review. *The International Journal of Human Resource Management*, 35(1), 154–182. https://doi.org/10.1080/09585192.2023.2221385

8. Redseer Strategy Consulting, India's Got Retail: A Tale of Fragmented Supply & Consolidating Distribution, March, 2025

9. Experience adapted from On Your Feet (OYF.com)

Chapter 5: Transparency Is the New Currency

1. HBR, The Impact of Employee Engagement on Performance

2. Clark, M. A., Robertson, M. M., & Young, S. (2019). "I feel your pain": A critical review of organizational research on empathy. *Journal of Organizational Behavior*, 40, 166–192; Ohm et al. (2020).

3. Yu R. Stress potentiates decision biases: A stress induced deliberation-to-intuition (SIDI) model. *Neurobiol Stress* 2016 Feb 12;3:83-95. doi: 10.1016/j.ynstr.2015.12.006. PMID: 27981181; PMCID: PMC5146206.

4. Birkinshaw, Julian and Cable, Dan (2017), *The Dark Side Of transparency*, McKinsey Quarterly

Chapter 6: Enter the Test Kitchen

1. Mcfarland, Colin, Design Like You're Right, Test Like You're Wrong, Medium, March, 2016

2. Geenway, Roger, Reflection Toolkit, The University of Edinburgh

Chapter 8: A Coalition of the Winning

1. Deci, E. L., & Ryan, R. M. (2000). The "what" and "why" of goal pursuits: Human needs and the self-determination of behavior. *Psychological Inquiry, 11,* 227-268. https://doi.org/10.1207/S15327965PLI1104_01

2. Watkins, Michael. *The First 90 Days: Critical Success Strategies for New Leaders at All Levels.* Harvard Business School Press, 2003.

3. Experience adapted from On Your Feet, OYF.com

Chapter 10: Check Yourself

1. Aberdeen research and Spiceworks, State of IT 2025: Insights on Budgets, Jobs, and AI, Nov. 2024

2. McKinsey and Company, How to identify employee disengagement, June 2024

Acknowledgments

Like every effort of this magnitude, there were a variety of individuals who contributed to its development. So many people offered us help, guidance, and support. We would like to express gratitude for all the individuals who took time to speak with us, answer our survey, and agree to be featured in this book. We would like to acknowledge the following individuals who went above and beyond through working with us to develop featured stories. These tales developed a level of resonance for readers to assess the story of transformation through the eyes of a Monster Slayer. We would like to acknowledge them as well as the support folks in the Marketing, Comm, and Legal departments that helped ensure the release of these stories for this book.

Shellye Archambeau
Andrew Nodes
Sanjay Srinavasta
Kristl Date-Dopps and Kathlyn Jones
Matt Meier
Shibashish Roy

Dean Carter

Benedetto Vigna

Laura Harshberger

Kelly Dowdy

Sameer Badlani

Tom Brandl

In addition, we would like to thank all the research assistants including Maitri Surti, Joannna Sam, and Kelly Zhou who helped us with the book, as well as our editor extraordinaire, John Fried.

—Keep on slayin'!

Index